In Mem
JANE AUSTEN,
youngest daughter of the late
Rev.ᵈ GEORGE AUSTEN,
formerly Rector of Steventon in this County
she departed this Life on the 18ᵗʰ of July 1817,
aged 41, after a long illness supported with
the patience and the hopes of a Christian.

The benevolence of her heart,
the sweetness of her temper, and
the extraordinary endowments of her mind
obtained the regard of all who knew her, and
the warmest love of her intimate connections.

Their grief is in proportion to their affection
they know their loss to be irreparable,
but in their deepest affliction they are consoled
by a firm though humble hope that her charity,
devotion, faith and purity, have rendered
her soul acceptable in the sight of her
REDEEMER.

Jane Austen Memorial Stone at Winchester Cathedral

David Gee 4 / Alamy Stock Photo.

This will give you some more
ammunition for when your dad
starts whining about J.A!
love
Grandad + Margaret

30 GREAT MYTHS ABOUT JANE AUSTEN

Claudia L. Johnson
Clara Tuite

WILEY Blackwell

Registered Office
John Wiley & Sons, Inc., 111 River Street, Hoboken, NJ 07030, USA

Editorial Office
The Atrium, Southern Gate, Chichester, West Sussex, PO19 8SQ, UK

For details of our global editorial offices, customer services, and more information about Wiley products visit us at www.wiley.com.

Wiley also publishes its books in a variety of electronic formats and by print-on-demand. Some content that appears in standard print versions of this book may not be available in other formats.

Library of Congress Cataloging-in-Publication Data
Names: Johnson, Claudia L., author. | Tuite, Clara, author.
Title: 30 great myths about Jane Austen / Claudia L. Johnson, Clara Tuite.
Other titles: Thirty great myths about Jane Austen
Description: First edition. | Hoboken, NJ : Wiley-Blackwell, [2020] |
    Includes bibliographical references and index.
Identifiers: LCCN 2020019244 (print) | LCCN 2020019245 (ebook) | ISBN
    9781119146865 (paperback) | ISBN 9781119146872 (adobe pdf) | ISBN
    9781119146889 (epub)
Subjects: LCSH: Austen, Jane, 1775-1817–Criticism and Interpretation.
Classification: LCC PR4037 .J63 2020 (print) | LCC PR4037 (ebook) | DDC
    823/.7–dc23
LC record available at https://lccn.loc.gov/2020019244
LC ebook record available at https://lccn.loc.gov/2020019245

Cover Design: Wiley
Cover Image: Portrait of Jane Austen, the "Rice Portrait", 1788–89 (oil on canvas), by Ozias Humphry (1742–1810) / Private Collection / Bridgeman Images

Set in 10/12pt Sabon by SPi Global, Pondicherry, India
Printed and bound by CPI Group (UK) Ltd, Croydon, CR0 4YY

10 9 8 7 6 5 4 3 2 1

CONTENTS

ABBREVIATIONS AND NOTE ON THE TEXT

All quotations from Jane Austen's novels and other works are taken from *The Cambridge Edition of the Works of Jane Austen* (2005–2008), General Editor, Janet Todd. They are indicated by parenthetical references in the text, with an abbreviated title and page number.

J   *Juvenilia*, ed. Peter Sabor (Cambridge: Cambridge University Press, 2006)

NA   *Northanger Abbey*, ed. Barbara M. Benedict and Deirdre Le Faye (Cambridge: Cambridge University Press, 2006)

SS   *Sense and Sensibility*, ed. Edward Copeland (Cambridge: Cambridge University Press, 2006)

PP   *Pride and Prejudice*, ed. Pat Rogers (Cambridge: Cambridge University Press, 2006)

MP   *Mansfield Park*, ed. John Wiltshire (Cambridge: Cambridge University Press, 2005)

E   *Emma*, ed. Richard Cronin and Dorothy McMillan (Cambridge: Cambridge University Press, 2005)

P   *Persuasion*, ed. Janet Todd and Antje Blank (Cambridge: Cambridge University Press, 2006)

LM   *Later Manuscripts*, ed. Janet Todd and Linda Bree (Cambridge: Cambridge University Press, 2008)

Quotations from Jane Austen's letters are taken from *Jane Austen's Letters*, ed. Deirdre Le Faye, third edition (Oxford: Oxford University Press, 1995).

ACKNOWLEDGEMENTS

Claudia L. Johnson would like to thank Princeton University in general and its Department of English in particular for the research and sabbatical support that made writing this book possible.

Clara Tuite would like to thank the University of Melbourne for the research leave that enabled work on the volume. She gratefully acknowledges the support of the Australian Government through a grant from the Australian Research Council that funded the research and editorial assistance of Jenny Lee and Caitlyn Lehmann.

To Jenny and Caitlyn, we are extremely grateful for their valuable suggestions and keen attention to detail. Caitlyn also provided assistance with illustrations and skillfully compiled the Index.

At Wiley Blackwell, we would like to thank former editor Emma Bennett for her enthusiastic commissioning of the book and guidance in the early stages of the project, and Mohan Jayachandran and Aneetta Antony for seeing the volume through production.

INTRODUCTION

All canonical authors are mythical creatures. They exist within the aura of their posthumous reputations – assessments, assumptions, facts, and fantasies that have accreted over time – sometimes taking on new associations as the social and historical conditions of readings and readers change. But some authors exercise a particularly powerful purchase on the imaginations of their readers over the centuries. Jane Austen is one of them. She has mobilized powerful, wishful, and sometimes contradictory ideas and feelings about issues as diverse as family, intimacy, taste, history, class, nationality, desire, manners, and society; and all these have contributed to forming the "myth" of Jane Austen, transforming her from Jane Austen into the beloved and sometimes despised figure of "Jane Austen."

Jane Austen is thus one of the most complex mythological creatures to inhabit the literary canon – continually invented and re-invented, as she is, by adoring critical readers and fans (and detractors) alike. It is Austen's ability to command re-readings that makes her such a compelling and commanding novelist – still – in the twenty-first century. One sign of Austen's greatness is precisely her ability to inspire the invention of myths. Indeed, mythmaking about Austen is a thriving and dynamic activity, sustained by a global community of readers. Austen's novels have always inspired a diversity of critical opinions, as well as continuations, remakes, parodies, biographical romances, and fantasies. For this reason, Austenian mythmaking is often surprising and unpredictable. One of its most intriguing features is a tendency to produce Austens that are diametrically opposed: Austen the Tory who is also a liberal feminist; Austen the husband-hunting butterfly who was also gay; Austen the acerbic satirist who is also a supreme romantic; Austen the master stylist who was also unconscious of her art.

Our volume takes its cues from previous volumes in this series in regarding the myth as a form of accepted belief (not necessarily untrue), and indeed as a particular body of knowledge (albeit one that is not strictly factual). Myths are dynamic and historically contingent, changing over time. Like Austen's works, these myths can claim greatness. A great myth is one with a powerful impact on how we read and re-read. In this volume, we examine 30 of the greatest, most compelling myths that have shaped our readings of Austen. In examining these myths, we are not embarking on a mission of dedicated myth-busting; nor we do set out to correct these myths as misreadings – though we fully acknowledge the wonderfully wild and often wacky world that Austen-mythmaking can be. Rather, in the spirit of inhabiting and celebrating these worlds of mythmaking, we explore the social, emotional, and imaginative lives of these myths and the readerly transactions they enable. (And we acknowledge that some of these myths are generated by Austen's writings themselves.) We seek to illuminate these myths as vital forms of engagement with the life, work, and reception of Jane Austen. In the process, we attempt to introduce readers to the dynamic history of Austen reception both within academic scholarship and in the opinions of the general public, across two centuries, including the period well before academic literary criticism as such existed. Indeed, it becomes apparent that Austen was formative in the development of literary criticism as a discipline. Along the way, we apply the most up-to-date scholarship to understand how myths continue to shape our appreciation of Jane Austen.

In this volume, we take 30 of what we regard as the most powerful myths about Austen and explore them as ways of illuminating Austen's work and the histories of her reception – evaluating their reach, significance, and stakes, and assessing the gains and losses they have brought. Most often these myths take the form of declarative statements, such as: "There is no sex in Jane Austen" or "Jane Austen was a star-crossed lover." At other times, however, the myths we discuss occupy a deeper level of the collective imagination and are not always fleshed out. In our discussion of "Regency Austen," for example, we explore not simply how Austen has been considered a novelist belonging to the Regency period but rather how she has in some sense been made equivalent to the Regency Period. In an exploration which ranges over the areas of Jane Austen's life and letters, her historical contexts, the texts, and their afterlives, Jane Austen's novels are central to our discussion. A separate essay is devoted to each of the six main novels, as well as the juvenilia (considered as a separate body of work). This is not an exhaustive representation of Austen's oeuvre. But it does treat the texts about which there has been heavy mythmaking. The posthumously published *Sanditon* and *The Watsons* are not the subject of separate essays, because they are perhaps not yet the subject of avid mythmaking. But this will surely change. One myth about Jane Austen that virtually everyone has had a hand in perpetuating is the story about the elegant minimalism of her oeuvre – six little gems. But counterintuitively, perhaps, it is a sign of the vastness of that oeuvre that there are still – miraculously – texts that are relatively unexplored and not yet associated with powerful myths, but which, as interest and fascination develops, will surely command the great Austenian myths of the future.

Myth

1

JANE AUSTEN HAD NO INTEREST IN FAME

This myth was hatched by Jane Austen's brother, Henry Austen, in the "Biographical Notice of the Author" that appeared with *Northanger Abbey* and *Persuasion* when they were posthumously published in 1818: "Neither the hope of fame nor profit mixed with her early motives."[1] According to this myth, Austen took up novel-writing in secret, merely as a leisure pursuit; she had no intention of publishing, but her brothers found the manuscripts and brought them to life as published works, with little involvement or investment from Austen herself.

The trouble with this account of Austen's "motives" is that it assumes she was not interested in being a professional writer. But this is problematic. To be sure, Jane Austen's name did not appear on the title-pages of any of the lifetime editions of her novels; and it was not until Henry's obituary notice appeared that Austen's novels were attributed to her in print. But her letters make it clear that being a published author – not just a writer – was important to her.

How and why did the myth come about? The mythmaking can be understood partly as the Austen family's attempt to deal with the increasing public interest in Austen and her writing that developed after her death. Cultured but religiously orthodox and occupying the fringes of the gentry, the family managed Austen's growing reputation by ensuring she would be remembered as a model of modest and devout femininity. According to the traditional view, "proper" women did not put themselves out in public for money, and the elite were traditionally ambivalent about writing for money as a form of lowering oneself to "trade."

This is not to deny that large numbers of women took up writing for money in this period. They did. But when they did so, they had to contend with traditional understandings of proper femininity as incompatible

30 Great Myths About Jane Austen, First Edition. Claudia L. Johnson and Clara Tuite.
© 2020 John Wiley & Sons, Inc. Published 2020 by John Wiley & Sons, Inc.

with publicity and therefore of fame almost as a form of social impropriety. Despite these social obstacles, the early nineteenth century witnessed an explosion of women's writing. Austen was among a vast number of women at this time who were challenging these traditional understandings by publishing their writing. But her family was ambivalent.

We should also consider the motivations of Henry Austen himself. Having been declared bankrupt in 1816, he probably sought some measure of recognition as the enterprising agent who conducted his sister's business dealings. So, paradoxically, his declaration of modesty on Jane's part was a likely claim for vindication, vying for attention himself. Although Henry portrayed himself as Austen's enterprising agent, who was assumed to have done most of the negotiations on her behalf, Austen met with her first publisher, Thomas Egerton, about a second edition of *Mansfield Park*; and in her later negotiations with James Stanier Clarke and John Murray, she acted as an increasingly confident literary professional.[2]

In addition to these familial considerations, fame itself must be understood as a complex and changing social form. Jane Austen was writing at a time when fame was undergoing immense change as a result of the emergence of celebrity culture. The market necessitated new strategies for managing fame recognition and the enhanced aura of the author, who had become a newly intriguing and spectacular figure. During the Romantic period, the literary institution transitioned from a patronage system (where authors were known to their readers) into a fully fledged market system (where authors' work was produced for an anonymous public). Paradoxically, the Romantic myth of the author as an inspired creator oblivious of financial interest coincided with the very moment when the author emerged both as the producer of a commodity and as a commodity herself.[3]

The emergence of the institution of literary property and the Romantic conception of authorship entailed new strategies of immortality, and new ways of managing fame. The practice of anonymity was one of these. Austen's first published novel, *Sense and Sensibility* (1811), was signed with that mystical pseudonym of female authorship – "BY A LADY" – which is also a declaration of anonymity. This paradox – where the signature that blazons anonymity also confers authorship – suggests that the authorial anonym can be regarded as an initiation into public authorship as well as a retreat from it. Accordingly, fame, anonymity, publicity, and secrecy can be viewed as different points along a continuum, thereby complicating and nuancing an absolute distinction between fame and anonymity.

Far from repudiating fame, the practice of anonymity is a form of managing it: not authorial erasure, but an empowering authorial strategy. As Catherine Gallagher argues, anonymous signatures should not be mistaken for real women: they are not ignored, silenced, erased, or anonymous women. Instead, they are literal nobodies: authorial personae, printed books, scandalous allegories, intellectual property rights, literary reputations, incomes, debts, and fictional characters. They are the exchangeable tokens of modern authorship that allowed increasing numbers of women writers to thrive as the eighteenth century wore on.[4]

Where is Austen located among these changing forms of fame? She relied on a range of measures to conceal her identity as an author, preferring it to be known only within her family. But she was proud of her developing oeuvre and took steps to link her novels to one another. Kathryn Sutherland notes that "each new novel invok[es] the assistance of its predecessors. Such assistance is strictly inconsistent with absolute anonymity; on the contrary, her title-pages map a knowable fictional space or estate: 'MANSFIELD PARK: A NOVEL. ... BY THE AUTHOR OF "SENSE AND SENSIBILITY," AND "PRIDE AND PREJUDICE."'"[5]

For Gérard Genette, the phrase "by a lady" is "a statement of identity precisely between two anonymities, explicitly putting at the service of a new book the success of a previous one and, above all, managing to constitute an authorial entity without having recourse to any name, authentic or fictive."[6] Austen's wish to maintain a degree of anonymity, and the fact that "in public she turned away from any allusion to the character of an authoress,"[7] does not make her any less professional about her writing or any less interested in seeking an appreciative audience for it.[8] Rather, it was simply that the particular "character of an authoress" Austen chose was that of the anonymous authoress.

Austen's desire to be a published writer – to take that extra step and turn her writing into a book to be sold and read – is evident in the efforts she took to be published and in her frustration over failed attempts. A striking example of both occurs in her "Advertisement, By the Authoress" to *Northanger Abbey*, which informs the reader about the circumstances of the novel's delayed publication, expressing a distinct irritation:

> This little work was finished in the year 1803, and intended for immediate publication. It was disposed of to a bookseller, it was even advertised, and why the business proceeded no farther, the author has never been able to learn. That any bookseller should think it worth while to purchase what he did not think it worth while to publish seems extraordinary. But with this, neither the author nor the public have any other concern than as some observation is necessary upon those parts of the work which thirteen years have made comparatively obsolete. The public are entreated to bear in mind that thirteen years have passed since it was finished, many more since it was begun, and that during that period, places, manners, books, and opinions have undergone considerable changes. (*NA*, 1)

Unloading her incredulity in this withering critique of the "bookseller" (Crosby & Co.) who purchased the original manuscript, Austen's appeal to the reader also functions – intriguingly – to mediate her transition from obscurity to fame.

Northanger Abbey was Austen's earliest drafted novel, yet by the time Austen wrote this preface and the novel made its belated entrance into the public domain, "the author" had already achieved no small measure of fame with three well-regarded novels, hence Austen's anxiousness over the delay which threatened the novel with instant obsolescence. That Austen would not live to see her first-written novel in print, and that it would appear posthumously with her last-completed novel (*Persuasion*), adds a further layer of irony to her eloquent outrage. In another untimely twist, the voice of the author so irked by the prospect of the novel's coming too late, and being changed beyond recognition from its "period," arrives as the voice of the author beyond the grave (all too soon). Prefacing the two novels in the first edition of the book itself is the "Biographical Notice of the Author" written by Henry – the text that publicly identifies "Jane Austen" as the author of her novels for the very first time.

If Austen spurned the more public forms of fame, she nevertheless *managed* her fame and recognition, like any other author. Just as "she turned away from any allusion to the character of an authoress," Austen also famously declined the opportunity to meet the famous French writer Germaine de Staël, who modeled a very different version of the "character of an authoress," courting public fame (*la gloire*) as though it were a duty: "demanding, in the name of the populace counting on your brilliance, the keenest attention to your own ideas."[9] Staël's wildly popular *Corinne, or Italy* (1807) was an autobiographical *roman à clef* that celebrated the new exalted Romantic fame in the figure of an *improvisatrice* applauded by her adoring crowds: "*Vive Corinne!*," "*vive le génie, vive la beauté.*"

Parodically channeling such love of *la gloire*, Austen joked to her sister Cassandra in early 1796, "I write only for Fame, and without any view to pecuniary Emolument,"[10] her pointed distinction between fame (a high-minded, honorable form of social recognition) and money (a dirty form of mere trade) parodying the rhetorically inflated conception of fame that Staël would later articulate. This letter was written before any of Austen's (or Staël's) novels were published, but at a time when *le génie* of the young Jane Austen was definitely out of its bottle and finding its groove, working on the early drafts of her mature novels and having already crafted splendid parodies of sensibility. *Love and Freindship* (c. 1792), for example, whose heroine Laura has a "sensibility too tremblingly alive to every affliction of my Friends, my Acquaintance and particularly … my own" (*J*, 104), dissected the conventions of earlier epistolary novels like Goethe's *The Sorrows of Young Werther* (1774) that were still being reproduced in later novels such as Staël's *Delphine* (1802).

Staël and Austen shared a publisher, John Murray, as well as his editor, William Gifford, who wrote of Staël, the daughter of Jacques Necker, France's Minister of Finance, and Suzanne Curchot (Madame Necker), the celebrated salon hostess: "The family of Oedipus is not more haunted and goaded by the Furies than the Neckers, father, mother, and daughter, have always been by the demon of publication. Madame de Staël will therefore write and print without intermission."[11] Like father like daughter, perhaps, but it seems a ceaseless *mésalliance* with "the demon of publication" was far more menacing in the female of the species. Austen was clearly much less demanding of her publisher and editor.

The task of managing the social entailments of fame – being known as an author (or "authoress") – was especially complex for women writers. Austen was keen to preserve a certain amount of anonymity but was not implacably opposed to people knowing once the secret got out.

Henry gave the game away after *Pride and Prejudice* was published. Henry asked her if she would like to meet a Miss Burdett, and Austen called his bluff: "I should like to see Miss Burdett very well, but … I am rather frightened by hearing that she wishes to be introduced to *me*. If I *am* a wild Beast, I cannot help it."[12] Evidence suggests that Austen not only resigned herself to having her identity known but also enjoyed the open secret and took pleasure in the speculation that was a consequence of her novels coming into the world under the cloak of anonymity.

Bearing witness to this enjoyment are Austen's reports of growing interest in her novels among friends and acquaintances, none of whom knew for sure that she had authored them. In a letter warning Cassandra that some of their neighbors might already know, she is both alarmed and excited at the prospect: "you must be prepared for the Neighbourhood being perhaps already informed of there being such a Work in the World, & in the Chawton World!"[13]

In a letter to her brother Frank, who was in the navy, Austen acknowledges that she has flirted with exposure by naming the ships in *Mansfield Park* after his ships:

> I was previously aware of what I shd be laying myself open to – but the truth is that the Secret has spread so far as to be scarcely the Shadow of a secret now – & that I believe whenever the 3ᵈ appears, I shall not even attempt to tell Lies about it. – I shall rather try to make all the Money than

all the Mystery I can of it. – People shall pay for their Knowledge if I can make them. – Henry heard P. & P. warmly praised in Scotland ... & what does he do in the warmth of his Brotherly vanity & Love, but immediately tell them who wrote it! – A Thing once set going in that way – one knows how it spreads! – and he, dear Creature, has set it going so much more than once.[14]

Once the dear creature had set her going, the wild beast clearly took pleasure in the recognition her novels were starting to receive, which would spread far wider than the Chawton world.

Notes

1 Henry Austen, "Biographical notice," in J.E. Austen-Leigh, *A Memoir of Jane Austen and Other Family Recollections*, ed. Kathryn Sutherland (Oxford: Oxford University Press, 2008), p. 140. This notice is expanded in the 1833 Richard Bentley edition of *Sense and Sensibility*.

2 See Kathryn Sutherland, "Jane Austen's dealings with John Murray and his firm," *Review of English Studies*, 64(263), (February 2013), pp. 105–126.

3 See Raymond Williams, "The romantic artist," *Culture and Society, 1780–1950* (London: The Hogarth Press, 1991).

4 Catherine Gallagher, *Nobody's Story: The Vanishing Acts of Women Writers in the Marketplace 1670–1820* (Berkeley, CA: University of California Press, 1995), p. xiii.

5 Kathryn Sutherland, *Jane Austen's Textual Lives: From Aeschylus to Bollywood* (Oxford: Oxford University Press, 2005), p. 232.

6 Gérard Genette, *Paratexts*, trans. Jane E Lewin (Cambridge: Cambridge University Press, 1997), p. 45.

7 Henry Austen, "Biographical notice," p. 140.

8 See Jan Fergus, "The professional woman writer," *The Cambridge Companion to Jane Austen*, ed. Edward Copeland and Juliet McMaster (Cambridge: Cambridge University Press, 1997), p. 12.

9 Staël, "On the love of glory," *Major Writings of Germaine de Staël*, trans. Vivian Folkenflik (New York: Columbia University Press, 1987), p. 157.

10 Jane Austen to Cassandra Austen, 14–15 January 1796, *Jane Austen's Letters*, ed. Deirdre Le Faye, third edition (Oxford: Oxford University Press, 1995), p. 3.

11 Quoted in Samuel Smiles, *A Publisher and his Friends*, 2 vols. (London: John Murray, 1911), I: 314.

12 Jane Austen to Cassandra Austen, 20 May 1813, *Letters*, p. 212.

13 Jane Austen to Cassandra Austen, 4 February 1813, *Letters*, p. 203.

14 Jane Austen to Francis Austen, 23 September 1813, *Letters*, p. 231.

Myth 2

THERE IS NO SEX IN JANE AUSTEN'S NOVELS

Virginia Woolf's famous quip – there are "25 elderly gentlemen living in the neighborhood of London who resent any slight upon [Jane Austen's] genius as if it were an insult offered to the chastity of their aunts" – says as much about Austen's stature as a genius in twentieth-century England as it does about a decided fixation upon her chastity.[1] The first step towards pondering this myth is acknowledging how much the reading public wants to believe it, because it is so patently counterfactual. Consider the frequency of pregnancy in the novels. Mr. Palmer in *Sense and Sensibility* despises his wife and cringes at her conversation and her motiveless laughter, yet she is pregnant with his child throughout much of *Sense and Sensibility* and the progress of her pregnancy has a lot to do with the comings and goings of Elinor and Marianne. In *Pride and Prejudice*, Mr. Collins is one of several gentlemen "in want of a wife," and after his marriage to Charlotte Lucas, and in due time (Austen is exceptionally accurate in the management of calendars), he announces that they are expecting a "young olive-branch" (*PP*, 403). In the first chapter of *Mansfield Park*, we learn that Mrs. Price is encumbered with an alcoholic husband and a "superfluity of children" (*MP*, 5) and the grand total of 10 children ties her with Mrs. Morland in *Northanger Abbey*. *Emma* narrates many stories concurrent with the heroine's, and one of these follows the life of Miss Taylor, who in the first chapter becomes Mrs. Weston and in the 53rd her "friends were all made happy by her safety" (*E*, 503) after she gives birth to a daughter, making the progress of her pregnancy one of the basic timelines developed by the novel.

30 Great Myths About Jane Austen, First Edition. Claudia L. Johnson and Clara Tuite.
© 2020 John Wiley & Sons, Inc. Published 2020 by John Wiley & Sons, Inc.

Manifestly, characters in Austen's novels have sex. So the myth that there is no sex in Jane Austen cannot pertain to sex *per se*. Nor can it really be about sex scenes, even though readers such as Lionel Stevenson have scoured the novels for kisses, only to discover that of the 16 mentioned, none occurs between lovers. Bodice ripping might be a staple of *contemporary* Regency fiction, but it is not featured in fiction written during the Regency period, Austen's included. Perhaps this myth pertains instead to something more like *sexiness*, to Austen's apparent refusal or inability to give a lot of narrative attention to characters in the throes of heterosexual passion. The *locus classicus* of this view is a letter Charlotte Brontë sent George Henry Lewes, who admired Austen greatly. Brontë complained that *Pride and Prejudice* contained "no glance of a bright vivid physiognomy, no open country, no fresh air, no blue hill, no bonny beck," but only "a commonplace face; a carefully fenced, highly cultivated garden, with neat borders and delicate flowers."[2] Writing about *Emma* two years later, Brontë was more specific about the kind of experience that happens *outside* those carefully regulated boundaries of mannerly behavior: "the Passions are perfectly unknown to her; she rejects even a speaking acquaintance with that stormy Sisterhood; even to the Feelings she vouchsafes no more than an occasional graceful but distant recognition … what throbs fast and full, though hidden, what the blood rushes through, what is the unseen seat of Life and the sentient target of Death – this Miss Austen ignores."[3] For Brontë, there is no yearning, no throbbing, no bodily longing, no *eros* in Austen's novels, and though Brontë and many readers after her find this absence unforgivable, many readers, as we have seen, actually commend the same perceived lack of emotional and physical turbulence and celebrate it as an effect of Austen's propriety.

But is it true? Let's consider the opposition Brontë develops between fenced (in) gardens and the open country, between the bordered and the unbordered. While Brontë assumes that passion that can only happen in their absence, Austen's novels show that a lot of erotic experience happens within the "carefully fenced" borders Brontë scorns. *Pride and Prejudice* is unembarrassed about some basics of physical attraction. Having rambled three miles to Netherfield through muddy lanes in order to visit her sister, Elizabeth Bennet arrives with her face flushed from exertion, Darcy feels "admiration of the brilliancy which exercise had given to her complexion" (*PP*, 36). Elizabeth seems noticeably to possess the "bright vivid physiognomy" Brontë is looking for, and Darcy finds Elizabeth's bodily vigor attractive. Further, well before Colin Firth/Darcy bared his extra-textual derrière in the BBC adaptation of *Pride and Prejudice* (1995), readers knew that the relation between

Darcy and Elizabeth was hot, and hot not despite the strongly felt presence of social rules but in no small part because of them. The early dialogues between them are striking, even thrilling, because they are marked by a welter of very strong emotions – resentment, pride, resistance, as well as attraction – that stay within the bounds of politeness, even as they also push against them. Suddenly asked to dance a reel by the very man who had pointedly and publicly disdained her, Elizabeth pauses before replying:

> "You wanted me, I know, to say 'Yes,' that you might have the pleasure of despising my taste; but I always delight in overthrowing those kinds of schemes, and cheating a person of their premeditated contempt. I have therefore made up my mind to tell you that I do not want to dance a reel at all – and now despise me if you dare."
>
> "Indeed I do not dare." (*PP*, 56)

Elizabeth's capacity to overcome her momentary confusion, to transform her resentment into wittily controlled banter, makes her provocation ("if you dare") more rather than less attractive, as Darcy gallantly submits ("Indeed I do not dare"), realizing that he is "bewitched" by her and in a state of "danger" as a result. The sexiness of such banter is intensified by the "limitations" imposed by polite converse. To be sure, the exchanges between Elizabeth and Darcy grow less polite, more intimate, and their composure less assured – they argue, they taunt, they insult each other, they expose each other's faults, pain, and weakness, and often while alone – but the pair never lose their status as the sort of lady and gentleman Brontë found so insipid. One would have to be willfully unimaginative – or insensate – not to recognize such exchanges as passionate, even vehement.

It seems wrongheaded, then, to debate whether there is or is not passion in Austen's novels. What is worth debating instead is whether or not Austen's novels valorize the containment over the release of that passion. As we have seen, *Pride and Prejudice* gives containment and self-command their erotic due, but other novels stage the debate far less conclusively. Although critics once upon a time argued that *Sense and Sensibility* sided emphatically with Elinor's polite reticence against Marianne's affective extravagance, readers now agree that Marianne's expansiveness makes her uniquely attractive in a world dominated by shallow, venal worldlings, and conversely, despite all her strenuous efforts of self-control, Elinor finds herself as desperately and as hopelessly in love with a man who is just as weak, though not so dishonorable, as Willoughby. When Anne Elliot in *Persuasion* finds herself preferring open dispositions to calculating ones, she is reprising the debates of Austen's earlier novel, and sharing that novel's impatience with the commonplace notions of propriety.

Whatever Brontë found, Austen's novels give a lot of attention to passion out of bounds, to the illicit. Take, for example, the two Elizas in *Sense and Sensibility*, whose characters and experiences are closely linked to Marianne. Brandon loves Marianne, as it happens, because she resembles the first Eliza, an orphaned heiress whom his father (her guardian) first locks up and then forcibly marries to his eldest son and heir in order to replenish the family wealth – and all this despite the passionate love Brandon and Eliza have for each other. Helpless, alone (Brandon decamped to the East Indies), and anchored to a vicious and possibly perverse husband – Brandon reports with tantalizing terseness that his brother "had no regard for her; his pleasures were not what they ought to have been") – Eliza "falls." She is seduced into adultery, divorced, cast off without enough money to live on, and left to spiral downward into poverty, vice, illness, and death. And this is only the beginning! Eliza has an illegitimate daughter, also named Eliza, who at the age of 17 finds herself, like Marianne (likewise 17, without a fortune and without male protection), seduced by the charming and feckless Willoughby, who then abandons her when he recollects that he really needs to marry a rich wife, only almost literally to stumble upon Marianne instead. And there's more. This Eliza, in turn, is pregnant with Willoughby's child and gives birth – want to bet that her child's name is Eliza? – and at novel's end we assume that mother and child are being supported by Brandon and his new wife, Marianne. Folded not very inconspicuously into the very fabric of *Sense and Sensibility*, then, we find a luridly sensationalistic mini-novel – with all the heightened passion, excess, and high drama one could want – that visibly impinges on the main plot. One might argue that all this passionate excess merely goes to recommend the superior merits of self-control over passion. But it's hard to make this argument stick, given that this narrative material assails the coldness and mercenariness of the ruling class and treasures the fervor it exploits and crushes.

Illicit passion also features prominently in *Pride and Prejudice*, though here it is accorded less dignity. Lydia Bennet is noisy, unmodulated, and coarse, and her "high animal spirits" – a vigorous bodily, libidinal energy – brook no control, no discipline. Granted that chasing after handsome men bespeaks an unregulated interest in sex, Lydia's bodily raucousness does not deserve the prestige Brontë associates with the term "passion," and it is likely that Lydia values Wickham as much for the status value of his red coat as for the attractions of his (unclothed) body.

And Wickham himself is a smarmy social animal whose principal interest is money. Sexual transgressors here, in other words, are not heroes whose ennobling passion places them above a shallow world's laws, but are banal subjects of that world at its most shallow. Mary Bennet proves her silliness when she takes her sister's disgrace as an occasion to set forth a "useful lesson," e.g. that "loss of virtue in a female is irretrievable – that one false step involves her in endless ruin – that her reputation is no less brittle than it is beautiful, – and that she cannot be too much guarded in her behaviour towards the undeserving of the other sex" (*PP*, 319). But in addition to being callow, Mary is simply wrong. The "spiteful old ladies in Meryton" (*PP*, 342) notwithstanding, the world actually does accept Lydia after Darcy intervenes and bribes Wickham into marrying her, and Lydia is pleased to note that marriage now entitles her to the benefits of precedence over her sisters.

Sexual transgression is carried to new levels in *Mansfield Park*. In this novel, the ordinary limits that constrain sexuality – call them lovers' vows – are extraordinarily permeable. Among the most obvious of these is the limit imposed by being betrothed. Maria Bertram metaphorizes this when she finds herself in the wilderness at Sotherton, fenced in and longing to step out:

> "I cannot get out, as the starling said." As she spoke, and it was with expression, she walked to the gate; [Henry Crawford] followed her. "Mr. Rushworth is so long fetching this key!"

> "And for the world you would not get out without the key and without Mr. Rushworth's authority and protection, or I think you might with little difficulty pass round the edge of the gate, here, with my assistance; I think it might be done, if you really wished to be more at large, and could allow yourself to think it not prohibited."

> "Prohibited! nonsense! I certainly can get out that way, and I will." (*MP*, 116)

As Henry Crawford realizes, Maria is speaking figuratively, for what Maria really wants is to break free from her engagement to the miserably dull but fabulously rich Mr. Rushworth. Henry is ready to help Maria over those prohibitive, restrictive fences here and near the end of the novel when they represent not merely engagement vows but marital vows. Adultery brings this novel to crisis, much as elopement had in *Pride and Prejudice*.

But other "fences" to sexual passion are resisted in this novel as well. In the first chapter, Sir Thomas worries that taking his penniless niece under his roof would encourage his sons to fall in love with her.

But Mrs. Norris instantly counters that the incest taboo would forestall any such attachment:

> "of all things upon earth, *that* is the least likely to happen, brought up as they would be, always together like brothers and sisters? It is morally impossible ... breed her up with them from this time, and suppose her even to have the beauty of an angel, and she will never be more to either than a sister." (*MP*, 7)

For a while at least, Mrs. Norris's confidence in the repressive force of the incest taboo is well founded: Tom and Edmund Bertram are not even a little attracted to Fanny. But on Fanny's side the prohibition has no discernible force. There are many reasons why the passion she bears for Edmund – and it is a passion, for she blanches and blushes, seethes, struggles, and trembles in its grip, alone and misunderstood – is a love that cannot speak its name: he is infinitely above herself, and decidedly in love with someone else, for starters. But she never seems to think that being raised as his sister places him off limits. On the contrary, fraternal and erotic love here are on a continuum together rather than fenced off from each other. Henry Crawford falls for Fanny, with whom he had only been casually flirting, when he witnesses the exquisite somatic pleasure she takes in William's company: he "saw ... the glow of Fanny's cheek, the brightness of her eye, the deep interest, the absorbed attention. The sensibility which beautified her complexion and illumined her countenance" (*MP*, 274), and he decides to transfer those fine feelings from the brother to himself. Crawford cannot do so because Fanny's affection is already fully engaged by Edmund, her other "brother" of sorts. One of the most troubling ironies of this novel is that Fanny's describes the culminating crime of adultery –

> both families connected as they were by tie upon tie; all friends, all intimate together! It was too horrible a confusion of guilt, too gross a complication of evil, for human nature, not in a state of utter barbarism, to be capable of! (*MP*, 511)

with the intense abhorrence one might expect from the violation of the incest taboo when it is, if nothing else, purely exogamous. By contrast, after the scandal breaks, Edmund embraces Fanny with the words "My Fanny – my only sister" (*MP*, 514).[4]

Given the rich prominence of passion inside and outside social restraints in Jane Austen's novels, given the sympathy her novels can adduce for heroines who permit themselves to nurse erotic feelings on which society frowns – heroines like Jane Fairfax, Elinor Dashwood, or Fanny herself – we might well ask: is this myth plain wrong? Is there anything it can tell us about Jane Austen that is true? Yes. Some readers have found her chilly because they want her to foreground or privilege the privacies of the dyadic relationship, when Austen is actually far more interested in dramatizing the social effects and implications of erotic desire. Austen's novels explore how characters understand, misunderstand, or manage their passionate feelings with respect to a wide range of other attachments and obligations that also make large and legitimate claims upon their desires. Should Anne Elliot disoblige her father and her friend by accepting the man she (also) loves? Should Fanny accept Henry Crawford out of gratitude to Sir Thomas and solicitude for her impecunious Portsmouth family? What does Marianne owe to social relationships outside her love for Willoughby? And so on. Once we reach the conclusion of her novels, such questions have been thoroughly examined, if not always conclusively, and the remaining business of getting the principals together for a proposal scene seems relatively perfunctory. While cinematic versions of Austen's novels work to produce climactic proposal scenes and to fill those scenes out with dialogue, blushes, and batted eyelids nowhere to be found in the novels themselves, Austen has little interest in intruding upon dyadic privacies, and her proposal scenes quickly segue from direct representation to reportage or to ellipses. What, the narrator asks, does Emma say when Knightley proposes? "Just what she ought, of course. A lady always does" (*E*, 470).

Notes

1 Virginia Woolf, *New Republic* (30 January 1924), https://newrepublic.com/article/115922/virginia-woolf-jane-austen, accessed 14 November 2019.
2 Letter of 12 January 1848 to George Lewes, printed in *Jane Austen: The Critical Heritage*, vol. 1, ed. B.C. Southam (London: Routledge & Kegan Paul: 1968), p. 126.
3 Ibid, p. 128.
4 For an excellent counterweight to my argument here about incestuous resonances, see Talia Schaffer, *Romance's Rival* (Oxford: Oxford University Press, 2016).

Myth 3

JANE AUSTEN WROTE ON LITTLE BITS OF IVORY

This is one of those rare myths about Jane Austen that Jane Austen herself seems not only to have originated but also to have insisted upon, repeatedly. The *locus classicus* of this myth is Austen's letter to her 18-year-old nephew, James Edward, who was at the time trying to write an ambitious historical novel. When two chapters of his manuscript evidently went missing, Austen assured him that she had not purloined them:

> What should I do with your strong, manly, spirited Sketches, full of Variety & Glow? – How could I join them on to the little bit (two Inches wide) of Ivory on which I work with so fine a Brush, as produces little effect after much labour.[1]

These lines are a regular feature in scholarship on Austen as well as in popular discussions of her among informed Janeites and among the general public. What Austen actually meant by them, however, is up for grabs. Did she actually admire his work? Had she sincerely compared it favorably to her own? Was she encouraging him? Was she flattering him? Was she mocking herself? Was she being so exquisitely ironic at his expense that he would not be able to detect that she was mocking him? Was she in some way concealing her greatness from herself?

One possible clue to her opinion about her nephew's grand, glowing, manly style may be found in Austen's responses to James Stanier Clarke, Librarian to the Prince Regent, who had urged Austen to write a novel not in the style of *Emma* (which Austen had just dedicated to the Prince Regent at his suggestion) but rather in the style of a historical romance: "any historical romance, illustrative of the history of the august House of

30 Great Myths About Jane Austen, First Edition. Claudia L. Johnson and Clara Tuite.
© 2020 John Wiley & Sons, Inc. Published 2020 by John Wiley & Sons, Inc.

Cobourg," he suggested fatuously, would be welcome, and she could then dedicate the novel to Prince Leopold. Austen famously demurred, saying that that she "could not sit seriously down to write a serious romance" without relaxing "into laughter at myself or other people," and accordingly be hanged before finishing the first chapter.

> No, I must keep to my own style & go on in my own Way; And though I may never succeed again in that, I am convinced that I should totally fail in any other.[2]

Though unequivocal, this reply still falls within the bounds of modesty. Privately, however, in her *Plan of a Novel* (1816), Austen ridicules grandiose novel-writing without reserve: the perfectly virtuous heroine and her father are chased away from their perfectly cozy village by perfectly villainous aristocrats and would-be ravishers, forced to move from one place to another to avoid capture by their relentless persecutors, until, "continually cheated & defrauded, worn down to a skeleton, & now & then starved to death," they are hunted out of "civilised Society," and finally retreat into Kamschatka, where the heroine's father expires "after 4 or 5 hours of tender advice and parental Admonition to his miserable Child." Inconsolable, she "crawls back towards her former Country – having at least 20 narrow escapes from falling into the hands of the Anti-hero," and after literally running into her hero "they are happily united" forever after (*LM*, 228–229). This material may not tell us exactly what Austen thought of her nephew's evidently short-lived aspirations to become a novelist, but it does tell us what Austen thought about novels to which her little bit of ivory was opposed. Novels on the grand scale, clearly, are not so much beyond her reach as beneath it.

In this sense, then, Austen's artistic commitment to composing on "a little bit (two Inches wide) of Ivory" is no myth at all. She is indeed, if not exactly a miniaturist, then at least a practitioner of the small-scale. And the scale refers to several qualities. To number – "3 or 4 Families in a Country village is the very thing to work on," Austen advised her niece Anna,[3] and this was advice she generally followed, keeping the number of her characters to a handful. Scale also refers to place. Those 3 or 4 families are in a "Country village" such as Highbury, but are well within bounds of each other's company even if they find themselves in Bath, Lyme Regis, or even London – in pointed contrast to *Plan of a Novel*, where the principals move again and again from place to place until they end up in Kamschatka. And scale refers to the register of emotions she frames.

Extraordinary incidents, high-blown sentiments, and exotic places have no room on two inches of ivory. In her self-imposed circumscription, it bears emphasizing, Austen parts company with virtually all of her contemporaries. Walter Scott self-deprecatingly compared his "Big Bow-wow strain"[4] to Austen's delicacy, but bow-wows are not gendered. Maria Edgeworth and Fanny Burney, whose novels Austen admired, were entirely at home in the great metropolis, and their novels are teeming with scenes from high life, and with dramatically charged incidents stretched over a wide canvas, while Mary Brunton's *Self-Control* (1811) features a heroine who is kidnapped deep into the wilderness of America and who escapes her tormenter by means of taking a canoe down the rapids of a river. Clearly, Austen deliberately decrescendos and delimits, and in doing so her achievement was, for her time, highly original. Early reviewers agree that Austen's novels are striking and wonderful precisely because they are in some sense scaled down.

Then why consider this little bit of ivory business a myth at all? Because the issue of scale very quickly morphs into what Donald Greene memorably called the "myth of limitation," *tout court*, "the one steady landmark in the swirling waters of Jane Austen criticism."[5] On the basis of their scale, Austen's novels were soon regarded in terms of everything they (supposedly) did or could not include. Dorothy Van Ghent described this "limitation" to a tee: Austen's novels are "limited to the manners of a small section of English country gentry who apparently have never been worried about death or sex, hunger or war, guilt or God," and our Table of Contents testifies to the durability of the myth Van Ghent embraced so uncritically.[6] In saying so, Van Ghent was merely restating the common refrain about Austen's exclusion of dramatic events. During the Victorian period, admirers and detractors often agreed about these mythic limitations, the former finding them charming and serene, and the latter finding them boring and uninspiring. It was not until the historical scholarship of the late 1960s and 1970s, particularly the pathbreaking work of Avrom Fleishman, Alistair Duckworth, and Marilyn Butler, that the large questions raised by social, political, and religious issues circulating in the novels became not only fully visible but now absolutely glaring![7]

As celebrated (or scorned) for her few inches of ivory as Austen has been, there has always been a minority countertradition that never considered Austen small-scale in the first place, some readers who have insisted not merely on Austen's greatness in some general sense but on her actual *grandeur*. Like Reginald Farrer, Caroline Spurgeon, also writing in the aftermath of World War I, celebrates Austen's sublime vastness. Austen's books, Spurgeon writes, are full of "the magic casements of fiction, its vistas [opening] on infinity." Note well that she doesn't say "views." She says *vistas*. *Vistas* afford limitlessly expansive views, and underscoring this, Spurgeon has them looking out onto *infinity* itself.[8] Not for Spurgeon those narrow boundaries – "two inches wide." And D.A. Miller's latter-day notion of Jane Austen's divinity posits a daunting, loftily rarefied Austen, one who creates a mundane world that has no place for her in it and who then proceeds, through the intimidating, formidable workings of her style, to surmount that world with the magnificence of a god.[9] Clearly, scale and import bear no necessary relation, and the small-seeming world of Austen has been sufficient to provide infinite astonishment to her readers. As the Earl of Iddesleigh, writing at the outset of the twentieth century, observed, for Austenians, we're the limited, delimited ones, narrow ones; we're the ones who are blinkered, while Austen is sublimity itself. "Ordinary life," as he put it, "was seen by [Austen] not dimly and partially as we see it but in all its actual vastness, and it was in this huge field that she worked with such supreme success. If the 'little bit of ivory' were only 'two inches wide,' those inches were not of mortal measure."[10]

Notes

1 Jane Austen to James Edward Austen, 16–17 December 1816, *Jane Austen's Letters*, ed. Deirdre Le Faye, third edition (Oxford: Oxford University Press, 1995), p. 323.

2 Jane Austen to James Stanier Park, 1 April 1816, *Letters*, p. 312.

3 Jane Austen to Anna Austen, 9–18 September 1814, *Letters*, p. 275.

4 From a journal entry of 14 March 1826, reprinted in *Jane Austen: The Critical Heritage*, vol. 1, ed. B.C. Southam (London: Routledge & Kegan Paul: 1968), p. 106.

5 Donald Green, "Jane Austen and the myth of limitation," in *Jane Austen Today*, ed. Joel Weinsheimer (Athens, GA: University of Georgia Press, 1975), p. 142.

6 Dorothy Van Ghent, *The English Novel: Form and Function* (New York: Harper & Row, 1961), p. 103.

7 See Marilyn Butler, *Jane Austen and the War of Ideas* (Oxford: Oxford University Press, 1975, rev. 1988); Alistair Duckworth, *The Improvement of the Estate* (Baltimore: Johns Hopkins University Press, 1971); Avrom Fleishman, *A Reading of Mansfield Park: An Essay in Critical Synthesis* (Minneapolis: University of Minnesota Press, 1967).

8 Caroline Spurgeon, "Jane Austen," in *Essays by Divers Hands: Being the Transactions of the Royal Society of Literature in United Kingdom* (London: Oxford University Press, 1927), p. 81.

9 D.A. Miller, *Jane Austen, or The Secret of Style* (Princeton, NJ: Princeton University Press, 2005).

10 Walter Stafford, 2nd Earl of Iddesleigh, "A chat about Jane Austen's novels," *Nineteenth Century*, 47 (1900), p. 820.

Myth 4

JANE AUSTEN'S JUVENILIA ARE SCRAPS WHICH SHE OUTGREW

The persistence of this myth is puzzling because everyone who cares for Austen's fiction desperately wishes there was more of it. Writers and directors, having produced film and TV versions of the novels over the past 30 years, have resorted to simply inventing more when faced with the apparent dearth of Austenian texts. *Becoming Jane*, *Lost in Austen*, *Death Comes to Pemberley*, *Miss Austen Regrets*, even *Pride and Prejudice and Zombies* feed the cravings of a public in search of another, a new Austen fix.

As Whit Stillman's exceptional 2016 adaptation of *Lady Susan* and the 2019 TV adaptation of *Sanditon* prove, there is more *real* Jane Austen to be read and enjoyed, lots more, if readers turned to Austen's youthful productions, which remain largely unknown to a general public despite the availability of wonderful scholarly and classroom editions. Referred to collectively as the "juvenilia" since some of them appeared for the first time in 1922 in an edition prefaced by G.K. Chesterton, these 27 pieces – described variously as novels, tales, odes, plays, scraps, some unfinished – were written from 1787 to 1793, when Austen was between the ages of 11 and 18 years old. Austen herself transcribed these pieces into three stationer's notebooks, entitling them *Volume the First*, *Volume the Second*, and *Volume the Third*, each complete with page numbers and tables of contents.

Volume the First
Frederic and Elfrida
Jack and Alice
Edgar and Emma
Henry and Eliza

30 Great Myths About Jane Austen, First Edition. Claudia L. Johnson and Clara Tuite.
© 2020 John Wiley & Sons, Inc. Published 2020 by John Wiley & Sons, Inc.

The adventures of Mr Harley
Sir William Mountague
Memoirs of Mr Clifford
The beautifull Cassandra
Amelia Webster
The Visit
The Mystery
The Three Sisters
To Miss Jane Anna Elizabeth Austen
A fragment – written to inculcate the practice of Virtue
A beautiful description of the different effects of Sensibility on different
    Minds
The Generous Curate
Ode to Pity

Volume the Second
Love and Freindship
Lesley Castle
The History of England
A Collection of Letters
To Miss Fanny Catherine Austen
The female philosopher
The first Act of a Comedy
A Letter from a Young Lady
A Tour through Wales
A Tale

Volume the Third
Evelyn
Catharine, or the Bower

That Austen esteemed these pieces is proven by the very existence of these volumes themselves, presented to us as if together they might constitute a magnum opus, a triple-decker novel, in the manner, say, of *Pride and Prejudice* or *Emma*. That she continued to value and to return to these works once she grew up is proven by the fact that she made occasional emendations in the first two decades of the nineteenth century, and even let a niece and nephew try their hands at finishing some as late as 1814–1816. And that these volumes continued to be valued as a family legacy is proven by the fact that Austen's sister Cassandra, the keeper of Austen's literary effects, treasured them after Austen's death and, upon her own, willed one volume each to her brothers and her nephew.[1]

Late-nineteenth- and early-twentieth-century Austenians emphatically did not share Austen's attachment to her youthful performances. James Edward Austen-Leigh's *Memoir of Jane Austen* (1869/1870) presented his dear aunt Jane as a prim, disembodied, and unpretending writer of realist novels from a quieter, gentler time. He describes juvenile Austen's work as "preliminary process"[2] – immature practice pieces, in short. In his second edition of his *Memoir* (1871), Austen-Leigh gives us a bit more information about Austen's early pieces, gallantly averring that they are of a "slight and flimsy texture" and therefore should not be "exposed" to the world, concluding that "the family have rightly, I think, declined to let these early works be published."[3] R.W. Chapman, who would eventually collect these pieces under the damning title *Minor Works*, also wistfully apologizes for the publication of *Volume the Second* in 1922, calling it an "act of espionage or exhumation." To be sure, the juvenilia were never vetted by Jane Austen for outright publication, but nor are they really drafts, perhaps unwisely rescued from the trash heap or fireplace or, worse, the grave.[4]

These paragons of sobriety must have been a bit scandalized – or at the very least nonplussed – by Austen's youthful works, which are hilariously rife with crime, vice, and outrages of every conceivable sort. In a "Scrap" from *Volume the Second*, for example, patricide is only the first among the "Errors" committed by "Young Lady, whose feelings [are] too Strong for her Judgement":

> I murdered my father at a very early period of my Life, I have since murdered my Mother, and I am now going to murder my Sister. I have changed my religion so often that at present I have not an idea of any left. I have been a perjured witness in every public tryal for these past twelve Years, and I have forged my own Will. In short, there is scarcely a crime that I have not committed (*J*, 222).

But the best part of this inventory of vice is the brilliantly fatuous deadpan with which it concludes: "But I am now going to reform" (*J*, 222). From homicide we turn to suicide in *Frederic and Elfrida*, where the sweet-tempered Charlotte, "whose character was an earnest desire to oblige every one" (*J*, 6), amiably accepts two successive proposals of marriage, and is so shocked to recollect her "double engagement" (*J*, 9) the next morning that she throws herself into a stream and floats Ophelia-like back to her village, "where she was picked up and buried" (*J*, 9) by her friends. In *Henry and Eliza*, cannibalism makes a cameo appearance, when the heroine, having escaped a dungeon with her two children, "began to find herself rather hungry, and had reason to think by their biting off two of her fingers, that her Children were in much the same situation" (*J*, 43). Alcoholism reigns supreme in *Jack and Alice*, the principals are often passing the bottle, arguing noisily and carried home, "Dead Drunk" (*J*, 16). And sex? In *Edgar and Emma*, Mrs. Wilmot tallies no fewer than 20 children, not counting "all the rest" (*J*, 36), who are at home; in *Sir William Montague: An Unfinished Performance*, the hero, in the course of five short paragraphs, falls in love with seven women (in addition to committing murder), and the sketch is "unfinished" only because his amorous impulses cannot be contained; and in *The History of England* the 15-year-old Austen tosses off the following bawdy "Sharade" on the word "carpet," about James I's homosexual attachment to Sir Robert Carr, his "pet": "My first is what my second was to King James the 1st, and you may tread on my whole" (*J*, 187).

As these snippets show, the young Jane Austen is jauntily irreverent. The keepers of "dear Aunt Jane's" flame seemed determined not to notice or to acknowledge this. But admirers underplayed it as well. Although G.K. Chesterton readily granted that Austen was "the very reverse of a starched or a starved spinster," he could not resist finally enlisting her into the cause of orthodoxy, celebrating with equal firmness her opposition to the French Revolution and her contentment with the "narrow domestic routine" of her life.[5] And even Virginia Woolf, who rightly identifies the distinct and penetrating sound of Austen's laughter, ultimately declares that laughter to be in the service of good sense: "Her fool is a fool, her snob is a snob, because he departs from the model of sanity and sense which she has in mind."[6]

But Austen's juvenilia are not normative and not normativizing. When the penniless but highfalutin hero of *Love and Freindship* nobly declares himself superior to the base need for food and drink – "And did you then never feel the pleasing Pangs of Love, Augusta? (replied my Edward). Does it appear impossible to your vile and corrupted Palate, to exist on Love?" (*J*, 111) – Austen isn't so much critiquing the excesses of sensibility as she is inciting them in the interests of producing more and more laughter. Later in this novella, when Edward dies in a coach accident, his grief-stricken wife runs mad with hallucinations that show her to be more than a little peckish: "Look at that grove of Firs – I see a Leg of Mutton – They told me Edward was not Dead; but they deceived me – they took him for a cucumber –" (*J*, 130). Sensibility in *Love and Freindship* – like all of the other forms of excess depicted in the juvenilia – is the engine of Austen's laughter, not the object of it.

Nowhere is the young Austen's indifference to moralizing more apparent than in *The Beautifull Cassandra*, written when she was 12. Weighing in at 465 occasionally misspelled words, its 12 chapters, each consisting of only one or two sentences, constitute a complete novel narrating the undaunted and slightly criminal adventures of the titular character who confounds all our expectations. The first person she meets, we're told in Chapter 3, "was the Viscount of —, a young man, no less celebrated for his Accomplishments and Virtues, than for his Elegance and Beauty." But nothing comes of this encounter – "She curtseyed & walked on" (*J*, 54) – because what really interests her is the ice cream we learn about in the next chapter:

CHAPTER THE 4th

SHE then proceeded to a Pastry-cook's, where she devoured six ices, refused to pay for them, knocked down the Pastry Cook & walked away. (*J*, 54)

By far Austen's unruliest heroine, the beautiful Cassandra flounces around London with unimpeded energy from one brief encounter to another, eating way too much ice cream (without paying), taking cab rides (without paying), encountering a handsome young lady (without speaking), and all to return home seven hours later to her mother's embrace, smiling with whispered satisfaction: "This is a day well-spent!" (*J*, 56). This is a "novel" that celebrates vitality, not good sense. And there is arguably more unalloyed pleasure, more real jouissance at its conclusion than there is in all of Austen's mature novels put together.

But finally it isn't the raciness or the boisterousness of the juvenilia that is most impressive. On the contrary, they are funny in part because of their breezy, unaccented matter-of-factness. What makes the juvenilia so fabulous and so enduring is their stylistic mastery, something Woolf was clearly referring to when she praised the "rhythm, shapeliness, and severity" of her sentences. The smallest units of signification – word choices, sentence structure – are tools which the young Austen brandishes in the interests of interrogation and critique. Sometimes she disrupts convention by going low with funny sounds – using place names like Pammydiddle or Crankhumdunberry – and sometimes by going high with diction, like using the phrase "gracefully purloined" instead of "filched" or merely "stole." As other times she uses parallel structure as to interrogate corrupt social equivalencies: "In Lady Williams every virtue met. She was a widow with a handsome Jointure & the remains of a very handsome face" (*J*, 14). This balanced placid-seeming but quite subversive sentence uses the term handsome in different senses to draw attention to what counts for "virtue" in the world – fortune (jointure) and good looks (face). Its exposure of shallow worldliness is intensified further by the word "remains," implying not only that Lady Williams's beauty has faded but also that she as an older woman is in some sense already dead, having no personal value apart from that jointure.

In the juvenilia, we can see the extent of Austen's indebtedness to eighteenth-century parody. Like Pope's *The Rape of the Lock*, which is a mock epic, or Swift's *Modest Proposal*, which mocks the rhetoric of political economy, Austen's juvenilia proceed from and in turn create a dazzling formal self-consciousness, a self-consciousness at once playful and deep. They ponder and expose the function, the hidden agendas, of fictional conventions and ritualized or formulaic language by strategically defamiliarizing it. In Austen's hands, literary discourse – genre, style, devices, plot structures, stock figures, diction, sentence structure itself – are exposed and interrogated. Consider, for example, what we expect from an opening sentence, like this one from *Frederic and Elfrida*:

> The Uncle of Elfrida was the Father of Frederick; in other words, they were first cousins by the Father's side. (*J*, 14)

Most opening sentences draw the reader in. Here Austen pulls off a stunning little reversal, producing with remarkable economy a marvelous brain twister that almost sublimely stymies any reader's attempt to determine who these characters are and what are their precise relations. Her practice here and throughout is to make itself subject to doubt as well as an agent of doubt, to invite re-examination, re-reading. In parodying what first sentences do, in short, she is making you less likely to read hers or anyone else's uncritically.

Sometimes Austen's formal parody explores the deeper valences of conventions, as in the following excerpt from *Jack and Alice*:

> A few days after their reconciliation Lady Williams called on Miss Johnson to propose a walk in a Citron Grove which led from her Ladyship's pigsty to Charles Adams's Horsepond. (*J*, 20)

Walking through the citron grove, we are for a moment not in the actual England (where citrus trees do not grow), but in the idealized world of pastoral serenity where elegant ladies might stroll arm in arm. Austen's sentence unfolds a series of codes that again seem straightforward, only to depart abruptly from expectations we didn't even suspect we were nursing by forcing into view what pastoral convention conceal: pigsties, horse ponds, the inelegant actualness of working farms. At times, the formal critique implicit in parody inevitably verges even farther onto ideological critique, as in the following excerpt from the beginning of *Henry and Eliza*:

> As Sir George and Lady Harcourt were superintending the Labours of their Haymakers, rewarding the industry of some by smiles of approbation, and punishing the idleness of others, by a cudgel, they perceived lying closely concealed beneath the thick foliage of a Haycock, a beautifull little Girl not more than 3 months old. (*J*, 38)

Again, Austen's parody begins by imitating its prototype so closely that we amble through the sentence quite contentedly. Who are Sir George and Lady Harcourt? George is the patron saint of England and the name of several generations of English kings. And the name Harcourt is archetypical in English lore: Harcourts are not just any stock characters. They are England's gentry Everyman-and-wife – venerable, figures in a national mythology, figures who had already been idealized in novels by the likes of Richardson and Fielding, and in plays of the period before Austen was born. And of course Sir George and his lady superintend their laborers: that's what they're supposed to do. But when we learn that they reward industry with *smiles of approbation* and punish idleness with a *cudgel*, something shocking starts to happen. We probably expected laggards to be punished with *stern glances* or *firm admonition*, but instead we are invited to imagine Sir George and his lady clubbing their tenants. Who would dare imagine Darcy or Knightley or Mr. Bennet doing this? Austen's abrupt deviance from conventional expectations thus teaches us something about relations which those conventions customarily exclude. Austen remembers this in *Mansfield Park*, when she tells us about Sir Thomas's plantation in Antigua, the structural equivalent of the pigsty and the cudgel here.

Austen's juvenilia are, then, laboratories in which the young author is gleefully exploring and mastering literary style, and though her large-scale parodies – like *Love and Freindship* – usually get the lion's share of our attention, she is just as interested in exploring smaller manipulations of style, such as this understatement from *Jack and Alice*: "Miss Simpson was pleasing in her person, in her Manners, & in her Disposition; an unbounded ambition was her only fault" (*J*, 14). At 14, Austen is already a master of prose triplet, and this sentence lulls us so comfortably that many readers actually miss the stunner in the second clause, which entirely reverses the placid vacuity of the first: a woman whose "only" fault is boundless ambition has quite a fault indeed, one which impinges on the manners and disposition initially affirmed! The delayed bombshell of understatement would remain one of Austen's favorite effects: as in "Only a novel" from *Northanger Abbey*, or Sir Thomas's more darkly inane thinking – or more precisely, not thinking – about Henry Crawford as a model fiancé: "He wished him to be a model of constancy; and fancied the best means of effecting it would be by not trying him too long." Or take, as another example, Austen's mastery of nonsense. "Preserve yourself from a First Love and you need not fear a second" (*J*, 18) from *Jack and Alice* is a perfect example of Austen's playful delight in inanity, but Austen's play with nonsense here certainly develops into the interest in mind-bending claptrap she explores in, say, *Mansfield Park*, when Mrs. Norris (having been told not to "urge" Fanny to act, seems to assent: "'I am not going to urge her,' – replied Mrs. Norris sharply, 'but I shall think her a very obstinate, ungrateful girl, if she does not do what her aunt and cousins wish her – very ungrateful, indeed, considering who and what she is.'" (*MP*, 172).

Reading some of these pieces for the first time, Virginia Woolf realized that even though the juvenilia surely entertained Austen's family circle, they were meant "to outlast the Christmas holidays," that she was even at 11 writing for posterity: "She was writing for everybody, for nobody, for our age, for her own; in other words, even at that early age Jane Austen was writing." In the wisecracking, in the sarcasm, and in the barbs of the youthful writing, there is a stunning audacity, virtuosity and, most of all, authority. The juvenilia are important then not only because they lead to Austen's mature work, though they do, but because so many of them are perfect works in their own right in which Jane Austen realizes and revels in her status, proudly signing herself to several of these pieces: "THE AUTHOR."

Notes

1 For the best account of the history of Austen's youthful writing see Peter Sabor's superlative Introduction to his edition of *Juvenilia* from *The Cambridge Edition of the Works of Jane Austen* (Cambridge: Cambridge University Press, 2006), pp. xiii–lxvii. For other splendid editions of the juvenilia see Margaret A. Doody and Douglas Murray's pathbreaking *Catherine and Other Writings*, and Kathryn Sutherland's facsimile online editions at the British Library.

2 J.E. Austen-Leigh, *A Memoir of Jane Austen and Other Family Recollections*, ed. Kathryn Sutherland (Oxford: Oxford World's Classics, 2002), p. 43.

3 Ibid, pp. 40 & 43. The one exception is Austen's hilarious but innocuous "The mystery," which Austen-Leigh included in this second edition.

4 *Times Literary Supplement* (15 June 1922), unsigned.

5 G.K. Chesterton, ed., *Love & Freindship and Other Early Works* (New York: Frederic A. Stokes Co., 1922), pp. xv, xvi.

6 Virginia Woolf, "Jane Austen at sixty," *The Nation* (15 December 1923), p. 433. This is a review of Chesterton's edition of *Love and Freindship*, and it is reproduced in *The Common Reader*, First Series. Subsequent citations to Woolf are drawn from this review.

Myth 5

JANE AUSTEN'S NOVELS ARE NATURALISTIC

That young lady had a talent for describing the involvement and feelings and characters of ordinary life which is to me the most wonderful I have met with.

(Walter Scott, journal entry, March 1826)

Jane Austen's novels are consecrated as miracles of nature, or rather miracles of the aesthetic consecration of nature – by which we mean that they are "true to nature," or naturalistic; lifelike; probable; embodying the principle of verisimilitude, aka "the appearance of being true or real."[1] All these terms can be understood through the broader rubric of realism, of which naturalism is just one form. Whether we call a work naturalistic or realistic, we are referring to an aesthetic style, a mode of representation, not nature or reality itself. The naturalistic artwork is a representation, which can never be the same as what it represents. And just as the naturalistic must be distinguished from nature itself, so should realism be considered an effect of the real, not "the real" itself. From this perspective, some would argue that Austen's "naturalistic" novels are more appropriately regarded as stylistic constructions. It is a matter of degree.

The story of Austen's canonization traces the gradual recognition and re-evaluation of the ordinary and the mundane as the supremely stylish. It is the unfolding of an enigma that was there from the beginning, articulated in embryonic terms in the earliest reviews, by Walter Scott and Richard Whately, who celebrated the "exquisite touch" and stylistic "compactness" with which Austen endows her representations of nature.[2]

Walter Scott's March 1816 unsigned review of *Emma* in the *Quarterly Review* (written in October 1815) is significant not only as the first important public review of Austen's work but also as the first to identify Austen's novels within a specific "class of fictions" – the style that came to be known as realism. For Scott, Austen's novel *Emma* is not just another book to review, but an event, an occasion for formulating a new kind of fiction "which has arisen in our own times, and which draws the characters and incidents introduced more immediately from the current of ordinary life than was permitted by the former rules of the novel."[3] Scott's reference to "rules" reminds us of how recently the novel had constituted itself as a genre and differentiated itself from romance. Within these "former rules," deriving from romance, "the novelist professed to give an imitation of nature, but it was, as the French say, *la belle nature*," an idealized vision of nature.[4] The new form of naturalism that Austen pioneers is about the commonplace, the ordinary, and the mundane. It takes its cues from real life and aims at being life-*like*. This is not just the real life and nature of the outside world but a highly particular inside world; part of an artistic program that can "proclaim a knowledge of the human heart" as it traces "the paths of common life."[5] Austen occupies a central place, then, in Scott's history of the genre.

Scott was the first to recognize Austen's fiction as pioneering a new style, which he claimed "reminds us something of the merits of the Flemish school of painting."[6] This school, which flourished from the early fifteenth to the seventeenth centuries, was associated with landscape and portrait genres, excelling in miniatures. Epitomizing the new style across both genres was Jan van Eyck's work, where according to a twentieth-century commentator, "the exquisite finish and minute attention to detail" confer "a quality of static, almost timeless monumentality" and where the "dispassionate recording of textures and the unified impression of unemphatic actuality achieve a perfection of realistic painting which was never surpassed."[7] Such paintings seem to embody what Franco Moretti called "the older, more vivid opposition between the everyday and the sacred;" in the early nineteenth century, this was superseded by a "semantic field of everydayness" that tended toward "a more colourless realm of the 'habitual', 'ordinary', 'repeatable'."[8] Something of that refined and spare monumentality has always been Austen's, poised as she is on the cusp of that drift to the "colourless" associated with later, less aestheticized, grittier forms of nineteenth-century realism.

At the other extreme is the hyper-aestheticized, decadent proliferation of detail associated with continental European realism. Austen's realism is not about this; hers never risks what Naomi Schor refers to as "the pathology of the detail,"[9] which conflicts with the laws of verisimilitude.

Indeed, as R.W. Chapman noted in 1922, Austen "knows all of the details, and gives us very few of them."[10]

All these later forms of nineteenth-century realism intersect with the form of naturalism exemplified by the French novelist Émile Zola, who emphasized the documentary and scientific resources of the novel form and its capacity for scientific representation. His works emphasized biology and heredity as primary influences upon human life and society, focussing on the so-called struggle for survival and identifying the human subject with "natural" or biological impulses. There are intriguing links between Austen and this late-nineteenth-century naturalism. In *Jane Austen's Novels* (1883), George Pellew explicitly links Austen with Zola, arguing that she "anticipated the scientific precision that the spirit of the age is now demanding in literature and art;" similarly, Arnold Bennett refers to *Mansfield Park* as "a fine novel" with "one or two pages of Zola's ... realism in it."[11]

Austen's Flemishness was a different kind of European style, in which the "subjects are not often elegant, and certainly never grand; but they are finished up to nature, and with a precision which delights the reader."[12] In a journal entry, Scott compared his own work (unfavorably) to Austen's: "the exquisite touch which renders ordinary commonplace things and characters interesting from the truth of the description and the sentiment is denied to me."[13]

But this very naturalism is itself an enigma. This distinction between the thing itself and the form of representation is central to the charm and paradox of Austenian realism. While the term "natural" awards praise, it also raises questions: how is it that the presentation of the natural should be an art? This tension becomes a source of evaluative intrigue that has informed Austen's reception from the nineteenth century.

Richard Whately's simple formula in his 1821 review, in a section of the *Quarterly Review* entitled "Modern Novels,"[14] neatly embodies this paradox when it praises Austen's fictions for "the art of copying from nature as she really exists in the common walks of life."[15] In this important review, Whately adopts Scott's Flemish figure as part of a detailed analysis of Austen's fiction in the landscape of earlier and contemporary fiction. This includes, among other things, a comparative account of Austen and Maria Edgeworth, on both religious and formal grounds. Whately, who was the Archbishop of Dublin, praises Austen's fiction for its religion (we sense it is there in her fiction – whereas in Edgeworth's fiction it is nowhere to be seen) and for the discretion with which the religion is made to reside in the novels. For Whately, "certainly no author has ever conformed more closely to real life, as well in the incidents, as in the characters and descriptions. Her fables appear to us to be, in their own way, nearly faultless;" he singles out "the minute fidelity of detail" and the "probability of incident" to "give fiction the perfect appearance of reality," thereby aligning Austen with "her great mistress, Nature" and, riffing on Scott's figure of the "human heart," recommending her work to anyone who delights in "the study of human nature."[16] The art of the probable is a key component of Austenian realism: Whately's review elaborates the art and nature paradox by noting that Austen's novels "have all that compactness of plan and unity of action which is generally produced by a sacrifice of probability: yet they have little or nothing that is not probable."[17]

In 1813, Annabella Milbanke, the future Lady Byron, wrote to her mother praising *Pride and Prejudice* as "a very superior work" without "any of the common resources of novel writers, no drownings, no conflagrations, nor runaway horses, nor lap-dogs and parrots, nor chambermaids and milliners, nor rencontres and disguises." Paradoxically, "common resources" are precisely those elements of the improbable used by traditional novels to create interest and excitement. Milbanke enthuses about Austen's novel: "I really think it is the *most probable* I have ever read."[18] Here, as elsewhere among Austen's nineteenth-century readers, in this routine and ritualistic invocation of the probable, we sense a relief at Austen's departure from those "former rules of the novel" that worked against the probable and natural in the service of an idealized fantasy of nature.

Whately piquantly conveys the emotional element of novel-reading – and a sense of the probable as one of its key pleasures – when he refers to "those sundry little violations of probability which are to be met with in most novels; and which so far lower their value, as models of real life,"[19] and which are clearly the obstacle to an experience of complete literary pleasure. It is as though it was only when Austen appeared that one could even recognize what literary pleasure might be and how these "sundry little violations" interfered with that pleasure. Austen's novels were invented it seems in order to absolve the genre of its tendency toward these "sundry little violations" – to brush them away like the memory of something unpleasant that had been tolerated as a matter of course but is now all happily in the past, washed away by Austen's clarity and finesse.

In his comparative analysis with Edgeworth, Whately emphasizes the crucial alliance between the natural and the probable in Austen's fiction: "for there is a distinction to be made between the *unnatural* and the merely *improbable*."[20] Edgeworth, like many other novelists, may have cracked one (the natural) but not the other (the probable). Both are necessary for perfect fiction. Catherine Gallagher argues that "earlier fictions could be distinguished from lies if they were manifestly improbable. Honest fictions, that is, were expected to distinguish *themselves* by their incredulity."[21] But this is not so with the new kind of realist fiction that emerges in the nineteenth century.

The terms of the canonical discourse around Austen's "naturalistic" fictions are familiar. Even so, precisely because of its very familiarity – that formula of transfiguring the real that Austen's novels have come to apotheosize – we tend not to ask the obvious question: why is it that "ordinary commonplace things and characters" might be in need of an "exquisite touch" to be interesting? Scott's revelatory frisson of excitement is clearly generated by the exotic conjunction of the ordinary and the wonderful, an effect of the commonplace suddenly made intriguing. But what else is going on here? Implicit but disavowed in these acts of praise is the assumption that the ordinary needs to be "worked," that some element of the real needs to be eliminated through a make-over of nature. The praise and pleasure are implicated in acts of exclusion, repudiation, and, even, disgust. The much later school of realism and naturalism took this seamy side of life head on.

Scott's 1815 review marks how new it was to consider the "common" as an appropriate subject of artistic representation at that time. It seems old habits of reading and viewing die hard. Part of the appeal of Joe Wright's 2005 cinematic adaptation of *Pride and Prejudice*, which transports Austen away from the "aristocratic" setting of previous versions (think of the 1940 version with Greer Garson and Laurence Olivier) to a more historically correct lower gentry milieu, is that it restores something of the "common" element of the original social milieu. As the director noted in an interview, "I like messiness. I think messy is beautiful;" of Lizzie Bennet, he said: "She's got her feet in the mud, and she's reaching for the stars."[22] The "common" was perilously close to the vulgar for much of the nineteenth century – meanings that Austen consciously plays with. As Claudia L. Johnson notes, "Elizabeth's wit is occasionally marked by an unabashed rusticity bordering on the vulgar."[23] *Mansfield Park*'s narrator refers to Fanny's "little rusticities" offending her sophisticated cousins at the big house. For Henry James, as a "painter of life," this applied to the artform of the novel itself, for "it is only by positively becoming exquisite that [art] keeps clear of becoming vulgar."[24]

Art and vulgarity, style and nature. Writing about *Pride and Prejudice*, G.H. Lewes put the paradox this way: "Take it to pieces, … and you will find that … all this ease of nature, which looks so like the ordinary life of everyday, is subordinate to principles of Economy and Selection."[25] This makes Austen sound like a practitioner of intelligent design. Written in 1860, Lewes's judgment mixes a Darwinian vocabulary of natural selection with a language of artistry and "artistic sense." Nevertheless, it helps illuminate the evolution of the theory and practice of artistic "omniscience," which concerns the question of authorial intention and design and is integral to the tension between art and nature. D.A. Miller calls the bluff of Austen's naturalism by calling up her intention: "The first secret of Austen Style [is that] its author hates style, or at any rate, must always say she does; she must always profess the values, and uphold the norms, of 'nature,' even as she practices the most extraordinarily formal art the novel had yet known."[26] The question of whether Austen herself was conscious of such intelligent design is the subject of our next myth.

Notes

1 Pam Morris, *Realism* (London: Routledge, 2003), p. 5.
2 Walter Scott, in *Jane Austen:* Emma: *A Casebook*, ed. David Lodge, revised edition (Macmillan, 1991), p. 41; Richard Whately, *Quarterly Review*, xxiv (1821), quoted in *Jane Austen: The Critical Heritage*, ed. B.C. Southam, vol 1. (London: Routledge & Kegan Paul, 1968), p. 95.
3 Scott, unsigned review in *Quarterly Review*, p. xiv (1816) in Southam, *Critical Heritage*, p. 59. An anonymous review that appeared soon after in the *Gentleman's Magazine* (September 1816) similarly places the novel in "the very highest class of modern Novels" (*Critical Heritage*, p. 72).
4 Scott, in Southam, *Critical Heritage*, p. 61.
5 Ibid, pp. 59, 64.
6 Scott, in Lodge, Emma: *A Casebook*, p. 41.
7 *The Oxford Companion to Art*, ed. Harold Osborne (Oxford: Oxford University Press, 1987), pp. 410, 411.
8 Franco Moretti, *The Bourgeois: Between History and Literature* (London: Verso, 2013), fn 4, p. 71.
9 Naomi Schor, "Details and decadence: End-troping in *Madame Bovary*," *Sub-Stance* 26 (1980), p. 27. On how excessive detail conflicts with verisimilitude or "aesthetic plausibility," see Schor's *Reading in Detail: Aesthetics and the Feminine* (New York: Methuen, 1987), p. 85.
10 R.W. Chapman, "Austen's methods," *Times Literary Supplement* (9 February 1922), p. 82.
11 George Pellew, quoted in *Jane Austen: The Critical Heritage 1870–1940*, vol. 2, ed. B.C. Southam (London: Routledge & Kegan Paul, 1987). p. 177; Bennett quoted by Southam in *Critical Heritage*, vol. 2, p. 115.
12 Scott, in Southam, *Critical Heritage*, vol. 1, p. 67.
13 Ibid, p. 106.
14 Whately, *Quarterly Review*, p. xxiv, quoted in Southam, *Critical Heritage*, vol. 1, p. 88.
15 Ibid, p. 88.

16 Ibid, pp. 95, 96, 96, 102, 105.

17 Ibid, p. 95.

18 Quoted in B.C. Southam, *Jane Austen:* Sense and Sensibility, Pride and Prejudice and Mansfield Park: *A Casebook* (Penguin, 1987), p. 153.

19 Whately, in Southam, *Critical Heritage*, vol. 1, p. 88.

20 Ibid, p. 89.

21 Catherine Gallagher, "Fictionality," *The Novel*, ed. Franco Moretti (Princeton, NJ: Princeton University Press, 2006), p. 338.

22 https://www.indiewire.com/2005/11/tackling-a-classic-joe-wright-on-pride-and-prejudice-77678/, accessed 16 May 2019.

23 Claudia L. Johnson, *Jane Austen: Women, Politics, and the Novel* (Chicago: Chicago University Press, 1988), p. 76.

24 Henry James, Preface to *Roderick Hudson*, in *Literary Criticism* (New York: Literary Classics, 1984), p. 1048.

25 Lewes, quoted in Southam, *Critical Heritage*, vol. 1, p. 175.

26 D.A. Miller, *Jane Austen, or The Secret of Style* (Princeton, NJ: Princeton University Press, 2003), p. 26–27.

Myth

6

JANE AUSTEN WAS UNCONSCIOUS OF HER ART

"Design! nonsense, how can you talk so!"
(Jane Austen, *Pride and Prejudice*, 1813)

The key to Jane Austen's fortune with posterity has been in part the extraordinary grace of her facility, in fact of her unconsciousness.
(Henry James, "The Lesson of Balzac," 1905)

An artist can never be fully conscious. But neither can he cut ice if he is not an unremittingly conscious executant.
(Elizabeth Bowen, 1936)

The myth that Jane Austen was unconscious of her art has been extraordinarily persistent and richly entangled with other great myths about Austen. Why is there such an investment in it and how did it come about? This great myth is perhaps best understood in relation to one of Jane Austen's greatest achievements: the turning of mere lifelikeness into novelistic art. Of that achievement, the critic G.H. Lewes wrote in 1847: "[T]ruth in the delineation of life and character [and] deep and lasting interest excited by anything like a correct representation of life … seems to us to be Art, and the only Art we care to applaud."[1] But what kind of art is the merely truthful? The myth of the unconscious Austen seems to pre-empt this question.

The truism that Austen drew perfectly from the society she knew limits a full appreciation of the complexity of her aesthetic practice and commitment to style. "Every thing came finished from her pen," her brother Henry opined in 1818, "for on all subjects she had ideas as clear as her expressions were well chosen."[2] The critic Mrs. Malden concurred, adding her own flourish, "Everything is finished to the highest point of finish."[3]

30 Great Myths About Jane Austen, First Edition. Claudia L. Johnson and Clara Tuite.
© 2020 John Wiley & Sons, Inc. Published 2020 by John Wiley & Sons, Inc.

The implication that Austen did not revise her work ignores the abundant evidence of her extant manuscripts, which show continual editing and revising. It also ignores the work of the editors who prepared her work for publication.[4] And it assumes that Austen did not engage with her literary predecessors and contemporaries. This diminishes Austen's contemporaries and circumscribes our understanding of her works, which were keenly engaged with her precursors and contemporaries throughout her long literary apprenticeship.

Let's start with the question of aesthetic practice. The myth that Jane Austen was unconscious of her art speaks to a tension between art and nature that informs the (somewhat counterintuitive) aesthetic ideal of an art that copies life. If art is "copying" nature, how can it be art? The myth of the unconscious Austen attempts to resolve this question by setting Austen's naturalness against the conception of art associated with writers such as Alexander Pope or Samuel Johnson, who imitated classical models. It aligns Austen's work with nature and without artifice, despite its high degree of "finish." In this sense, the unconscious Austen is implicated in the Romantic myth of the author as being divinely inspired: William Wordsworth's figure of the poet's "spontaneous overflow of powerful feelings;" Samuel Taylor Coleridge's account of Kubla Khan having arrived in a dream; William Blake's self-styling as a visionary bard.[5]

Furthermore, the Romantic prerogative for inspiration belonged to poets, not novelists, who had a harder case to make for the art of their form, and mainly to male poets at that. The poet and novelist Mary Robinson was perhaps the best-known contemporary woman writer to assume the mantle of inspiration; she claimed to have written "The Maniac" after dosing herself with laudanum and to have woken the next morning "unconscious of having been awake while she composed the poem."[6] But Robinson was a poet and the exception that proves the rule, as well as a canny player of celebrity culture in a way that Austen never was. Interestingly, there is never a hint that Austen's presumed "unconsciousness" was divinely inspired, although her nephew speaks about his aunt's writing as "this mystic process."[7]

The idea that Austen was somehow "unconscious" of her art maintains the notion of Romantic inspiration without compromising the key feature of copying from nature. Yet that element of copying also compromises originality and divine inspiration. This contradiction is celebrated in paradoxes about Austen's "art-concealing art," in which "no labour has been spared, and yet nothing is laboured."[8] It is a complex matter, in which gender plays a part. For many later male practitioners of the novel genre – Gustave Flaubert, Honoré de Balzac, and Henry James – lay claim to a Romantic, divinely inspired mode of authorship.

Tellingly, Henry James made his 1905 pronouncement about Austen's "unconsciousness" and its "extraordinary grace" in an essay on the French novelist Honoré de Balzac (both a realist and a Romantic), whose art he hymned as "the mystic process of the crucible, the transformation of the material under aesthetic heat."[9] Gracefulness is an emphatically feminine requirement, aligned with the beautiful and distinguished from masculine sublimity. "To be graceful," Edmund Burke wrote in his *A Philosophical Enquiry into the Origin of Our Ideas of the Sublime and Beautiful* (1757), "it is requisite that there be no appearance of difficulty."[10] This gendering provides an instructive insight into the limitations that hedged female artistry.

For much of the time from the eighteenth century to the mid-nineteenth, it was considered unladylike (and morally compromising) to assume a public platform and write – much less to arrogate the mantle of a divinely inspired celebrant of art. This is why some women writers, such as George Eliot and George Sand, took male pseudonyms. The idea that Austen was "unconscious" of her art falls short of granting her the lofty prerogative of being inspired, but it recognizes a woman writer as an artistic celebrant, without compromising the decorum required of her.

Writing in the 1930s, at the height of the modernist consecration of the novel as an artform, Elizabeth Bowen steers a course for Austen that combines inspiration and consciousness: "An artist can never be fully conscious. But neither can he cut ice if he is not an unremittingly conscious executant."[11]

In a typically tortured attempt to grapple with the figure of the woman artist and the challenge she presented to feminine decorum, Henry James implies that for Austen to be conscious would be somehow graceless. While he knew and socialized with women artists, James never presents them in his fiction. There are women of the house – artistic interior decorators and even collectors – and artist manquées, but never women who actively pursue an artistic vocation: suffering for one's art as a profession or vocation is a purely masculine prerogative. Even George Sand, of whom James is extremely fond and to whom he attributes some capacity for Romantic magic, is merely "a great *familiar* magician," and her "touch," he hastens to add, "never vulgar or vulgarizing."[12]

Where James attributes to Balzac a "mystic process" of "aesthetic … transformation," he imagines Austen as engaging in absent-minded "wool-gathering," but later picking up her "dropped stitches … as little touches of human truth, little glimpses of steady vision, little master-strokes of imagination."[13] According to this sly tableau, Austen's great "fortune with posterity" was to have had a minor art recognized as a great artist's "master-strokes." On this reckoning, Austen's novels nod off on the minor art of mimicking nature, then belatedly pick up the stitches with "little master-strokes of imagination." Austen got lucky twice, in degree and kind, when what was merely a craft became recognized as great art.

This brings us back to the question of art as a form of copying, likeness, correctness, and truthfulness. For here, even appreciative readers such as Lewes and James regard Austen's artfulness as being circumscribed – as though the merely correct is all a female artist can aspire to. This is not the high-Romantic model of the artist struck by bolts of inspiration. In applauding correctness, these critics seem to make a counterintuitive case for an art almost completely lacking in creativity or imagination. But this would be to underestimate the premium placed on the ideal of the everyday and the familiar (see Myth 5); for in this realm too there is scope for magic, as evidenced by the "Victorian tendency to invest Austen's very mundanity with magical quaintness."[14]

The myth of an unconscious Austen is intimately related to the myth of a provincial Austen: sheltered in the countryside, taking her inspiration from nature, writing only about what she saw, and using this, and this only, as her guide. Not venturing out into the public, nor much beyond the villages of Steventon and Chawton, this Jane Austen inhabited Bath very reluctantly (see Myth 8). Much like Shakespeare, she was a sheltered provincial genius, about whom little was known. Though not exactly a village rustic, Austen is in this reading a genteel woman who lived a sheltered life while turning out beautifully polished sentences without much care. This myth has vestiges of the traditional reluctance to associate gentlewomen with labor, commerce, or publicity – all of which are part of being a published author – and as such is invested in traditional preconceptions about Austen's class position as a genteel woman, a woman of the gentry.

The Harvard scholar George Pellew (an acquaintance of Henry James) busted this myth back in 1883, when he wrote:

> [I]t is ... surprising enough, that in the early part of the century, when Gothic tales and romantic poetry formed apparently the chief part of purely literary reading, a young girl living in a remote parsonage should have composed stories of such truth to nature, and such witty discrimination of character, that reputable critics have called her Shakespearian; but it would be truly miraculous, if this work had been done by the unaided force of original genius, without any connection of agreement or disagreement with previous writers, or with contemporary thought.[15]

Nevertheless, most readers would probably argue that Austen's work is still miraculous even if she *was* aware of previous writers and contemporary thought. Virginia Woolf suggests that Austen's art is a combination of hard work *and* the miraculous. In her reading of the unfinished *The*

Watsons as one of "the second-rate works of a great artist [that] offer the best criticism of [her] masterpieces," Woolf speculates about the process of overcoming difficulties, had Austen lived to revise the manuscript: "How it would have been done we cannot say – by what suppressions and insertions and artful devices. But the miracle would have been accomplished."[16]

Far from being a homely songbird, Austen was an acutely attentive stylist who worked long and hard on her writing. The clearest, most eloquent riposte to our myth lies in her unfinished manuscripts, which show Austen in the act of styling and editing her own work. In the nineteenth century, before R.W. Chapman's complete edition of her novels (1923) and the previously unpublished writings (1925–1954), there was no textual evidence for the assumption that Austen did not revise her work; ever since then, the textual evidence of Austen's commitment to revision has mounted, especially in the past two decades, with new developments in textual study and textual editing and important new editions of Austen that show her at work as she revises her writings.[17]

What can the manuscripts tell us about Austen's way of working and her art? Particularly instructive is the case of *Persuasion*, with its rewritten ending and two cancelled chapters. In *Jane Austen's Literary Manuscripts*, B.C. Southam responds directly to Henry James's version of the myth. Of *Persuasion*, he writes:

> We feel the inevitable rightness in her handling of the novel's conclusion; yet this achievement was not, in the act of creation, a swift and effortless performance, but a triumph of rethinking through trial and error. … Apparently James knew nothing of the two [cancelled] chapters; indeed, it provides a signal example of that conscious art which James was always seeking.[18]

In 1939, Mary Lascelles, who revised Chapman's edition of Austen in the 1960s and wrote an important early critical study significantly entitled *Jane Austen and Her Art* (1939), also analyzed Austen as a stylist – and one acutely conscious of her art – in relation to both her MSS revisions and her engagement with her contemporaries.

Lascelles singled out Austen's "discreet use of idiosyncrasy in speech," which she achieved by revising her manuscripts. In *The Watsons*, Lascelles shows Austen substituting "little vulgarisms and colloquialisms for unaffected formal speech – as to indicate the peculiar tone of the speaker."[19] In the revisions to the *Sanditon* MS, Lascelles spots how "a little button of absurdity is fastened on top of Sir Edward's pretentious vocabulary by the substitution of 'anti-puerile' for 'sagacious' in his description of the ideal novel-reader – that is, of himself."[20] (See Figure 1.)

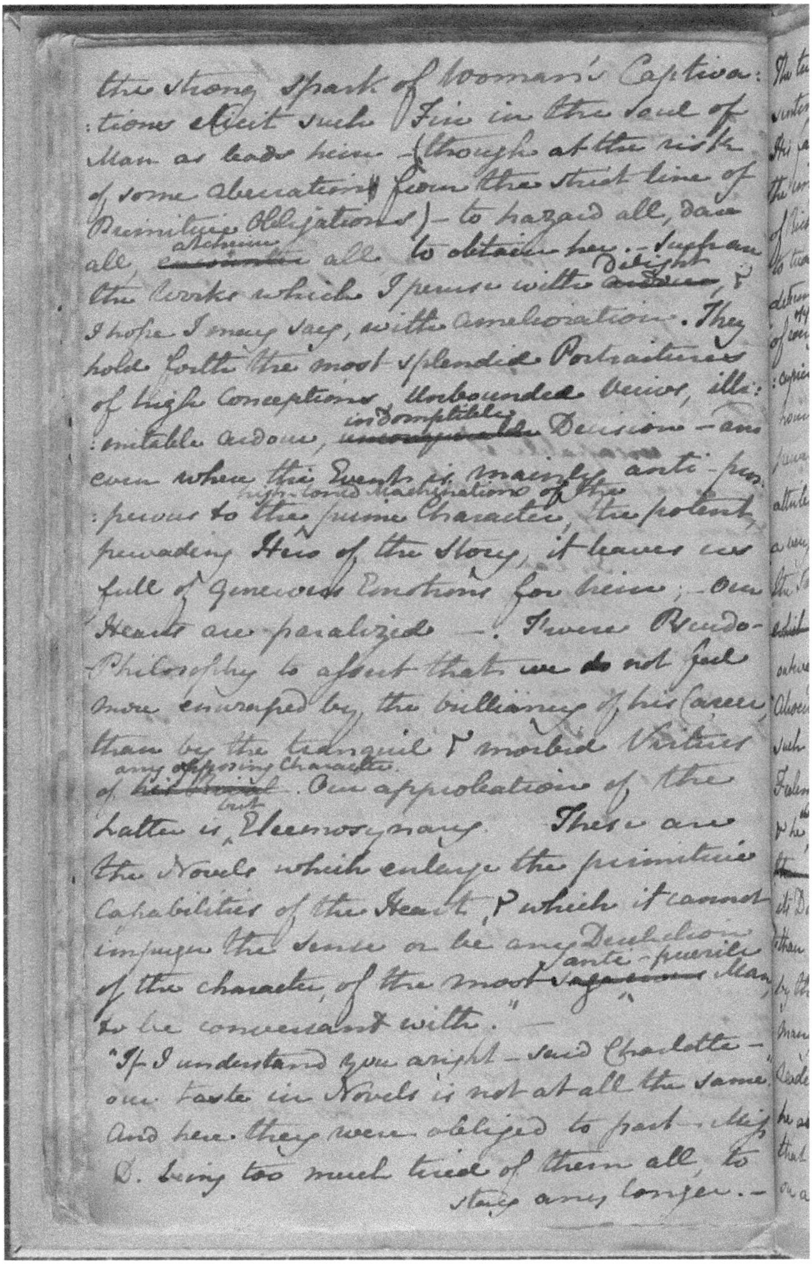
the strong spark of Woman's Captiva:
:tions elicit such Fire in the Soul of
Man as leads him – (though at the risk
of some aberration from the strict line of
Primitive Obligations) – to hazard all, dare
all, attchieve all, to obtain her. – Such are
the Works which I peruse with delight, &
I hope I may say, with amelioration. They
hold forth the most splendid Portraitures
of high Conceptions, Unbounded Views, illi:
:mitable Ardour, indomptible ~~unconquerable~~ Decision – and
even where the Event is mainly anti-pros:
:perous to the high-toned Machinations of the prime Character, the potent,
pervading Hero of the Story, it leaves us
full of Generous Emotions for him; – our
Hearts are paralized –. T'were Pseudo-
Philosophy to assert that we do not feel
more enwrapped by the brilliancy of his Career,
than by the tranquil & morbid Virtues
of any opposing Character. Our approbation of the
Latter is but Eleemosynary. These are
the Novels which enlarge the primitive
Capabilities of the Heart, & which it cannot
impugn the Sense or be any Dereliction
of the character, of the most anti-puerile ~~sagacious~~ Man,
to be conversant with." –
"If I understand you aright – said Charlotte –
our taste in Novels is not at all the same.
And here they were obliged to part – Miss
D. being too much tired of them all, to
stay any longer. –

Figure 1 Austen's *Sanditon* MS, booklet 2, folio 21v. The Library, King's College, Cambridge.

The art of being true to nature is of course not the same thing as mere copying and reproduction. Austen's art is so much more than that. Her consummate skills as an ironist and a satirist mark another dimension of her artistry. We might usefully adopt Linda Hutcheon's theory of parody here: "parody is repetition with critical distance, which marks difference rather than similarity;" and it is "irony's edge" that "gives parody its 'critical' dimension in its marking of difference at the heart of similarity."[21] In Austen's repetition with difference, there is a world of aesthetic transformation. It is always repetition with some kind of magical difference – hence the "exquisite touch" that creates a new form of realism.[22]

This is particularly striking in Austen's mastery of dialogue, which is precisely repetition with a twist. Let's consider this in more detail. In an illuminating discussion of Austen and Frances Burney, who was also known as having a gift for social observation, Lascelles notes the particularity of novelistic dialogue as distinct from the direct narration or first-person narration of journal-letter form, which was Burney's preferred form. Despite her "gift of mimicry," Burney is weaker on dialogue and unable to capture "the fine point of interaction between character and circumstance," when she abandons the first-person narration of *Evelina* (1778) in *Camilla* (1796); Lascelles argues that the diarist's ability as a diarist to "select shrewdly and remember faithfully ... the idiosyncrasies of speech," "may become a snare ... when she turns novelist" and uses third-person form.[23]

Austen's dialogue, on the other hand, has a subtlety that enables her characters to parody one another, as in Emma's "outrageous parody" of poor Miss Bates. Lascelles argues:

> Mannerism, especially when it takes the form of recurrent word or phrase, is by no means easy to represent; there is but a hair's breadth between the point at which the reader delightedly recognizes it as a revealing habit of speech, and the point at which its iteration begins to weary him. But even as Mr Elton's "Exactly so" is ready to catch the attention ... and before it can threaten tediousness, Emma transfixes it by her mimicry beyond the need of repetition.[24]

"Transfixes it by mimicry beyond the need for repetition:" this tells us everything about the aesthetic and ultimately transfiguring powers of Jane Austen's art.

Paradoxically, it is not the known and expected but the "tingling shock of the unexpected which will create the illusion of the living voice."[25] This is Austen's cutting of ice as "an unremittingly conscious executant," enacting the "mystic process of the crucible, the transformation of the material under aesthetic heat."

Notes

1 *Jane Austen: The Critical Heritage*, vol. 1, ed. B.C. Southam (London: Routledge & Kegan Paul, 1968), p. 124.

2 Henry Austen, "Biographical notice" (1818), in J.E. Austen-Leigh, *A Memoir of Jane Austen and Other Family Recollections*, ed. Kathryn Sutherland (Oxford: Oxford University Press, 2008), p. 141.

3 S.F. Malden [Mrs Malden], "Austenolatry," *Eminent Women Series*, 1889 (quoted in *Jane Austen: The Critical Heritage 1870–1940*, vol. 2, ed. B.C. Southam (London: Routledge & Kegan Paul, 1987), p.189).

4 See Kathryn Sutherland, "Jane Austen's dealings with John Murray and his firm," *The Review of English Studies*, 64(263), (2012), pp. 105–126.

5 William Wordsworth, Preface to *Lyrical Ballads* (1800), *The Prose Works of William Wordsworth*, vol. 1, eds. W.J.B. Owen and J.W. Smyser (Penrith, CA: Humanities E-Books, 2009), p. 146.

6 *Mary Robinson: Selected Poems*, ed. Judith Pascoe (Peterborough, Ontario: Broadview, 2000), pp. 122–123.

7 J.E. Austen-Leigh, *A Memoir of Jane Austen and Other Family Recollections*, ed. Kathryn Sutherland (Oxford: Oxford University Press, 2002), p. 82.

8 John Mackinnon Robertson, quoted in Southam, *Critical Heritage*, vol. 2, p. 192.

9 Henry James, "The Lesson of Balzac" (1905), *Literary Criticism: French Writers, Other European Writers, The Prefaces to the New York Edition* (New York: Library of America, 1984), p. 130.

10 Edmund Burke, *A Philosophical Enquiry into the Origin of our Ideas of the Sublime and Beautiful* (1757), ed. Adam Phillips (Oxford: Oxford University Press, 1990), p. 107.

11 Elizabeth Bowen, 1936, in *Jane Austen: Critical Assessments*, ed. Ian Littlewood, vol. 2 (Mountfield: Helm Information, 1998), p. 259.

12 James, review of George Sand, Letters, *Literary Criticism*, p. 737, 735.

13 James, "Lesson of Balzac," p. 118.

14 Claudia L. Johnson, *Jane Austen's Cults and Cultures* (Chicago: Chicago University Press, 2012), p. 91.

15 George Pellew, 1883, quoted in Southam, *Critical Heritage*, vol. 2, p. 177.

16 Virginia Woolf, "Jane Austen," *Collected Essays*, 2 vols, ed. Leonard Woolf (1925; London: Chatto & Windus, 1966), 1: 147.

17 Key events here are the Cambridge University Press edition and Kathryn Sutherland's online editions of Austen's unfinished works and manuscripts. See *Jane Austen's Fiction Manuscripts* at janeausten.ac.uk.

18 B.C. Southam, *Jane Austen's Literary Manuscripts: A study of the novelist's development through the surviving papers* (London: The Athlone Press, 2001), pp. 86–87.

19 Mary Lascelles, *Jane Austen and Her Art* (London: Oxford University Press, 1939), p. 99.

20 Ibid, p. 100.

21 Linda Hutcheon, *A Theory of Parody: The Teachings of Twentieth-Century Art Forms* (New York: Methuen, 1985), p. 6; and *Irony's Edge: The Theory and Politics of Irony* (London: Routledge, 1994), p. 4.
22 "Exquisite touch" is Walter Scott. For more, see Myth 5.
23 Lascelles, *Jane Austen and Her Art*, p. 98, 97, 97.
24 Ibid, pp. 96, 96–97.
25 Ibid, p. 98.

Myth 7

NORTHANGER ABBEY IS A SPOOF ON GOTHIC FICTION

It is certainly true that *Northanger Abbey* spoofs the Gothic novels that were so popular early in Austen's career, so this myth can take us part way toward an understanding of the novel. Composed in 1798–1799, when Gothic fiction was at the height of its popularity, *Northanger Abbey* features many characters who explicitly refer to Gothic classics such as Ann Radcliffe's *Mysteries of Udolpho* (1794) and *The Italian* (1797), and Matthew Lewis's *The Monk* (1796), but Catherine Morland's friend, Isabella Thorpe, gives her of a list of seven equally "horrid" novels: "Castle of Wolfenbach, Clermont, Mysterious Warnings, Necromancer of the Black Forest, Midnight Bell, Orphan of the Rhine, and Horrid Mysteries. Those will last us some time" (*NA*, 33). There was a time when readers assumed that Austen, keen to ridicule the fashionable taste for Gothic fiction, simply made up these evocatively lurid titles. But in the 1920s, novelist and bibliophile Michael Sadleir discovered that these were actual novels, all but one published by Minerva Press, which specialized in publishing Gothic and sentimental novels for and by women. Sadleir's research proved not only the widespread popularity of Gothic fiction but also the depth of Austen's familiarity with it and of her reliance on the audience's familiarity as well. Indeed, by the 1790s, the Gothic novel had become so familiar and its plot material so predictable, that it was often the butt of critical satire. An anonymous letter about "Terrorist Novel Writing" printed in *The Spirit of the Public Journals for 1797* proffers a "Recipe" for a Gothic novel which directs the would-be author to *Take* –

30 Great Myths About Jane Austen, First Edition. Claudia L. Johnson and Clara Tuite.
© 2020 John Wiley & Sons, Inc. Published 2020 by John Wiley & Sons, Inc.

An old castle, half of it ruinous,
A long gallery, with great many doors, some secret ones,
Three murder bodies, quite fresh,
As many skeletons, in chests and presses,
An old woman hanging by the neck; with her throat cut,
Assassins and desperadoes, *quant suff.*
Noises, whispers, and groans, threescore at least.

This list of "ingredients" is to be mixed in the form of "three volumes, [and] to be taken at any of the watering places before going to bed."[1] In some ways the parody here seems similar to some of the spoofing in *Northanger Abbey*. Catherine, for example, can't get her mind off the skeleton of Laurentini in *The Mysteries of Udolpho*. Henry, himself a parodist of sorts, jokingly encourages the gullible Catherine to look for other horrors that a building such as "what one reads about" may produce – such as "peals of thunder" and "frightful gusts of wind"; remote and dimly lit bedchambers walled with "sliding panels and tapestry"; hidden doors "secured by massy bars and a padlock"; ponderous chests and cabinets "which no efforts can open"; heart-stopping excursions through secret subterraneous corridors disclosing the obligatory "dagger … drops of blood … [and] instrument of torture" (*NA*, 161–163), Catherine is being set up to form Gothic expectations that Henry – and Austen – know will be disappointed. Northanger Abbey, far from moldering into a sublime pile, is fully modernized, "improved", and spruce, its pointed windows admitting the reassuring brilliance of sunlight. The bedchamber into which Catherine is ushered is comfy, with no lurid tapestries or moldy velvet drapery in sight. The chest she discovers contains neatly folded hats and bonnets rather than the human remains of murder most foul, and the black cabinet is impossible to pry open only because Catherine herself had locked rather than unlocked it to begin with. Once open, it is discovered to contain not the memoirs of a mysterious sufferer but a laundry list.

But Catherine's misadventures don't stop with these disappointments, which remain private. Cherishing the "hope" – and Austen is winking at us by writing "hope" instead of "fear" – that Northanger Abbey will turn up "some awful memorials of an injured and ill-fated nun" (*NA*, 144–145), Catherine observes the coldness of Henry's father and quickly surmises that he murdered his wife. Henry had already poked fun at Catherine's love of Gothic novels, but when he learns that they are not mere amusements for her, as they are for him, and that she actually takes them seriously as representations of life, his punishment of Catherine is quick and severe:

> "If I understand you rightly, you have formed a surmise of such horror as I have hardly words to—Dear Miss Morland, consider the dreadful nature of the suspicions you have entertained. What have you been judging from? Remember the country and the age in which we live. Remember that we are English, that we are Christians. Consult your own understanding, your own sense of the probable, your own observation of what is passing around you. Does our education prepare us for such atrocities? Do our laws connive at them? Could they be perpetrated without being known, in a country, like this, where social and literary discourse is on such a footing; where every man is surrounded by a neighborhood of voluntary spies, and where roads and newspapers lay every thing open? Dearest, Miss Morland, what ideas have you been admitting?" (*NA*, 203)

In this passage, which is something of a touchstone in readings of *Northanger Abbey*, Henry is stupefied for an instant, unable to utter the "horror" that Gothic novels invite Catherine so easily to believe: that a modern Englishman, a law-abiding Christian living in full view of neighbors could be suspected of killing his wife. According to Henry, Catherine's suspicion is not merely absurd, but culpable, as if "admitting"– allowing herself to entertain – suspicions against the General are tantamount to a treasonous lack of faith in the modern laws and institutions of England itself. And Catherine accepts this chastisement. She runs off "with tears of shame" (*NA*, 203), blaming herself for the extravagance of her Gothicizing imagination: "charming as were all Mrs. Radcliffe's works, and charming even as were the works of all her imitators, it was not in them perhaps that human nature, at least in the midland counties of England, was to be looked for."

So far so good. But the problem with believing *Northanger Abbey* to be a "spoof" is that it assumes the novel has only this single gag: to set Catherine up and watch her fall for one ridiculous Gothic exaggeration after another. But, if *Northanger Abbey* were an anti-Gothic novel, establishing its norms of sanity, moderation, and good sense by invoking, ridiculing, and reversing the excesses of books such as Radcliffe's, then the novel would end here, and it does not. Within three chapters, the General throws Catherine out of his house, because (we later learn) she is discovered not to be as rich as he had imagined. This act falls short of the grandeur of murder, to be sure, but it is actually quite an homage to Radcliffe, in whose novels the quest for wealth and status is the general mainspring of the drama. To underrate the seriousness of the General's behavior toward Catherine is to imply that gentlemen are not to be judged on the basis of their callous violence to vulnerable girls, which Gothic novels emphatically insist on doing. General Tilney's expulsion of Catherine is grossly uncivil in the deepest sense, exhibiting insolence toward inferiors, indifference to the good opinion of neighbors, and contempt for the rules of hospitality and gentlemanliness, all the decencies Henry Tilney had associated with the safeguards of English authority at its most benign. By the novel's end, Catherine concludes that Gothic novels actually taught her what no one and nothing else could: "in suspecting General Tilney of either murdering or shutting up his wife, she had scarcely sinned against his character, or magnified his cruelty" (NA, 256). The terms of Catherine's conclusion deserve our attention, for Austen has turned the table on us: having found herself, like all good Gothic heroines, obliged to endure a villain's wrath alone, Catherine vindicates Gothic hyperbole, and it is Henry rather than Catherine who looks like the naive, credulous one.

Northanger Abbey is a youthful work, but it is in no way an immature or minor one. On the contrary it is Austen's most explicitly ambitious novel and was intended to be her first published work, but it did not appear until December 1817, after Austen's death. In 1803, then called *Susan* and later *Catherine*, it was revised and sold to a publisher, but it never appeared, and Austen was obliged to buy it back in 1816. Austen was aggrieved by the novel's nonappearance and intended to publish it again. At least one reason why Austen valued this novel throughout her career is that it is a defense of the novel itself, of particular novelists such as Burney and Edgeworth. But also a defense of Ann Radcliffe as well, for Catherine and Isabella are obviously reading *her* works in Chapter 5 when the narrator breaks in and tells us that novels are works "in which the greatest powers of the mind are displayed, in which the most thorough knowledge of human nature, the happiest delineation of its varieties, the liveliest effusions of wit and humour are conveyed to the world in the best chosen language" (NA, 31).

As this "intrusion" makes clear, *Northanger Abbey* is a metafictional novel, a novel about novels, about writing novels, and about reading them. The opening line announces: "No one who had ever seen Catherine Morland in her infancy, would have supposed her born to be an heroine" (NA, 5), and this is a jibe at readers like ourselves, who might find that Catherine falls "miserably short of the true heroic height" (NA, 9) only because we have clichéd ideas about what the heroic looks like and where to find it. Accordingly, we as well as Catherine have to learn how to recognize the heroically Gothic outlines of her story as we learn how to read properly. Catherine, of course, seems a wholly naive reader, of both her world and her novels. She is comically endearing in part because she is as haunted and perplexed by the social mysteries of Bath as she is by those of Udolpho. She starts out as a reader content with surfaces: she believes exactly what people and books say, as though they were completely transparent. Isabella professes a lofty disdain for the maneuvers of men, and Catherine simply overlooks her coquettish and mercenary pursuit of them; her brother declares that rattles like John Thorpe are favored by women, and so Catherine suppresses her own irritation in his company; General Tilney professes an indifference to money, so Catherine does not believe he will object to Isabella's poverty.

Catherine may be trustful – from the start we are told that "youth and diffidence" (*NA*, 44) mark her mind – but she is not stupid. Before long, her confidence ruptures. Once the disparity between profession and fact becomes too conspicuous for her to overlook, she begins to experience her world as a troubling and baffling place, and to become, in short, a Gothic heroine beset by mysteries. She cannot "avoid a little suspicion" (*NA*, 53) of Isabella's duplicity; she feels "astonishment" (*NA*, 62) – which along with awe and terror are mandatory Gothic sentiments – at Thorpe's exaggerations and contradictions; she is "distressed, but not subdued" (*NA*, 98) by the heartless attempts of her brother and friends to coerce her into breaking her engagement with the Tilneys; and she is "puzzled" (*NA*, 131) by the constraint Henry and Eleanor suffer in their father's company. The Gothic novel is before all else devoted to dramatizing the intuition of horrible truths concealed beneath surfaces, to exposing how persons and institutions you trust (Church, parents, police, fathers, mothers) coerce and betray us in the interests of greed and dominion. Austen uses Gothic fiction to expose a truth about daily life in Regency England.

But one of the novel's least-appreciated jokes is the fact that Catherine is unable to imagine herself to be the Gothic heroine she is. *We* are able to perceive John Thorpe's boorish determination to force Catherine on a carriage ride with him despite her refusal – a refusal that prompts him merely to laugh and smack his whip – as a variant on the standard Gothic abduction scene. The Gothic frame established from the outset of the novel to which Catherine, of course, has no access – invites *us* to conclude that Gothic modulations may intensify the horror of daily life, but they do not distort them. Instead, they help us to recognize and to understand them as the ordeals they are.

Opposing the "alarms of romance" to the "anxieties of common life" (*NA*, 206) and seeming to side artistically with the latter, the novel finally brings them into an illuminating and troubling conjunction. The Gothic novel defamiliarized the common so as to bring its alarming strangeness into view. But by the time Austen took up her pen, Gothic strangeness itself had become so familiar as to be dismissed as convention alone, and as a result it needed itself to be defamiliarized. In adapting the fictional norms of Gothic to Regency England, Austen was thus rehabilitating them. Even Henry Tilney enjoyed Gothic novels: "*The Mysteries of Udolpho*, when once I had begun it, I could not lay down again" (*NA*, 108). But Austen's claims for fiction go well beyond the pleasure of a good "read." She writes fiction the better to examine "strange" truths about familiar life, sharpening our discernment and enlarging our understanding by obliging us to be attentive readers of books and worlds that we, like Henry Tilney, erroneously think we already understand. In so doing, *Northanger Abbey* makes good its assertion that novels are works "in which the greatest powers of the mind are displayed." What an audacious way to start one's career.

Note

1 Reprinted in *Gothic Documents: A Sourcebook, 1700–1820*, eds. E.J. Clery and Robert Miles (Manchester: Manchester University Press, 2000), p. 184.

Myth

8 THE BATH JANE AUSTEN KNEW AND LOATHED

Jane Austen's Bath was a ferocious old dowager. Forget Lady Catherine de Bourgh, it was Bath who made Jane Austen quake. That's the legend at least. In December 1800, when George Austen announced he wished to retire to Bath and informed the family that they were to move there, Jane was so "greatly distressed," in one account, that she actually fainted.[1] Austen's parents had been married in Bath, which is one reason her father might have wanted to return, late in life, to this happy place; another reason was the prospect of securing husbands, and possibly marital bliss, for his daughters. Jane Austen herself hated Bath, and the notorious spa town was no good for her writing. Or so the story goes.

In fact, Bath was a sustaining and inspiring site that Austen drew upon throughout her career from the get-go: it was the setting for *Northanger Abbey*, her first drafted novel (originally written in 1798–1799), and for *Persuasion*, her last fully completed novel. The inland spa town was the inspiration too – however indirectly as a kind of displaced setting – for *Sanditon*, her last (incomplete) novel, set by the sea. And it was Bath where, in 1804, Austen drafted her mid-career fragment *The Watsons*, the threshold novel positioned halfway between the Steventon and Chawton periods in Austen's life and career, and the novel-in-progress which, when Jane Austen left Bath, she never returned to. But is Bath to blame for that?

To be sure, *Persuasion*'s Anne Elliot comments less than flatteringly on "all the white glare of Bath" (*P*, 35). The town could also be wet and overcast, as Austen herself complains: "Well, here we are at Bath; it has rained almost all the way, & our first view of Bath has been just as gloomy as it

30 Great Myths About Jane Austen, First Edition. Claudia L. Johnson and Clara Tuite.
© 2020 John Wiley & Sons, Inc. Published 2020 by John Wiley & Sons, Inc.

was last November twelvemonth."[2] Austen wrote this letter in 1799, before the move, when she was visiting with her mother and brother Edward, accompanying him as he took the Bath waters to treat his gout. Far from fear and loathing, it's nearer the mark to say that the tone is one of mild if habituated annoyance ("just as gloomy" as a year ago), and that Austen was a bit underwhelmed or wryly amused by Bath. Hate is too unsophisticated a term for the complex flows of feeling – however ambivalent – that the spa town aroused in Jane Austen:

> We stopt in Paragon as we came along, but … it was too wet & dirty for us to get out. … a Gentleman in a Buggy, who on a minute examination turned out to be Dr Hall – & Dr Hall in such very deep mourning that either his Mother, his Wife, or himself must be dead. …

> I have some hopes of being plagued about my Trunk; – I *had* more a few hours ago. … but at any rate, the Trunk cannot be here till tomorrow – so far we are safe – & who knows what may not happen to procure a further delay. …

> We are exceedingly pleased with the House; the rooms are quite as large as we expected, Mrs Bromley is a fat woman in mourning, & a little black kitten runs about the Staircase. We have two very nice rooms, with dirty Quilts & everything comfortable. I have the outward & larger apartment, as I ought to have; which is quite as large as our bed room at home, & my Mother's is not materially less. …

> There was a very long list of Arrivals here, in the Newspaper yesterday, so that we need not immediately dread absolute Solitude – & there is a public Breakfast in Sydney Gardens every morning, so that we shall not be wholly starved. … I like our situation very much.[3]

Austen could and did "like" Bath on occasion. Certainly, she is harassed on arrival by the problem of lost luggage, but them's the breaks for any traveler. She is "exceedingly pleased with the House" – whose rooms are curiously both "nice" and "dirty" – but hers is spacious and "comfortable": "I like our situation very much." There is also a sense of social possibility – however eccentric – and however much, coincidentally, this little snatch of a social parade, in the personages of Dr. Hall and Mrs. Bromley, is fashioned into a procession of mourning (a topic on which Austen's letters have form – see Myth 23).

The reference to a "list of Arrivals … in the Newspapers" brings the prospect of sociability, for which Austen readies herself by "marking my Silk Stockings."[4] It also anticipates a moment in Austen's later work – when the announcement of new arrivals triggers Sir Walter and Elizabeth's pursuit of the Dowager Viscountess Dalrymple (see Myth 25).

Jane Austen herself responds differently to the prospect of social interaction; and, despite what seems like straightforward approval of the abundant opportunities for socializing on offer at Bath, there is also a hint of irony in the suggestion that "we need not dread absolute Solitude" – as though "Solitude" may be precisely what Austen wants.

Whatever happened when Austen received the news in December 1800 about the move to Bath – whether she received it as a fatal blow, or not – she had pretty clearly accustomed herself to the scheme a month later when she wrote "there is something interesting in the bustle of going away, & the prospect of spending future summers by the Sea or in Wales is very delightful. – For a time we shall now possess many of the advantages which I have often thought of with Envy in the wives of Sailors or Soldiers."[5] Again, we see that the seeds for *Persuasion* were sown early in Austen's life.

Nevertheless, seven years later, on 1 July 1808, Austen was happy to have left Bath and commemorated the event when she wrote, "It will be two years tomorrow since we left Bath for Clifton, with what happy feelings of Escape!"[6]

When all is said and done, Austen seems to have felt a lot of different things about Bath. There may not be a lot of extant letters from Bath, but the ones that have survived attest to a varied palette of emotions. The Bath that Austen produces across her letters and works is a rather complex beast, of many moods and often rather melancholy (fused with "the wistfulness of all professional beauties"),[7] rather than the terrifying termagant of legend (for which, in any case, Austen was more than a match).

Of Bath's changed fortunes as a ci-devant seat of power, Jan Morris wrote in 1975:

> A thousand years ago the first coronation of a King of England took place in Bath, but since then the monarchs, the presidents and the premiers have come here only for pleasure, escape or lesser ceremony – an emperor in exile, a queen in search of pregnancy, a prime minister electioneering, a king comforting the victims of war.[8]

Nevertheless, "if Power is not an attribute of Bath, Authority distinctly is – not the authority of political regimes, but the authority of manners."[9] Perhaps it's this "authority of manners" that makes Bath and Jane Austen seem like a match made in heaven (see Myth 27).

For despite all this mythic animosity on Austen's part, the fortunes of Austen and Bath have been linked together, for better and worse. Whatever Austen herself thought, her fans have had no such mixed emotions. They love Bath, primarily (if perversely enough) through its association with Austen.

For many years, the unofficial guidebook to Jane Austen and Bath warned readers about Austen's aversion to Bath:

> No admirer of Jane Austen and her works should be without some knowledge of the City of Bath and of the considerable part that it played in her life – this despite the fact that it was by no means a favourite place of hers, and that she so much preferred country life to that of the town.[10]

This opening line tells us all we need to know in a nutshell about why the myth that Jane Austen disliked Bath has been so persistent. For some admirers, the thought of Austen as actually enamored of such a mobile and fashionable place as Bath impugns their vision of Austen as the complete country gentlewoman.

This tendency to assume that Austen disapproved of Bath stems, like other myths, from a desire to identify Austen exclusively with the country. But this is to deny Austen's rather precarious class position (see Myth 25), her own mobility and status as a drifter on the fringes of elite society. For she occupied the fringes of the gentry in the country and at Bath; this marginal status was more pronounced in Bath because the family was not surrounded by as many other relatives there to support them, as they were in the country, and, more to the point, because they were poorer financially after George Austen's death.

As far as family networking goes, the Austen family's circumstances were very different from the Elliots in *Persuasion*. They too had repaired to Bath as a form of retrenchment (like the Elliots, if on a much smaller scale). But whereas the Elliots force themselves on their relatives, the Dalrymples, the Austens had the slightly disturbing experience of having to maintain contact with a relative with whom they would have preferred *not* to associate: their aunt, Jane Leigh-Perrot, who was arrested, convicted, and imprisoned of shoplifting (and seems, what's more, to have been guilty – a kleptomaniac). This unfortunate event interposed itself between the trip to Bath with Edward and her mother at the end of 1799 and the family move there in early 1801. Shortly after Austen returned to Chawton, her aunt was arrested. Once the Austen family arrived in Bath to live, Jane and Cassandra narrowly escaped having to be the family representatives who visited and supported their aunt in prison.

Upon his retirement George Austen drew an income of up to £600 a year from his clerical livings and an annuity, which paid for the rented house in Bath and three servants. That this was not a lot is suggested by the fact that the family moved to a cheaper house. After George Austen's death in January 1805, the women were forced to live on only £450 a year between them. This made them dependent upon Jane Austen's brothers (who provided most of this money), putting them in similar circumstances to the Dashwood women in *Sense and Sensibility*.

Even so, Bath was full of excitements and adventures, and a range of cultural opportunities (a fact which our myth encourages us to ignore): theatre, music, conversation, books from circulating libraries – all of this was at Austen's fingertips and makes its presence felt in the novels. There was a lot of fun to be had in Bath, as *Northanger Abbey* effusively shows. And despite the fact that this was an early novel in Austen's career, the conversations its characters have about novels and manners are highly sophisticated. For all Catherine Morland's quixotism and naivete, and for all Jane Austen's reputation as a critic of supposedly foolish Gothic novels, *Northanger Abbey* is the most self-reflexively engaged with contemporary fiction of the six major novels (see Myth 7). Austen's novel, and her characters, depend on Bath as a particular kind of setting for the display of literary knowingness and urbane sophistication.

It's a matter of tone, like the different kinds of satires of Bath that thrived in Austen's day. Indeed, many of the original guidebooks of the period were in fact satires. In a range of verse epistles in the style of Christopher Anstey's *New Bath Guide* (1766) – such as John Cam Hobhouse's *The Wonders of a Week at Bath* (1811), George Watson Taylor's *The Cross-Bath Guide* (1815), and N.T.H. Bayly's *Epistles from Bath* (1817) – Bath was a site of folly or vice, according to the respective Horatian or Juvenalian modes. Jane Austen's own epistles are more in the spirit of the Horatian tradition, which regards Bath as a site of folly rather than vice. Just as it would be a mistake to confuse a gentler Horatian satire, like Christopher Anstey's *New Bath Guide* (1766), with a judgy Juvenalian satire, so too would it be incorrect to assume that Austen's response to Bath was too sternly disapproving.

So often, Austen's tone is one of wry amusement at the randomness and oddity that Bath life habitually occasioned: "We took a very charming walk … up Beacon Hill … We had a Miss North & a Mr Gould of our party; – the latter walked me home after Tea; – he is a very Young Man, just entered of Oxford, wears Spectacles, & has heard that Evelina was written by Dr Johnson."[11] Besides, the existing genre of Bath satires makes Bath a rhetorically available target – so it's not just Austen. And Bath itself is on the make; that's the point of the satires. While appearing as the haughty dowager, "the Bath of the persistent legend," "the Bath that Jane Austen knew and loathed," as Jan Morris writes, is merely "a Somerset borough of the middle rank."[12]

The twentieth-century writer Angela Carter had a similarly fraught relation to Bath, where she spent a productive period during the 1970s (writing her most important collection of stories, *The Bloody Chamber*), despite the fact that many assume she languished there. Like Austen, Carter had mixed feelings about Bath, as dramatized by her rendition of the Jekyll-and-Hyde character of its main architectural attraction, the Royal Crescent: "The front – a soft yellow façade, with the strange two-dimensional quality of a dreamscape. The back – with its shantytown of loos, and bathrooms and ductwork. ... The skull beneath the skin."[13] Carter in fact challenged Austen's iconic status as one of the patron literary mascots of Bath, and disapproved of Austen's blue plaque, believing that Mary Shelley had a stronger claim on the city's blue plaque, for having written most of *Frankenstein* there.

Today, there is not only a Jane Austen plaque but also a portrait, a waxwork, and plans for a bronze statue, as well as a dedicated Jane Austen Centre at 40 Gay Street, Bath. The center offers "a permanent exhibition that explores Jane's time in Bath and the influence that this beautiful city had on her books, characters and personal life;" and it has commissioned a "New Jane Austen Portrait," by Melissa Dring, a forensic artist who has worked for the FBI, that "shows Jane at the time she lived and worked in Bath, suffused with a gentle ambient glow of pale golden Bath stone."[14]

Whether we see a vista suffused with a harsh white glare or a warm golden glow, or indeed a kaleidoscopic vision of both, it is perhaps impossible to imagine any other way of looking at Bath than through the variegated shades of Austen-tinted glasses.

Notes

1 R.W. Chapman, *Jane Austen: Facts and Problems* (Oxford: Clarendon Press, 1948), p. 46.
2 Jane Austen to Cassandra Austen, 17 May 1799, *Jane Austen's Letters*, ed. Deirdre Le Faye, third edition (Oxford: Oxford University Press, 1995), pp. 39–40.
3 Ibid, pp. 39–41.
4 Ibid, p. 41.
5 Jane Austen to Cassandra Austen, 3–5 January 1801, *Letters*, p. 68.
6 Jane Austen to Cassandra Austen, 30 June–1 July 1808, *Letters*, p. 138.
7 Angela Carter, "Bath," *Nothing Sacred: Selected Writings* (London: Virago, 1982), p. 73.

8 Jan Morris, "Introduction," *Bath: An Architectural Guide*, by Charles Robertson (London: Faber, 1975), p. 11.
9 Ibid, p. 11.
10 Jean Freeman, *Jane Austen in Bath* (Alton: Jane Austen Society, 1983), p. 1.
11 Jane Austen to Cassandra Austen, 2 June 1799, *Letters*, p. 43.
12 Morris, *Bath*, p. 9.
13 https://angelacarteronline.com/2018/01/30/angela-carter-and-bath/, accessed 17 August 2019.
14 https://www.janeausten.co.uk/the-jane-austen-portrait/, accessed 24 June 2019.

Myth 9

JANE AUSTEN'S WRITING IS EASY TO UNDERSTAND

Like so many myths about Jane Austen, this one has the standing of a general truth, and it would seem perverse to contest it. Austen's prose has always been presented to us with adjectives like transparent, concise, elegant, limpid, lucid, lapidary, and most of all clear. Among modern critics, Roger Gard has described this position most straightforwardly. Austen's genius is "clarity;" her points are "obvious;" there is "no ambiguity" in the novels; and "the reader is never long unsure about what has happened, and never finally unsure how to take it."[1] In championing the ease of Austen-reading, Gard understood himself to be defending Austen from academics (like ourselves – who violate Austen with heavy prose and silly over-complications) and to be giving Austen back to common readers, who have found comfort and reassurance in the intelligibility of her prose and of the world it describes. When the biographer and critic Goldwin Smith remarked, "There is no hidden meaning" in Austen, he was praising her marvelous transparency and describing why so many people enjoy her.[2]

In many ways it certainly is productive to consider the ease of Austen's prose. Unlike Austen's novels, Defoe's *Robinson Crusoe* and *Moll Flanders* have no chapter breaks, and the unbroken torrent of his prose can nonplus modern readers. Fielding's novels have chapters aplenty, but the effusion of classical references challenges readers unfamiliar with Latin and Greek. And the sheer volume of Richardson's *Clarissa* and *Sir Charles Grandison* put off readers whose reading habits have been trained on shorter and shorter units of prose. Austen certainly did bring an exceptional degree of economy to the English novel. No reasonable person would seriously compare *Mansfield Park* to, say, *Finnegans Wake* or *Gravity's Rainbow*.

30 Great Myths About Jane Austen, First Edition. Claudia L. Johnson and Clara Tuite.
© 2020 John Wiley & Sons, Inc. Published 2020 by John Wiley & Sons, Inc.

But the ease and transparency of Austen's prose should not be exaggerated. Indeed, she is often deliberately very hard to understand on the simplest level of sense. A few examples from Austen's early work will illustrate this. Consider the opening sentence of *Jack and Alice*, written probably when Austen was 14:

> MR. JOHNSON was once upon a time about 53; in a twelve-month afterwards he was 54, which so much delighted him that he was determined to celebrate his next Birthday by giving a Masquerade to his Children & Freinds (*J*, 13).

Like parody in general, this beginning is conventional and unconventional at the same time, unfolding codes that first seem to proceed in an orderly way only to swerve into trouble. Austen starts with the familiar *once upon a time*, the apparent purpose of which is to locate us securely in a narrative present. To our bewilderment, however, by mid-sentence we have transported not one but two years and after – or is it before? – the "beginning." When does the story really begin? Only after reading the sentence a few times are we able to orient ourselves temporally, and even then our re-examination is likely to turn up fresh doubts generated by the phrase *about 53* that we might have glided over the first time, and these doubts threaten to overturn the entire sentence. What could *about 53* mean – 53 give or take a year? If so, Mr. Johnson might be *about 53* two years later, when at 55 he invites folks to the masquerade. Austen's playful difficulty here calls attention to what George Eliot in *Daniel Deronda* more portentously calls "the make-believe of a beginning." If first sentences in classic novels are supposed to give us some orientation, to clarify time, place, and relationships, then Austen has thrown us for a loop by purposely contriving very difficult sentences and in the process delighting in the creation of confusion.

One more example of calculated difficulty taken from Austen's early work, once again from *Jack and Alice*, shows Austen's interest in difficulty at the level of the sentence:

> Tho' Benevolent & Candid, she was Generous & sincere; Tho' Pious & Good, she was Religious & amiable, & Tho' Elegant & Agreable, she was Polished & Entertaining. (*J*, 14)

This is quintessential Austen, a microcosm of her mature art. Of course, it is a parody of the balanced, subordinate sentence structure we associate with Samuel Johnson, the purpose of which is to master complexity, to order contrarieties into a harmoniously settled whole. But here, instead of holding contrasting elements in equipoise through the power of anti-thetical parallel structure, each clause throws us off balance because the structural elements are equivalencies not opposites. Austen writes a sentence that asks to be understood in one relatively clear way only to end up confounding us, obliging us to think hard.

From the very outset of her career, then, Austen is committed to vexing, disrupting, stymying the process of sense making, to slowing us down. Austen's sentences often seem to ask us, in other words, to be taken for simple and clear only to pull a bait and switch, confounding our assumption that we already know what she is about to say. In her mature novels, take sentences like: "He was not an ill-disposed young man, unless to be rather cold hearted, and rather selfish, is to be ill-disposed" from *Sense and Sensibility* (*SS*, 5). This would not be out of place in the *Juvenilia*, and like Austen's earliest works they seem to unfold placidly, as if on their way to saying one simple thing, only to end up saying quite another, obliging us to do a double-take, to dwell in perplexity.

If we think of Austen's difficulty rather than her simplicity at all, we're likely to refer to the mobility of her irony, and for good reason:

> It is a truth universally acknowledged that a single man in possession of a good fortune must be in want of wife (*PP*, 3).

could not possibly offer this lofty proposition straight. And most readers take delight in working out that Austen must actually mean something very like the opposite of what she is saying here. The "universal truth" is actually a very local, personal opinion, "fixed in the mind" of Mrs. Bennet in particular. And this truth is not that wealthy men are "in want" of a wife, but that Mrs. Bennet's daughters are "in want" of single, wealthy men. We might further enjoy the littler irony that such men – the ones who typically own land – become the "property" of families seeking to marry off their daughters. All this is fine and good. But if we read the novel closely, we will soon learn that men who possess good fortunes are indeed "in want" of a wife, and have come into the neighborhood with the intention of getting one. Mr. Bingley, having made his fortune, is now ready to settle down, and he happily falls in love with one of the first women he meets: Jane Bennet. Mr. Collins comes to Netherfield with the expressed intention of finding a wife, and he makes his way through two candidates before settling on a third. We might even say that Darcy is "in want" of a wife, though he does not seem to know it yet. And the business of "wanting" a wife also clearly applies to men who do not have fortunes. Colonel Fitzwilliam almost apologetically confides to Elizabeth that younger sons cannot follow their hearts in marriage but needs must marry women of fortune. And driven by purely mercenary aims, Wickham goes after a rich Miss King, before being intercepted by Lydia and eloping with her. So: is the joke really on Mrs. Bennet and her ilk after all? Like virtually all of Austen's irony, her opening sentence here is dynamic: it means many things, and some of them are contradictory. This isn't simple.

What difference does it make whether we regard Austen as simple or difficult? For starters, if we begin reading Austen's novels from the acknowledgment of their difficulty rather than their clarity, then the trouble experienced by her heroines in simply knowing what's happening will be more conspicuous. Lord David Cecil – another great believer in Austen's clarity – writes, "There are those who do not like [Jane Austen], as there are those who do not like sunshine."[3] This may be true, but it is obscurity rather than sunshine that so often prevails in Austen's novels. In *Sense and Sensibility*, the words *astonishment, wonder, and amazement* pepper every page as the plot confronts both heroines with suitors whose motives, histories, and hearts baffle them. Using this discourse of the Burkean sublime, Austen knocks her characters' minds up against what they cannot compass, what arrests their capacities for understanding. Neither Elinor nor Marianne have any way of knowing the past histories of Edward Ferrars or Willoughby.

All of Austen's novels bring their protagonists to crises of intelligibility, and, it's worth stressing, only admirable characters find themselves in quandaries. No such crises are in the cards for the likes of Mr. Collins, for example. We cannot imagine him confounded, at a loss. And Austen's irony always falls heaviest on know-it-alls, on those who think they get things, like Henry Tilney, who, with Johnson's *Dictionary* and Blair's *Lectures on Rhetoric*, never grasps that Catherine is in a sense correct about his father's villainy. Similarly, Emma's sturdy resistance to perplexity is part of this novel's fun. For readers coming to the novel for the second, third, umpteenth time – the novel is most delicious when Emma is in the throes of the sublime without knowing it! Thus we see her struggling – briefly – to account for Mr. Elton's "strange" indifference to Harriet's sore throat, his "strange" attentions to herself, until clobbered with his proposal she succumbs: "I am very much astonished, Mr. Elton," she gasps. "My astonishment is much beyond any thing I can express", (*E*, 141) and finally, "she was too completely overpowered to be immediately able to reply" (*E*, 142), that blow of astonishment momentarily depriving her of speech.

But the real benefit of approaching Austen as a difficult rather than a simple writer is that we become more inclined to slow down and marvel at her artfulness. Austen's most ambitious and successful exercise in difficulty is the virtually unreadable, unendurable discourse of Miss Bates in *Emma*. When we encounter Miss Bates in movies, she is a diminutive bore. But on the page, when she is represented by long blocks of unbroken prose, she is fearsome to behold. We fall, helpless, bewildered, stymied before the boundless volume of her associative nattering, that seems to go on and on and on, verging on infinitude. Miss Bates's speech overpowers our attention, makes us want to turn away, to skip, to blink, *not* because it is inane or stupid – only those who've never read her speeches through could possibly think so – but on the contrary because it is because it is *difficult*; because it contains too much information – particularly concerning the lower "sets" at Highbury – for our brains to process and to integrate. Miss Bates's blather is generally seen as the very antithesis of the Austenian. While one is excessive, the other is economical; while one is unstructured and torrential, the other is concise and clipped. We are not equating the novelist's prose with the character's, though many have seen the unmarried Miss Bates, taking care of an aging mother and interesting herself in what the world regards as trivia, as an Austen surrogate. But we are suggesting that it is very instructive to accept the challenge of their difficulty.

Characters and readers alike are more alert and more discerning when they acknowledge the difficulty of making sense. Confounded by Henry Tilney's polite indirection concerning his rakish brother, Catherine Morland protests, "I cannot speak well enough to be unintelligible" (*NA*, 135). Henry rejoins, "Bravo! An excellent satire on modern language" (*NA*, 135). And some readers, who regard Henry Tilney as Austen's mouthpiece, believe that he is saying something like this: let's leave confusion and obscurity aside, and speak with clarity and transparency, like civilized men and women. But unlike the often too-transparent Catherine Morland, Austen, as I hope I've suggested, can speak well enough to be unintelligible. If there is comfort and consolation in Austen's clarity, there is pleasure and infinite amazement in her difficulty as well.

Notes

1 Roger Gard, *Jane Austen's Novels: The Art of Clarity* (New Haven, CT: Yale University Press, 1994), p. 12.
2 *Jane Austen: The Critical Heritage 1870–1940*, vol. 2, ed. B.C. Southam (London: Routledge & Kegan Paul, 1987), p. 190.
3 David Cecil, *Poets and Story-Tellers* (London: Constable, 1949), p. 99.

Myth
10

SENSE AND SENSIBILITY IS A SATIRE ON SENSIBILITY

The story of this myth goes something like: this novel sets up an opposition between sensibility (Marianne Dashwood) and sense (Elinor Dashwood) – between (in other words) an advocacy on behalf of powerful, individual feeling over an adherence to polite, if restrictive, social forms, between the practice of excess on one hand and containment of excess on the other, between ardor and caution. And, the myth continues, the novel obviously champions sense over sensibility, much as *Northanger Abbey* has been seen obviously to privilege Henry Tilney's common-sense faith in the beneficence of English society over Ann Radcliffe's dark intimations about social violence. Marianne is shown to be wrong. Betrayed in love, she learns her lesson, while Elinor is rewarded with the man she has always truly loved, though with due self-control.

It's not hard to see how this myth came about. *Sense and Sensibility* bears the hallmarks of Austen's early writings – an absorption in the popular literature of the time, a strong delight in the absurd, and a love of burlesque – and Marianne is often on the receiving end of Austen's humor. Marianne sallies out onto the steep downs to indulge her love of nature, despite signs of a storm to come. But no sooner does she cry out with delight, "Is there a felicity in the world … superior to this?" than she is met with a cloud burst and a driving rain full in her face (*SS*, 49). This looks like a pretty blunt take-down, as do many other instances where the narrator pokes fun at Marianne's emotionality. In the first volume in particular, Marianne is frequently mocked by the narrator. Sometimes that mockery is playful, as when Marianne decides to respect Colonel Brandon's pleasure in her music even though

30 Great Myths About Jane Austen, First Edition. Claudia L. Johnson and Clara Tuite.
© 2020 John Wiley & Sons, Inc. Published 2020 by John Wiley & Sons, Inc.

it amounted not to that ecstatic delight which alone could sympathize with her own ... and she was reasonable enough to allow that a man of five and thirty might well have outlived all acuteness of feeling and every exquisite power of enjoyment. She was perfectly disposed to make every allowance for the colonel's advanced state of life which humanity required. (*SS*, 42)

The sarcasm here is gentle, even indulgent, as this 17-year-old generously condescends to acknowledge that a gentleman of 35 might enjoy music deeply if undemonstratively. At other times, however, the narrator's mockery is heavy and punitive, as when Marianne's indulges her sorrow after Willoughby leaves the neighborhood:

> Marianne would have thought herself very inexcusable had she been able to sleep at all the first night after parting from Willoughby.... She got up with a headache, was unable to talk, and unwilling to take any nourishment; giving pain every moment to her mother and sisters, and forbidding all attempt at consolation from either. Her sensibility was potent enough! (*SS*, 96)

As these instances show, "sensibility," far from liberating one from restrictive codes of social behavior, actually prescribes and proscribes certain behaviors just as much as ordinary politeness does. The impetuous Marianne considers herself free from common constraints but her behavior closely follows its own kind of script. It is a strict script, and it is sometimes a selfish one as well.

One of the problems with this myth, however, is that the novel is entitled "Sense *and* Sensibility" not "Sense *or* Sensibility." As Margaret Doody has suggested, the title teases us into an opposition the novel confounds.[1] Austen is a complex writer, more interested in interrogating oppositions than in prescribing one side. Marianne's romantic faith in Willoughby, for example, may be rhapsodic, but it is hardly delusional. Willoughby (unlike, say, Wickham) is a respected gentleman known in the neighborhood; he courts Marianne assiduously in full view of their friends and acquaintances, who all agree with Marianne that his intentions are as honorable as they are transparent. And what's more, they – and Marianne – turn out to be right. Willoughby began his relationship with Marianne as an idle, predatory flirtation, but disarmed by her trust in himself, he came to love her truly. This is a pyrrhic victory for sensibility, for Willoughby turns out to love money and comfort more, but the novel still legitimates Marianne's sense of reality. Similarly, when Marianne finds Edward's reserved manners toward Elinor contrary to what a lover's manners should be, we may once again smile at her romantic clichés, but she is absolutely correct: there *is* something holding Edward back. Elinor confidently attributes his reserve to his disapproving mother, but the plot has one over on her as well, though not so mockingly. Like Willoughby, Edward is also encumbered with a secret life, a previous engagement. The double plot of *Sense and Sensibility* thus puts these two sisters not in opposing positions but in parallel ones. Neither sister has access to knowledge about their suitors' pasts or grounds for suspecting that they lack such knowledge. It makes no difference whether one holds back with Elinor's modest caution or hurries forward with Marianne's dauntless ardor: both sisters risk crushing disappointments.

It is not the merits of sense and sensibility themselves that this novel explores but the social context in which these different ways of managing one's emotional life play out. Of all Austen's novels, *Sense and Sensibility* is the most attuned to social criticism of its time. Like characters in the political fiction of the 1790s, when "Elinor and Marianne" was drafted, characters here are conscious of how ideology, an only apparently natural system of priorities, practices, and attitudes, delimits all our social behavior, and the novel assails dominant ideology for privileging – for giving more authority, standing, money, status – to the greedy, mean-spirited, and pedestrian. Whereas didactic novels in the 1790s teach young women the social codes they must adopt if they are to live as dutiful wives and well-behaved daughters, integrated into their communities, this novel makes those codes, customs, and communities themselves the subjects of its harsh interrogation.

Sense and Sensibility opens with a knot of relatives vying for property, calling attention to how systems of inheritance militate against stable and nurturing relations. Unlike the openings to the other novels, the first sentence here begins two generations before the novel starts. As soon as Austen introduces the Dashwood relatives and their incomes she reports: "The old Gentleman died," bequeathing his estate first to his nephew, Mr. Henry Dashwood – the father of Elinor and Marianne – and then "to his son, and his son's son" (*SS*, 4), depriving Henry Dashwood of the power to settle even a portion of his inheritance upon his wife and daughters. This patrilineal succession is at once commonplace and arbitrary, given that the wealth and property already in his possession, the Norland estate, is "not so really important" to John Dashwood "as to his sisters" (*SS*, 4). But "the old Gentleman" leaves property to the male infant because, having once or twice tickled the old man's fancy, the male child "outweigh[s] all the value of all the attention which, for years, he had received from his niece and her daughters" (*SS*, 5). To anyone acting *within* patriarchal ideology "the old Gentleman's" choice appears perfectly natural: male children *are* privileged: that's the way life is. But Austen invites us to stand far enough outside that ideology to see it as capricious. Austen's critique continues when the sisters' conscientious father, gasping on his deathbed, makes his son promise to provide for his widow and daughters. This promise is solemnly pronounced, but John

Dashwood gives his sisters no support, no shelter, no subsistence, all on the grounds that his son is the only proper object of his solicitude. Here, the patrilineal succession of wealth and property is shown to restrict rather than enable moral feeling. The vulnerability of the Dashwood sisters, the abrupt downward social mobility they experience, is the result of the established customs that leave them in the lurch.

Reading *Sense and Sensibility* as a critique of Marianne's sensibility has made it too easy to overlook elements of the plotting that vindicate Marianne's impatience with commonplace customs. Consider, for example, the extraordinary inset tales of the two Elizas. In *Sense and Sensibility*, men have secrets that women don't know about. Brandon's secret is about the two Elizas, mother and daughter. At the age of 17 the first Eliza, a rich orphan, is forced by her uncle, Brandon's father, to marry his eldest son and replenish the family's coffers: "Her fortune was large, and our family estate much encumbered" (*SS*, 233). Eliza's longstanding love for Brandon himself – a second son, outside the line of inheritance – is cruelly prohibited, and Eliza is locked up until she submits: "She was allowed no liberty, no society, no amusement, till my father's point was gained" (*SS*, 233). Miseries follow her in her married life. Brandon does everything to exonerate Eliza, short of pardoning adultery outright: "Can we wonder that with such a husband to provoke inconstancy, and without a friend to advise or restrain her … she should fall?" (*SS*, 234). Deprived of her patrimony, Eliza is not given a "legal allowance … adequate to her fortune, nor sufficient for her comfortable maintenance" (*SS*, 234), and is left after her divorce "to sink deeper in a life of sin" (*SS*, 235) and illness. Eliza's fate testifies to the failures of the status quo. As an orphan and an heiress, Eliza should melt the honorable breast of a good man, a man of sensibility. Like so much of the central matter in *Sense and Sensibility*, Eliza's story indicts the cold-heartedness and avarice of rich families. Though Brandon is generally read as a quiet hero, his own fixation on the first Eliza's spectacular demise actually places him in the same boat as Willoughby, who fantasizes that Marianne is thinking of him as she is dying. Men of feeling and worldly men without feeling alike are found wanting.

But there is another Eliza, an illegitimate daughter. When 17 she too, in the absence of responsible paternal protection, falls to predators. While Willoughby is idly waiting for the death of Mrs. Smith so he can inherit his own money, he has nothing better to do than prey on women. The women available are unprotected – like Eliza and later like Marianne Dashwood herself, also 17. Willoughby is completely unrepentant about debauching Eliza and abandoning her and his child by her. Like Brandon's father and brother, Willoughby needs money to support the habits of his class: "it had been for some time my intention to re-establish my circumstances by marrying a woman of fortune" (*SS*, 363). Thus he seduces Eliza out of boredom, and abandons her out of avarice, even blaming her for being so forward and coarse as to have yielded to his seduction in the first place.

The most striking thing about the tales of the two Elizas is their redundancy. One Eliza would have sufficed as far as the immediate narrative purpose is concerned, which is to discredit Willoughby with a prior attachment. But the presence of two vulnerable, wronged women points to broader crimes, and their common name has a generalizing effect, reflecting on the "good guy" Edward as well. He too forms an attachment to Lucy Steele out of gentlemanly idleness, and then entangles himself with Elinor. Though not the cad that Willoughby is, he is hardly a prize. In contrast to the Darcys and Knightleys of this world, gentlemen in this novel lack the rectitude and forthrightness with which Austen endows exemplary gentlemen when she wishes.

Sense and Sensibility is a novel about secrets that frustrate the hopes and hearts of both sisters, and no degree of caution on one hand or openheartedness on the other can preserve them. To be sure, the way each sister bears the twists and turns to which the novel subjects them is important. If Austen seems at times to give Marianne the short end of the stick, it is because her intensity makes her even more vulnerable. Indeed, Marianne seems to wear that vulnerability like a badge of honor. This is, after all, the only novel by Jane Austen in which a heroine almost dies, and Marianne later admits that her death would have been self-slaughter. And if Marianne "learns" a lesson in this novel, it is not to feel less but to feel more, more not for one person but for more people – such as her sister and mother, and all the persons who have been solicitous for her. Marianne's ardor is, as Brandon testifies, to be treasured, and the real object of Austen's satire here is the coldness of the world, not the rhapsodic enthusiasm of her heroine.

Sense and Sensibility is a disenchanted novel. Once its force is acknowledged, Austen's canon looks different. The sobriety of *Mansfield Park* won't seem odd. The venturesomeness of *Persuasion,* with its weariness with prudence, and its impatience with manor houses, will look more like a continuation rather than a reversal of the arc of her career. And Austen's most popular novel, *Pride and Prejudice*, will seem exceptional among all the novels in the harmony and felicity it accomplishes. Marianne changes her opinions about second attachments, but she is never obliged to surrender to the "commonplace," and in permitting her to withdraw from the world, *Sense and Sensibility* grants her the highest happiness it can imagine.

Note

1 See Margaret A. Doody's introduction to the *Oxford World's Classics* edition of *Sense and Sensibility* (Oxford: Oxford University Press, 1990), pp. vii–xlvi.

Myth

11

JANE AUSTEN WAS THE BEST-SELLING NOVELIST OF HER TIME

The global Jane Austen phenomenon is so entrenched in the twenty-first century that we may well wonder: was there ever a time when Jane Austen was not a best-seller? Yes, there was – when Austen was alive. Contrary to the myth, Austen was not the best-selling novelist of her day. Many of her contemporaries were far more popular: Maria Edgeworth, Walter Scott, Frances Burney, Elizabeth Inchbald, Ann Radcliffe, and Amelia Opie all achieved greater fame and fortune in their lifetimes than Jane Austen.

It was not until the decades after her death that Austen became more widely read. In 1832, her novels featured in a series of cheap, illustrated reprints of *Standard Novels* published by Richard Bentley, but these were not best-sellers: Austen's work was still read mostly by a small but appreciative middle-class readership. A broader popular appeal started to grow in 1883, with Routledge's cheap issues followed by a Sixpenny Series commencing in 1886. But it was not until the twentieth century that Austen approached the vast popular appeal of a best-selling author. Her fortunes were buttressed by critical appreciation in the academy, and her novels attained stratospheric popularity late in the twentieth century thanks to their dazzling new afterlife in the popular BBC TV and film adaptations of the mid-1990s.

Her spectacular global dominance now as both a popular best-seller and an icon of the academic canon tends to obscure an understanding of how Jane Austen's name accrued fame and fortune and how her reputation has changed over time. This has to do not only with her contemporaries' reading

30 Great Myths About Jane Austen, First Edition. Claudia L. Johnson and Clara Tuite.
© 2020 John Wiley & Sons, Inc. Published 2020 by John Wiley & Sons, Inc.

tastes but also with the changing fortunes of the novel genre itself. What books, and what kinds of books, were popular, and why? Who were the best-selling novelists of Austen's day? Is popularity the same thing as financial success? What other factors inform financial success? All of these questions are part of the story.

Despite Austen's increasing professionalism during her career, she earned much less in her lifetime than contemporaries such as Maria Edgeworth (£11 062, 8s, and 10d) or Frances Burney (£4280).[1] Edgeworth – who pioneered the regional novel and the Irish national tale – was the best-selling novelist of Austen's day and the most popular novelist in Britain in the 1800s and early 1810s. As Marilyn Butler notes, "From 1800, when she published *Castle Rackrent*, to 1814, when Scott published *Waverley*, Maria Edgeworth was easily the most celebrated and successful of practising novelists. ... Her publishers paid her up to £2000 for a single work, a remarkable sum before Scott did even better; [in contrast] Murray offered Jane Austen a conditional £450 for *Emma*" – an offer she refused.[2] By the mid-1810s, Edgeworth's reputation was eclipsed first by Scott and then by Austen.

Austen herself was a fan of Edgeworth. In a letter to her niece, Anna Austen (herself an aspiring novelist), Austen jokes about Scott, who had just made his move from poetry to the novel with the hugely popular *Waverley*: "Walter Scott has no business to write novels, especially good ones. – It is not fair. – He has Fame & Profit enough as a Poet, and should not be taking the bread out of other people's mouths. – I do not like him, & do not mean to like *Waverley* if I can help it – but fear I must."[3] Edgeworth, however, she regarded differently: "I have made up my mind to like no Novels really, but Miss Edgeworth's, Yours & my own."[4] So much did Austen admire Edgeworth that she sent her a copy of *Emma* when it was published in 1816.

Edgeworth was also an important influence on Scott, as he acknowledged in the Preface to *Waverley*. Nevertheless, Scott had some advice for Edgeworth: "The rats won't go into the trap if they smell the hand of the rat-catcher," suggesting that Edgeworth's writing tended toward the didactic, meaning designed to instruct (for better), and pedantic (for worse).[5] Yet despite its reputation for didacticism, Edgeworth's work was appreciated for its eye for local color and ear for regional speech and lively dialogue (the dialogue, ironically, being what Scott and other contemporary reviewers would soon appreciate in Austen).

Another popular – and didactic – genre was the conduct novel. Modern readers find it difficult to appreciate conduct novels, and hence tend to underestimate their popularity. But from the 1790s to the Regency, conduct novels such as *A Gossip's Story* (1796), by the counter-revolutionary

Mrs. Jane West, and Mary Brunton's *Self-Control* (1811) and *Discipline* (1814), were enormously popular. Spanning this period, Frances Burney's *Camilla* (1796) joins the theme of education to self-control, and she returns to the subject in *The Wanderer* (1814). In a letter to her sister Cassandra, Austen writes: "I often wonder how *you* can find time for what you do, in addition to the care of the House." She extends the compliment to Jane West: "And how good Mrs. West could have written such Books ... with all her family cares, is still more a matter of astonishment!"[6] Indeed, it was only because Cassandra, Mrs. Austen, and Martha Lloyd (Frank Austen's second wife) agreed to manage the Chawton household that Jane Austen herself had time to write.

In April 1811, Austen jokes about trying to get a copy of Mary Brunton's *Self-Control*, which had just been published, and being "half afraid of finding a clever novel *too clever* – & of finding my own story & my own people all forestalled."[7] Her "own story" was *Sense and Sensibility*, her first published novel, which had gone to press in January 1811 and was published in November 1811 on commission by Thomas Egerton. The first edition sold out and brought Austen £140 as well as the copyright. In a letter written after she had read *Self-Control*, she jokingly suggests that she need not have worried: "I am looking over Self Control again, & my opinion is confirmed of its' being an excellently-meant, elegantly-written Work, without anything of Nature or Probability in it."[8] As Kathryn Sutherland notes, "The extraordinary contemporary success of Brunton's improbable moral tales of independent heroines would continue to irk Austen through the 1810s and in her mind at least invite unwanted association with her own all too probable compositions."[9] These qualities in Austen's work would soon earn high praise from her early reviewers, Walter Scott and Richard Whately (see Myth 5).

Austen's novels now epitomize the subtlety of a highly aestheticized form of fiction that is a world away from earnest didacticism. Nevertheless, Austen took her cues from the conduct novel – if only to move away from it. For one of Austen's achievements was to write a kind of conduct novel which, while endorsing values such as self-regulation, was both so "natural" and aesthetically stylized as to transform the conduct genre beyond recognition.

The question of which books were best-sellers raises the question of *how* books were sold. How were they published? How did they circulate? In the eighteenth century, there were generally four options available to writers who sought renumeration for publishing: (1) by subscription, (2) by sharing net profits, (3) by selling copyright, and (4) on commission, where the author paid the expenses of publication while the publisher distributed the copies and took a commission on all copies sold.

Many books were published by subscription, where the printing was financed by contributions, usually from wealthy and influential individuals who offered advance payment for their copies. Burney's *Camilla* was published by subscription in 1796. It had a print run of 4000 copies and sold as a set of five volumes for 21 shillings. There were more than 11 000 subscribers, including members of the royal family, the titled aristocracy, and upper income groups, subscription libraries, and book clubs, and numerous individual readers, including "Miss J[ane]. Austen, Steventon."[10] When Austen's father, the Reverend George Austen, approached the publisher Cadell on her behalf with the manuscript of "First Impressions" (the original title of *Pride and Prejudice*), he flattered the publisher by invoking Burney's *Evelina* as a preceding work by another young woman who had appeared "under a respectable name."[11] (It is also possible that Austen first encountered her new title as a phrase in Burney's *Cecilia*.)

In 1800, few newly published books were sold to individual readers. New books were expensive luxuries out of reach of any but the richest members of society. Most people with incomes of less than £10 000 a year accessed their literature through libraries, and libraries were the main sales channel for new books. Austen acknowledged this reality that most readers were borrowers, not buyers. After the first edition of *Mansfield Park* sold out, she writes to her niece Fanny Knight that her brother Henry had asked her to London to agree to a second edition, and she says, "I am very greedy & want to make the most of it." A couple of days later she writes: "We are to see Egerton today, when it will probably be determined" whether the second edition would go ahead. "People are more ready to borrow & praise, than to buy ... but tho' I like praise as well as anybody, I like what Edward calls *Pewter* too."[12] When borrowing predominates over buying, sales do not tell the whole story of an author's popularity; for while borrowing meant reduced sales, it multiplied readers.

A number of factors inform sales; and, for all their significance, sales alone (and earnings) do not reflect popularity. In purely financial terms, Hannah More, the author of best-selling conduct novels and counter-revolutionary and religious tracts, was the most successful writer of the Romantic period, but most of her earnings came from supporters' subsidies rather than the market itself.[13] Many of those supporters were institutions, such as the Church and loyalist associations. Indeed, "the whole machinery of moral reform" connected More's fictional parables of laboring people to a larger counter-revolutionary and loyalist reform movement, implicating her in "a complex and frankly promotional set of references to her activity."[14]

Another factor that influences lifetime earnings is the length of an author's publishing career. Austen's writing life was comparatively brief: seven years, whereas Edgeworth published for 38 years and Burney a remarkable 55. When Austen died in 1817, her star was on the rise; had she lived longer, she would have substantially increased her earnings and financial success.

In a poignant document entitled "Profits of my Novels," Austen charts her meager earnings. The list notes a "Residue" of £13, 7s from the first edition of *Mansfield Park*, and the amount of £12, 15s "received from Egerton, on 2d. Edit: of Sense &S", while the "First Profits of Emma" were £38, 18s, and then "From Egerton" she received £19, 13s for the "2d ed. S&S."[15] The second edition of *Mansfield Park* was a failure (published, as it turned out, by Murray, not Egerton); and *Emma*, which was competing with the second edition of *Mansfield Park*, returned a negligible profit. Austen sold the copyright for *Pride and Prejudice* to Egerton for £110, less than the £150 she wanted. As a result, Jan Fergus notes, she "did not profit from her most popular novel as she should have done. ... Had Austen published such editions for herself, she would have made about £475."[16] Austen probably began her final work, *Sanditon*, as an attempt to stave off the financial collapse that faced the Austen women after the bankruptcy of her brother Henry, the banker. When Austen finally began to earn some money from her writing, she invested it prudently in the Bank of England's "four per cent stock." "She made three deposits of £15 each, but never lived to enjoy any of the money – the first withdrawal was made by her sister Cassandra to help pay for her funeral."[17]

The "best-seller" is a certain kind of literary entity, then: one that generates fortune and renown at the moment of first publication. But such renown can obscure other kinds of notice that are just as important (if not more so) in the long term. The cult of the best-seller tends to ignore the fact that different readers encounter the same book at different times and in different places. Not everyone read Austen at the same moment or in the same place. Like Austen's fame and fortune, these discoveries came in their own time. The most inspired and inspiring readers of Austen were not all in London during the Regency. Many came later, and many more are sure to come.

Notes

1 See Jan Fergus, "The professional woman writer," *A Companion to Jane Austen*, ed. Claudia L. Johnson and Clara Tuite (Oxford: Wiley Blackwell, 2009), p. 47.

2 Marilyn Butler, *Maria Edgeworth: A Literary Biography* (Oxford: Oxford University Press, 1972), p. 1.
3 Jane Austen to Anna Austen, 28 September 1814, *Jane Austen's Letters*, ed. Deirdre Le Faye, third edition (Oxford: Oxford University Press, 1995), p. 277.
4 Jane Austen to Anna Austen, 28 September 1814, *Letters*, p. 278.
5 Maria Edgeworth to Mrs. Ruxton, 19 December 1825, *The Life and Letters of Maria Edgeworth*, ed. Augustus J.C. Hare (London: Edward Arnold, 1894), vol. 2, p. 484.
6 Jane Austen to Cassandra Austen, 8–9 September 1816, *Letters*, p. 321.
7 Jane Austen to Cassandra Austen, 29 May 1811, *Letters*, p. 186.
8 Jane Austen to Cassandra Austen, 11–12 October 1813, *Letters*, p. 234.
9 Kathryn Sutherland, *Jane Austen's Textual Lives: From Aeschylus to Bollywood* (Oxford: Oxford University Press, 2005), pp. 226–227.
10 See William St Clair, *The Reading Nation in the Romantic Period* (Cambridge: Cambridge University Press, 2004), p. 584.
11 George Austen quoted in J.E. Austen-Leigh, *Memoir of Jane Austen*, ed. R.W. Chapman (Oxford: Clarendon Press, 1926), p. 137.
12 Jane Austen to Fanny Knight, 30 November 1814, *Letters*, p. 281, 287.
13 St Clair, *Reading Nation*, p. 162.
14 Kevin Gilmartin, *Writing Against Revolution: Literary Conservatism in Britain, 1790–1832* (Cambridge: Cambridge University Press, 2007), p. 59.
15 "Profits of my novels," *Jane Austen's Fiction Manuscripts: A Digital Edition*, ed. Kathryn Sutherland (2010), https://janeausten.ac.uk/manuscripts/pmprofits/1.html, accessed 25 November 2019.
16 Jan Fergus, *Jane Austen: A Literary Life* (London: Macmillan, 1991), p. 140.
17 Maev Kennedy, "Jane Austen to star in Bank of England literary links exhibition," *Guardian* (16 July 2017).

Myth 12

REGENCY AUSTEN

"'Welcome to the Regency era! I expect my guests to eschew all things modern.'" So says Mrs. Wattlesbrook, hostess of the Regency theme park Austenland in Jerusha Hess's magnificent film *Austenland* (2013). Indeed, the film's "Regency era" is not only a period style and place but also licenses a riot of anachronisms, embodied mainly in the character of Miss Elizabeth Charming, who continually strays beyond the Regency, lurching lasciviously into the Victorian age and calling "'Tally Ho!'" as she goes. Drenched in Regency costume and period detail, *Austenland* dramatizes the delirious meeting between then and now that is so often summoned by the words "Jane Austen and the Regency."

These five words conjure an entire geo-aesthetic world. Jane Austen and the Regency go together like young bloods and tilburies in a Georgette Heyer romance. Or do they? When did this coupling come about? How did Jane Austen and the Regency become so inextricably linked? Readers and critics are hard-wired to a vision of Jane Austen as an exemplar of Regency style, but this proverbial association is somewhat perverse, if only because the period was named after a man Austen despised. Nevertheless, she dedicated *Emma* to him in 1815. How did all this transpire?

Strictly speaking, the British Regency refers to the period from 1811 to 1820, when George III had been deemed unfit to govern because of mental illness, and the throne was assumed by his oldest son, George, Prince of Wales, as Regent. After his father's death in 1820, the Regent was crowned George IV. In a looser sense, the "Regency" refers to the first few decades of the nineteenth century, "when the scandals, fashionable lifestyles, and artistic tastes of George IV and his brothers were in the ascendant."[1]

30 Great Myths About Jane Austen, First Edition. Claudia L. Johnson and Clara Tuite.
© 2020 John Wiley & Sons, Inc. Published 2020 by John Wiley & Sons, Inc.

In 1788, after George III's first bout of madness, the possibility of a Regency was first debated by Parliament, and the Prince of Wales began jockeying for position. Just as its temporal reach exceeds official dates, the Regency's geographical reach encompasses the global realm of empire. The first Regency Crisis coincided with the founding of the colony of New South Wales in Australia, and the Regent became a kind of symbolic aegis of the new colony. One of the ships that transported convicts to New South Wales between 1820 and 1841 was called the *Prince Regent*.

After Britain's long engagement in the French Revolutionary and Napoleonic Wars (1793–1815) came a period of postwar economic crisis, unemployment, dislocation, and radical dissent. In this sense, the Regency pivots around the Battle of Waterloo (1815), which marks the transition from war to peace. E.P. Thompson, the great historian of the working class, describes the next four years as "the heroic age of popular Radicalism."[2]

Basically, the Regency names a structure designed to manage political crisis, but it is inherently unstable, drawing attention to the instability of monarchy itself. For the radical Tom Paine, writing in 1792, regency exposed the inherently theatrical and illegitimate status of monarchy:

> Who then is the Monarch, or where is the Monarchy? If it is to be performed by a Regency, it proves it to be a farce. A Regency is a mock species of Republic, and the whole of Monarchy deserves no better description.[3]

The Regency is also marked by a sense that it is a supplement – added to remedy a deficiency; the dissolute son substitutes for his mad father, like a prosthesis or artificial body part. From 1811, the Regent's wig and palpably false bushy whiskers "became objects of caricature in their own right," Dorothy George observes in her history of British political caricature.[4]

Unlike his father, who was healthy-living and sober, the Regent was a dissolute dandy with a reputation for drinking, fast living, and womanizing, before and after his arranged marriage in 1795 to Caroline of Brunswick. (Jane Austen's brother Frank played a part in these events, when, as senior lieutenant in the *Lark*, he accompanied the naval squadron that brought Princess Caroline of Brunswick from Cuxhaven to England for her marriage to the Prince of Wales.[5])

The proposed Regency was contentious because many feared the prince would wreak havoc with his intemperate lifestyle and lack of interest in governing. His misdemeanors made the Regency a byword for scandal. But scandal's centrality to Regency culture was also associated with the new, meritocratic institutions of modernity and their imperatives of calculated risk, ambition, and political and social careerism.[6] Lightly sketched in Austen's novels, these trends are minutely detailed in the contemporary genres that emerged to anatomize the new alliance between scandal and celebrity: "silver fork" novels, the "royal" scandal fictions published by J.F. Hughes, London social "season" novels, and a range of genres documenting fashionable and criminal subcultures, including crime novels and popular slang dictionaries where "flash" words and phrases help map the giddy array of new social types that flourished in the period.[7]

The caricaturist Richard Dighton's *City Characters* (1824) and *West End Characters* (1825) illustrated the difference between the city fashion of men of business and an emergent dandyism embodied by the followers of George "Beau" Brummell, including the Regent, who was a follower of Brummell's fashion and a personal friend. Brummellian dandies were the protagonists of silver fork novels such as Thomas Lister's *Granby* (1826), Isaac Disraeli's *Vivian Grey* (1826), and Edward Bulwer-Lytton's *Pelham* (1828) and *Paul Clifford* (1830), which fascinated middle-class readers with their crossings between gentlemanly high life and criminal low life.

Austen casts her Regency dandy figures in the characters of Henry Tilney, Robert Ferrars, Frank Churchill, and Sir Walter Elliot. Tom Bertram, too, is a kind of Regent-as-dandy figure. Roger Sales argues that the Regency crisis of 1810 to 1812 and the subsequent scandals "provide an important but neglected context for Austen's Regency writings," convincingly suggesting that *Mansfield Park*, written during these years, "contains its own regency crisis when Sir Thomas Bertram has to visit his plantations in the West Indies," and when "Tom's style of rule has similarities with that of the Prince Regent."[8]

Georgette Heyer's Regency romances, while embracing period detail and historical correctness with enthusiasm, are more in line with the generic tradition of Regency silver fork novels than with Austen's realism. In *Regency Buck* (1935), Heyer's first Regency novel, Brummell himself makes a cameo appearance – one of several historical figures who feature, including Queen Charlotte and the Duke of Clarence (later William IV), who proposes to the heroine, Judith Taverner.

With the Prince Regent as the inaugural celebrity royal, the Regency names the emergence of political scandal as a new social and media currency. Foremost among the Regent's personal scandals was the Queen Caroline affair, a protracted, grubby episode that began about 1802, when the Prince of Wales publicly accused his wife of adultery, and culminated in 1820 with Caroline's so-called trial in the House of Lords and the new king's efforts to prohibit her from his coronation and prevent her being crowned queen. But his allies' public scandal-mongering to malign the queen backfired. She drew public support from people of all classes and political stripes – particularly women, including Jane Austen.

The Regency is a recurring theme in Austen's letters. In January 1809, she reports on the rumors that a Regency would be declared after the king's relapse into madness: "The Regency seems to have been heard of only here; my most political Correspondants make no mention of it. Unlucky, that I should have wasted so much reflection on the subject!"[9] There were more unlucky times after rumor became reality. In February 1813, she mentions a letter of grievances from Princess Caroline to her husband that had been published by the princess's Whig supporters in the *Morning Chronicle* (reprinted in the *Hampshire Telegraph*):

> I suppose all the World is sitting in Judgement upon the Princess of Wales's Letter. Poor Woman, I shall support her as long as I can, because she *is* a Woman, & because I hate her Husband.[10]

Unfortunately for Austen, there was more to come, and at closer quarters. In November 1815, she was in London visiting Henry, who was ill, and had arranged to meet John Murray to discuss the publication of *Emma*. Henry's doctor knew the prince's physician and informed him that Miss Austen was in town, as the prince liked her novels. The prince's librarian, the Revd. James Stanier Clarke, visited Austen at Henry's home and issued her with an invitation from the prince to visit Carlton House. Austen obliged, and the unctuous Clarke (whom D.W. Harding refers to as one of the first "admirer-victims" of Austen's "regulated hatred") suggested she might like to dedicate her next work to the Regent.[11] When Austen asked for clarification, Clarke replied that it was "certainly not *incumbent*" on her, but Austen felt honor-bound to heed the prince's wish.[12] Reluctantly, she went ahead with the dedication, which took up a whole page of paper, and also paid for the Regent's copy to be bound.

So Austen dedicated *Emma* to the Regent, though she despised him and pitied his wife. An anti-Regent Regency Austen, then? This suggests a more tangled conception of "Regency Austen," where literary style and politics do not inhabit separate spheres.

In fact, Regency politics and style connect in intriguing ways. The war accelerated scientific and technological innovation: this was immediately apparent in postwar speculative building booms, the remodeling of London by the Prince Regent in collaboration with John Nash, and the emergence of a distinctive Regency architectural and design aesthetic, which often hybridized neo-classical and oriental styles, in the work of architects like Nash and interior designers such as Thomas Sheraton, Thomas Hope, and George Smith, the prince's "Upholsterer Extraordinary." Nash's iconic Brighton Pavilion (1815–1820), commissioned for the Regent, was the apotheosis of the tent-like structures that pervade Regency architecture, epitomizing "the final reconciliation of the Regency house with its surroundings" and the transformation of traditional relations between public and private.[13] The innovations by Nash and his collaborators and followers still mark London and the institutions that shape it.

The Regency was also associated with the development of inner-city living and the transformation of West End London into a pleasure ground for wealthy young things like Willoughby's heiress, Miss Grey, in *Sense and Sensibility*. Albany, the residential complex in the heart of exclusive Mayfair, was transformed from the Duke of York's house in 1802 into the first serviced apartments in London. Lord Byron lived there during his "Years of Fame," as did Matthew "Monk" Lewis (author of *The Monk*, a Gothic sensation that *Northanger Abbey*'s John Thorpe calls a "tolerably decent" novel). From 1943, Georgette Heyer, the queen of Regency romance, lived there in resplendent middle-age, until she could no longer manage the stairs.[14]

In *Sense and Sensibility*, Marianne and Elinor visit Gray's, the fashionable jeweler's, in Sackville Street off Piccadilly; this is one of only two actual London shops referred to in Austen's novels (the other is Broadwood's, where *Emma*'s Frank Churchill buys a pianoforte for Jane Fairfax). Here Austen sets her consummate satirical portrait of the dandy Robert Ferrars, a young man "adorned in the first style of fashion" – the only man in a shop full of women – purchasing a tooth-pick case and recalling James Gillray's famous caricature of the Regent picking his teeth with a fork (see Figure 2).[15] Austen drills down into the Regency world of conspicuous consumption and nails the dandy's curious self-absorption in the commodity, as Ferrars ignores the other customers while "deciding on all the different horrors of the different toothpick-cases presented to his inspection" (*SS*, 251).

In Heyer's *Regency Buck*, we are reminded that *Sense and Sensibility* is itself a commodity – a book – when it makes an appearance in Hookham's Library in Bond Street. (Famous books, like famous people, make casual appearances in Heyer's Regency world.) Heyer's heroine picks up a copy after she has returned Maria Edgeworth's *Tales of Fashionable Life* – the switch a telling detail in itself (see Myth 11). She then cannily reads her cousin Bernard Taverner a passage about mercenary relations and the marriage market:

Figure 2 James Gillray, *A Voluptuary Under the Horrors of Digestion* (1792). © The Trustees of the British Museum.

"He seems a most gentleman-like man; and I think, Elinor, I may congratulate you on the prospect of a very respectable establishment in life."

"Me, brother! What do you mean?"

"He likes you. I observed him narrowly, and am convinced of it. What is the amount of his fortune?"

A laugh assured Miss Taverner that this passage had struck her cousin just as she believed it must.[16]

In this homage to Austen, the scene quoted from *Sense and Sensibility* is the moment when the unworthy John Dashwood comes to visit his sisters "with a pretence at an apology" (*SS*, 253). On the point of making his departure, he notices the "gentleman-like man," Colonel Brandon, then hangs around to meet him and concocts the notion that Brandon fancies Elinor. Not only is Dashwood proven wrong (Brandon likes Marianne), but his vulgar enquiry after Brandon's worth reveals his self-serving fantasy of passing responsibility for his sisters on to other men.

In Heyer's canny scene of reading, Bernard Taverner's self-incriminating nervous laughter prepares the reader for his later unmasking as a Regency villain (like John Dashwood, seemingly kind but actually sinister). For all the novel's name-dropping, Heyer pays tribute to Austen in a very different way. She names the novel but not the author, relying on the reader to make the connection. Indeed, for once, the historical personage is pointedly *not* named; Miss Taverner goes on to say, in Heyer's best-worst Austenese, "Surely the writer of that must possess a most lively mind?"[17]

The Regency lives on in the novels of Austen and Heyer, as well as in the enduring sites that were the center of Regency London. Hookham's Bookshop didn't last beyond 1871, but Hatchards still stands in Piccadilly. Established in 1797, it is Britain's oldest bookshop, and still selling copies of Austen's novels today.

Notes

1 Iain McCalman, "Regency," *An Oxford Companion to the Romantic Age: British Culture 1776–1832*, ed. Iain McCalman (Oxford: Oxford University Press, 1999), p. 671.

2 E.P. Thompson, *The Making of the English Working Class* (Harmondsworth: Penguin, 1977), p. 660.

3 Tom Paine, *Rights of Man*, ed. Claire Grogan (Peterborough, Ontario: Broadview Press, 2011) p. 211.

4 Dorothy George, *English Political Caricature*, vol. 2 (Oxford: Clarendon Press, 1959), p. 130.

5 See George Holbert Tucker, *A Goodly Heritage: A History of Jane Austen's Family* (Manchester: Carcanet Press, 1983), p. 169.

6 Marlon Ross, "Scandalous reading: The political uses of scandal in and around Regency Britain," *Wordsworth Circle* 27(2), (1996), pp. 103–112.

7 On the silver fork genre, see Edward Copeland, *The Silver Fork Novel: Fashionable Fiction in the Age of Reform* (Cambridge: Cambridge University Press, 2012); on other Regency genres, see Clara Tuite, "Celebrity and scandalous fiction," *English*

and British Fiction 1750–1820, eds. Peter Garside and Karen O'Brien (Oxford: Oxford University Press, 2015), pp. 399–403.

8 Roger Sales, *Austen and Representations of Regency England* (London: Routledge, 1994), p. 71.

9 Jane Austen to Cassandra Austen, 10–11 January 1809, *Jane Austen's Letters*, ed. Deirdre Le Faye, third edition (Oxford: Oxford University Press, 1995), p. 163.

10 Jane Austen to Martha Lloyd, 16 February 1813, *Letters*, p. 208.

11 See D.W. Harding, "Regulated hatred" (1940), reprinted in *20th Century Literary Criticism: A Reader*, ed. David Lodge (London: Longman, 1984), p. 272.

12 Quoted in Park Honan, *Jane Austen: Her Life* (New York: Fawcett Columbine, 1989), p. 368.

13 Donald Pilcher, *The Regency Style 1800 to 1830* (London: Batsford, 1947), p. 44.

14 Teresa Chris, *Georgette Heyer's Regency England* (London: Sidgwick & Jackson, 1989), p. 28.

15 John Wiltshire, *The Hidden Jane Austen* (Cambridge: Cambridge University Press, 2014), p. 39.

16 Georgette Heyer, *Regency Buck* (London: Pan, 1959), p. 113.

17 Ibid, p. 113.

Myth

13 ONLY WOMEN READ JANE AUSTEN

On the face of it this seems more like a truth universally acknowledged than a myth. All of the anecdotal data we've mustered concerning enrolments with undergraduate courses and reading clubs and Jane Austen societies on three continents confirm that many more women than men seem to read and enjoy Jane Austen's novels. In college and university classrooms, lots of factors come into play – the particular professor, course offering, and requirements; the changing demography of humanities and English literature students; and the age of the cohort – but generally women on Austen courses outnumber men by a ratio of about 10:1. A similar ratio holds outside the academy. A carefully conducted and analyzed poll undertaken in 2008 for the Jane Austen Society of North America showed that of 4501 respondents 96% were women.[1] Now, these figures and these impressions do not suggest that women are necessarily more insightful or devoted readers of Jane Austen, but they do confirm the general sense that Austen is particularly attractive to women. The book covers of the novels themselves, typically featuring sumptuous early-nineteenth-century portraits of intelligent-looking young women, both emerge from and in turn reproduce this impression, as do the tons of movie and TV adaptations, spin-offs, and vlogs marketed for women. Add to this the fact that special editions of Jane Austen's novels are presently sold, along with other "cute" accessories, by the worldwide woman's clothing and accessory chain Anthropologie, and the case seems closed.

But to our ears at least, numbers don't tell the whole story. When we relate them, a faint but discernible note of chagrin, and even defensiveness, sounds in our voices, expressive not merely of regret that more men and boys aren't reading Jane Austen but of anxiety that somehow

30 Great Myths About Jane Austen, First Edition. Claudia L. Johnson and Clara Tuite.
© 2020 John Wiley & Sons, Inc. Published 2020 by John Wiley & Sons, Inc.

Austen herself has lost some prestige as a result. Does the fact that Austen's readership nowadays seems predominantly female mean that Austen is somehow "narrow" or possibly even frivolous? Does it suggest that Austen has been absorbed into "chick lit" – frothy, commercially successful fiction in which plucky, if variously challenged but (as the expression now goes) "relatable," heroines overcome embarrassments, weight, and wardrobe problems, girlfriend issues, and job troubles, only to snag the men of their dreams in the end? While men simply pass over chick lit as not for them, many women have also pooh-poohed it as glib and meretricious. Once upon a time, Jane Austen was the darling novelist of high culture, the first novelist whose works were edited, it was observed, according to the strictest principles of textual scholarship, and mentioned in the same breath as Shakespeare himself for her powers of characterization. But if *Bridget Jones's Diary* is the grandmother of chick lit, then there is no doubt that it – like Harlequin romances before it – derives its precious DNA from *Pride and Prejudice*. Many Austen readers and scholars are uneasy about this offspring.

Austen herself partially anticipated uneasiness about this sort of anxiety and she moved quickly to defy it. In *Northanger Abbey*, which was to have been her first published novel, Jane Austen placed herself in an emerging canon of distinctively female novelists whose works critics then sneered at as trash engulfing the literary marketplace. Austen flouts their scorn, and she goes on the offensive. Reviewers and representatives of the high tradition are the clichéd and second-rate ones, so blinded by their allegiance to the Augustan male tradition that they would rather keep anthologizing snippets from Goldsmith, Milton, Pope, Prior, Sterne, Addison, and Steele than read novels which have "only genius, wit, and taste to recommend them" (*NA*, 31). That little word "only" packs the power of Austen's ironic punch: she's bragging. And it is not just the novel in general but the emergent *female* tradition of the novel Austen touts here as she praises novels by Frances Burney, Maria Edgeworth, Ann Radcliffe, and – it follows as night from day – herself, since hers is the novel we are in the act of reading. Austen's position is clear: these female-authored novels are works in which "the most thorough knowledge of human nature, the happiest delineation of its varieties, the liveliest effusions of wit and humour, are conveyed to the world in the best-chosen language" (*NA*, 31). Austen was not shy in her advocacy of women writers and women readers. Her novels elevate the ordinary world of manners, courtship, family, and neighborhood tittle-tattle, and cumulatively they show that any intelligent woman, perhaps even Bridget

Jones, might provide matter sufficient for a novel, *if* – and this is a big *if*, of course – her ponderings, struggles, and choices were narrated with the same intensity of discrimination as Jane Austen.

But with all of this readily granted up front, the fact is that Jane Austen emphatically did *not* understand herself to be a "woman's novelist" or her novels to be women's literature, and we should be wary of imposing our own late-twentieth and early-twenty-first-century economies of gender on her works as they were composed and received over the past two centuries. In Jane Austen's novels and in Jane Austen's world, the subject of marriage and its attendant concerns – such as the acquisition and transmission of wealth and property, the achievement of status, the formation of intra-family alliances, and of course the relation of all of the foregoing to love, esteem, and affection – were not cordoned off as the province of women. Indeed, that famous first sentence of *Pride and Prejudice* – "It is a truth universally acknowledged, that a single man in possession of a good fortune must be in want of a wife" – is so celebrated for its irony that we tend to overlook that it is actually true: all the eligible men in this novel *are* aiming to make a good marriage, however differently they may define it, and the women are as well. Although the novel was (as Austen knew only too well) considered a lightweight genre, it was also a "polite" one, meaning that it was accessible to a mixed rather than sexually segregated audience of readers.

Men dominated English letters at the time, and it should come as no surprise that men were Austen's first intensely enthusiastic champions. They never appear to be put off or somehow excluded by the trials and tribulations of female protagonists, but instead celebrate her artistry, her uncommon capacity to create compelling interest in the affairs of ordinary life, without recourse to marvelous or sensationalist events or effects. Accordingly, men such Sir Walter Scott, Archbishop Richard Whately, Thomas Macaulay, W.F. Pollock, and George Henry Lewes, to name only a few, were eloquent in praise of Austen's attention to detail, her irony, her subtlety, her realism, her characterization. Women writers, by contrast, particularly those who reached more conspicuously for grandeur, expansiveness, or dramatic intensity in their works, were decidedly chillier about Austen's novels – Madame de Staël dissed them as "vulgaire," Charlotte Brontë damned them as narrow, and George Eliot as second-tier. To be sure, many women loved Jane Austen (Margaret Oliphant, Virginia Woolf) and many men despised her (Mark Twain, D.H. Lawrence), but in its most influential forms, enthusiasm for Jane Austen in the late nineteenth and early twentieth centuries was a conspicuously, though not exclusively, male concern shared by prominent publishers, professors, and literati, such as Montague Summers, A.C. Bradley, Lord David Cecil, Sir Walter Raleigh, R.W. Chapman, and E.M. Forster, among others.[2]

If it seems self-evident to us today that women like Jane Austen because her novels are romantic love stories, it seemed just as obvious to Reginald Farrer in 1917 that women *dis*like Jane Austen because her novels were not romantic enough: Jane Austen "will always" seem "insipid to the large crowd of readers, chiefly women ... because they read fiction principally as an erotic stimulant, and judge its merits accordingly, by the ardor of its descriptions and expressions."[3] Instead of reading Austen's novels as gender-specific love stories, Farrer contends that her "heroes and heroines and subject-matter are, in fact, universal human nature, and conterminous with it".[4] We're rightly suspicious of the universalizing discourse of human nature, because of the hierarchies, exclusions, and biases it conceals. But this discourse can have the benefit of enabling sympathy and identification across gender lines. Farrer can readily sympathize with Fanny Price or Catherine Morland or Lady Russell, because he does not regard Jane Austen's novels to be about them *as women* in the first place: "a breaking heart is a breaking heart, no more no less, whether it find vent in the ululations of Tamburlaine, or in the 'almost screamed with agony' of Marianne Dashwood."[5] For Farrer, then, as for his World War I generation, Austen's novels could be treasured in part because male readers, especially soldiers, could read the poise, modesty, reticence, local attachment, and self-control under pressure evinced by her heroines not as distinctively female virtues but as qualities that spoke directly to them as well. As the shell-shocked hero of Kipling's World War I story "The Janeites" puts it, describing the Austenian reading club he belonged to in the trenches, "You take it from me, Brethren, there's no one to touch Jane when you're in a tight place."[6]

Historically speaking, Jane Austen has not been a woman's novelist, and she only became so since the mid-twentieth century. During the late 1940s and 1950s the fashion industry would run ads for a "Jane Austen dress," for gowns with "a Jane Austen air," for white organdies having "a faint flavor of Jane Austen," both feminizing and mass-marketing Austen for female consumers in an entirely unprecedented way. There have certainly been gains to this development, as women readers and viewers find in Austen's works material with which to understand and to affirm their experiences as women and to share that understanding with other women. But insofar as this habit of reading Austen's novels as essentially about and for women has excluded a category of readers who once found pleasure, consolation, and insight in them, who can doubt that it has caused a loss as well?

Notes

1 Jeanne Kieffer, "Anatomy of a Janeite: Results from *The Jane Austen Survey 2008,*" *Persuasions On-Line*, 29 (Winter 2008), p. 1.
2 Devoney Looser presents a powerful counterargument to this claim, showing the extensive participation of women as well as men in the "making" of Jane Austen. See the *Making of Jane Austen* (Baltimore: Johns Hopkins University Press, 2017). For a fuller discussion of Janeism as a male "cult" see my "Austen cults and cultures" in *The Cambridge Companion to Jane Austen*, 2nd edition, eds. Edward Copeland and Juliet McMaster (Cambridge: Cambridge University Press, 2012), pp. 232–248.
3 Reginal Farrer, "Jane Austen, *ob.* 18 July 1817," *Quarterly Review* (July 1917), reprinted in *Jane Austen: The Critical Heritage 1870–1940*, vol. 2, ed. B.C. Southam (London: Routledge & Kegan Paul, 1987), p. 252.
4 Ibid, p. 250.
5 Ibid, p. 250.
6 Rudyard Kipling, "The Janeites," *Debits and Credits* (Garden City, NY: Doubleday), p. 146.

Myth

14

AS *PRIDE AND PREJUDICE* SHOWS, ALL AUSTEN'S NOVELS ARE LOVE STORIES

Writing to her sister Cassandra on 4 February 1813, a week after *Pride and Prejudice* was published, Jane Austen admitted to "fits of disgust" at what would prove to be her most popular novel:

> The work is rather too light & bright & sparkling; – it wants shade; – it wants to be stretched out here & there with a long Chapter – of sense if it could be had, if not of solemn specious nonsense – about something unconnected with the story; an Essay on Writing, a critique on Walter Scott, or the history of Buonaparte – or anything that would form a contrast & bring the reader with increased delight to the playfulness & Epigrammatism of the general stile.[1]

We may be sure that Austen did not intend to disown the novel, which she had recently described as "my own darling Child."[2] Besides, the novel was well received. The *Critical Review* enthused over its love plot: "Elizabeth's prejudice and dislike gradually subside; and the *sly little god* shoots one of his sharpest arrows very dexterously into her heart."[3] But Austen herself was that "sly little god," and she had reservations.

Austen's letter suggests that she wanted her readers to acknowledge and appreciate something more – something beyond love, romance, and the happy ending. Austen is anxious that the "story" might overwhelm the "style." What was it that Austen wanted us to see that is "unconnected with the story"? What is the "shade" the work lacks?

---

30 Great Myths About Jane Austen, First Edition. Claudia L. Johnson and Clara Tuite.
© 2020 John Wiley & Sons, Inc. Published 2020 by John Wiley & Sons, Inc.

Let's start with the novel's "Epigrammatism." There is no better example of the novel's playful style than its magisterial opening sentence:

> It is a truth universally acknowledged, that a single man in possession of a good fortune, must be in want of a wife (*PP*, 3).

The sentence encapsulates in miniature a paradoxical quality of all Austen's works: the combination of airy simplicity with sparkling self-consciousness. It simultaneously reproduces a cliché – the gnomic, sententious assertion – while parodying it. The irony in *Pride and Prejudice* has a particular quality. Austen's word of choice, "Epigrammatism," invokes the subtlest form of irony, the "pointed" mode of expression (*OED*), where "pointed" means indirect – playful, ironic, self-conscious, self-reflexive.[4] The "Epigrammatical" opening sentence predicts the whole novel, which allegorizes an entire genre.

The third-person narrator utters what seems to be an uncontroversial statement of fact in a cool, omniscient tone. But we know from the moment this statement is uttered that all is not as it seems; the sentence means something different from what it says, and the novel is distancing itself from its own language. Austen has a knack of "saying things in such a way that they are also unsaid."[5] This irony transforms the seemingly assured statement of fact into a series of questions. Is it a truth universally acknowledged that a single man with a fortune must be in want of a wife? Is this novel ratifying that universal law? Are all Austen's novels love stories? To which we would answer, yes, all Austen's novels are love stories, but that's not all they are. Austen's marriage plots are not only about love; they are also about social harmony, and the love story is an allegory of class alliance and social mobility.

That there may be more to *Pride and Prejudice* than its love story is signaled by the novel's opening dialogue between Mr. and Mrs. Bennet, with its ironic counterpoint between realism and romance. It ironizes Mrs. Bennet's marriage plans, which involve a new arrival in the locality, Mr. Bingley:

> "Is he married or single?"

> "Oh! Single, my dear, to be sure! A single man of large fortune; four or five thousand a year. What a fine thing for our girls!"

> "How so? How can it affect them?"

> "My dear Mr. Bennet," replied his wife, "how can you be so tiresome! You must know that I am thinking of his marrying one of them."

"Is that his design in settling here?"

"Design! nonsense, how can you talk so! But it is very likely that he *may* fall in love with one of them, and therefore you must visit him as soon as he comes." (*PP*, 4)

So, the opening sentence, which seems to reproduce a truism, sets up the ironic enquiry that informs the novel, creating the "shade" Austen wishes to extend to her reader.

One function of the novel's opening sentence – indeed, its opening chapter – is to develop this epigrammatic irony. It draws the reader's attention to *Pride and Prejudice*'s generic status as a romance, a courtship novel whose business is getting its characters married; at the same time, it ironizes readers' expectations of these love-story genres. From the outset, Austen distances herself from her own novel and its language. Part of the novel's charm is that its narrator ironizes the match-making – as though she were Mr. Bennet – while also accomplishing the marriage that has been Mrs. Bennet's aim from the get-go.

But is that all there is? As Mr. Bennet might ask about his creator, "Is that her design in writing the novel?" To which we might reply, "Design! nonsense, how can you talk so! But it is very likely that these characters *may* fall in love." As we know, they do.

Austen deploys irony to deal with the embarrassment of having to reproduce a cliché, as her novel moves inexorably (if breezily) toward the outcome written in the stars by the gods of romantic fiction. Nevertheless, the novel disavows and frustrates this ending in various ways, especially through Mr. Bennet's "indolence," which is a structural feature of the narrative as well as an instance of Austen's innovative "delineation of domestic scenes" as pieces of realism, focusing on the ordinary, the mundane, and the probable (see Myth 5).

Early reviews of *Pride and Prejudice* celebrated Austen's creation of character. The *Critical Review* remarked, "On the character of Elizabeth, the main interest of the novel depends," while also observing that Mr. Bennet "presents us with some novelty of character; a reserved, acute, and satirical, but indolent personage, who sees and laughs at the follies and indiscretions of his dependents, without making any exertions to correct them."[6] Novelty of character here is not just amusement or interest, but is tightly bound within the aesthetic design of the whole. This "indolent personage" is both a character and a structural feature – the antithesis of his wife, for whom the "business of her life was to get her daughters married" (*PP*, 5).

Mr. Bennet represents a principle of self-reflexivity, delaying what, according to our myth, is the sole business of the novel. At one point he says to Elizabeth, "Are you out of your senses, to be accepting this man? Have you not always hated him?" (*PP*, 417). The novel draws its readers into the shade of his invocation of hate, a very dark feeling, like Austen's disgust for her novel.

Ultimately, however, marriage proves to be the "business" of the novel, accomplishing Mrs. Bennet's lifework. This happy ending is the perfect outcome of the genre. Why would Austen wish to distance herself from these expectations, even as she participates in them? The answer may be that she was embarrassed by the genre's low "cultural capital" at the time.[7]

For most of the eighteenth century, as the institution of literature was being invented and a literary canon created, lyric poetry was at the top of the generic hierarchy and the novel was near the bottom. All novels were romances, considered to be trash and pulp. For most of Austen's career, the novel was associated with women readers, romance, day-dreaming, and sexual licentiousness. There was wide debate about the uses and abuses of the genre. Most of Austen's other novels engage this lively cultural debate in some way. Austen offered a critique of sentimental literary conventions in her first published novel, *Sense and Sensibility*. In *Northanger Abbey*, she addresses her readers directly in defense of novels: "Yes, novels; – for I will not adopt that ungenerous and impolitic custom, so common with novel writers, of degrading by their contemptuous censure the very performances, to the number of which they are themselves adding" (*NA*, 30). As Marilyn Butler notes, when Austen jokes that *Pride and Prejudice* wants "an Essay on Writing" or "a critique of Walter Scott" to temper its lightness, her "recipes" are self-consciously "absurd," but the point is a serious one.[8] Austen is emphasizing the importance of an element of self-reflexive critique in a novel. This element of critique could also be the "shade" Austen "wants" – specifically for *Pride and Prejudice* but more generally for her version of the novel form.

Was Austen's disgust warranted? If she wanted her readers to find shade in her love story, history suggests they have been very receptive. Some have even detected darkness in the novel. And, for many, there is nothing more to be done "to bring the reader with increased delight to the Epigrammatism of the general stile": the magic has already been accomplished by the novel's black comedy, long relished by its readers. What more could they want?

D.W. Harding underscores the conjunction of light and shade in his account of the scene in which Mr. Collins proposes to Elizabeth. The scene is "comic fantasy, but … also, for Elizabeth, a taste of the fantastic nightmare in which economic and social institutions have such power over the values of personal relationships that the comic monster is nearly able to get her."[9] The "light & bright & sparkling" flip-side of this "fantastic nightmare" is the dream come true of marriage with Darcy; but here too the romance is often shaded.

The romance between Elizabeth and Darcy can be read as a political allegory. Both protagonists represent particular social classes: Elizabeth's middle-class "prejudice" is pitted against Darcy's aristocratic "pride." The scene in which he proposes is riven by oppositions between "Darcy's abominable pride" and Elizabeth's "anger." The protagonists are simultaneously individualized and socialized. Darcy's pride is the pride of an entire class. Likewise, Elizabeth's prejudice enacts middle-class resentment at upper-class arrogance. The fireworks of negotiating a settlement that is symbolized through marriage establish a kind of social contract between the classes. The "prejudice against pride" that spurs the novel's romantic drama resolves class conflict by creating a new alliance between the middle classes (or bourgeois or landless gentry) and the aristocracy (or landed gentry) (see Myth 25). Austen's magic lies in how she combines a focus on politics with romance. Her love story is also an allegory about class and history.

Soon after *Pride and Prejudice* was published, Annabella Milbanke, who went on to marry Lord Byron, observed that it was "not a crying book."[10] This distinguished it from existing novels. There is "half an hour" when Elizabeth "sat down and cried" after Darcy's first proposal, but then she begins to reflect (*PP*, 216). Austen highlights her reason, self-possession, and capacity for self-evaluation. Elizabeth also has taste, preferring Pemberley to its evil twin Rosings; this is another reason why the novel endorses her upward social mobility – and happy acquisition of a rich and handsome husband.

Austen shows all this through the new narrative technique of free indirect discourse, which brings the reader into the interior life of her complex new heroine, who can think *and* feel, and who has a curious bond with her sly, sardonic (if "indolent") father. In this, *Pride and Prejudice* offers its readers an exciting sense of the development or "novelty" of character, supported with detail and a complex play of narratorial sympathy for and distance from a complex female protagonist. Austen's form of the novel elevated the genre into a powerful cultural medium; it endowed what was considered a trashy cultural form with aesthetic elegance, emotional intelligence, ironic complexity, and satirical bite.

Pride and Prejudice re-casts the pleasures of romance by dramatizing how the "*sly little god* shoots one of his sharpest arrows very dexterously into [Elizabeth's] heart." Of course, the sly little god also shoots one into Darcy's. In the 1995 BBC TV adaptation, this happens in the famous "wet-shirt" moment, when Darcy, "the master," is momentarily overcome after being surprised half-naked by Elizabeth and her aunt and uncle, who are visiting his property as tourists. But the wet-shirt moment only happens on TV. In the novel, they both blush: "Their eyes instantly met, and the cheeks of each were overspread with the deepest blush"

Figure 3 *Pride and Prejudice* released by Pulp! The Classics (2013), with cover art by David Mann; cover design by Elsa Mathern. Reproduced with permission of the Licensor through PLSclear.

(*PP*, 278). The point is that it is mutual. This is deeply romantic but also politically strategic, suggesting "a conservative yearning for a strong, attentive, loving, and paradoxically perhaps, at times even submissive authority."[11] By showing the master of the estate momentarily overcome – losing his proud composure and sharing a blush with his beloved – Jane Austen's novel registers historical and political change through social gesture and the body. Perhaps this is another kind of "shade" or darkness. An ambivalent emotional charge drives Elizabeth and the romance, "bringing the reader with increased delight" to the style.

The novel combines the high and the low, aesthetic precision, satire, social commentary, and the pleasures of romance. This is a love story, but also a story of the novel's evolution from romance to realism. Its status as both classic high literature and "pulp" romance is playfully signaled by the cover image of Colin Firth's Darcy as the brooding, Byronic hero in a 2013 bicentennial faux-pulp edition, "Pulp! The Classics" (see Figure 3), which brands itself as a high and low re-mix of Austen, conjoining pulp and classic literary fiction in a way that dramatizes and knowingly exploits *Pride and Prejudice*'s crossover appeal.

The fact that *Pride and Prejudice* does both – transforming the romance novel in the direction of a new realism while enacting that mode of fairytale romance – is what gives this novel its particular magic, and why it is so popular as the leading example of Austen's oeuvre. Austen ushered the novel genre into the domain of social respectability and aesthetic credibility, laying down its possibilities as an artform. Her work is so dominant now because her novels – especially *Pride and Prejudice* – straddle the literary classic and popular romance. That it does both is the marvel and the miracle of this novel.

Notes

1 Jane Austen to Cassandra Austen, 4 February 1813, *Jane Austen's Letters*, ed. Deirdre Le Faye, third edition (Oxford: Oxford University Press, 1995), p. 203.
2 Jane Austen to Cassandra Austen, 29 January 1813, *Letters*, p. 201.
3 *Critical Review* (1813), quoted in *Jane Austen: The Critical Heritage*, vol. 1, ed. B.C. Southam (London: Routledge & Kegan Paul, 1968), p. 46.
4 "Epigrammatic," *Oxford English Dictionary* online: www-oed-com.
5 D.A. Miller, *Narrative and Its Discontents* (Princeton, NJ: Princeton University Press, 1981), p. 31.
6 *Critical Review*, p. 46.
7 On "cultural capital," see Pierre Bourdieu, "The forms of capital" in *Handbook of Theory of Research for the Sociology of Education*, ed. John G. Richardson (New York: Greenwood Press, 1986), pp. 241–258.

8 Marilyn Butler, *Jane Austen and the War of Ideas* (Oxford: Oxford University Press, 1989), p. 197.
9 D.W. Harding, "Regulated hatred" (1940), reprinted in *20th Century Literary Criticism: A Reader*, ed. David Lodge (London: Longman, 1984), p. 268.
10 Annabella Milbanke, quoted in Southam, *Critical Heritage*, p. 8.
11 Claudia L. Johnson, *Jane Austen: Women, Politics, and the Novel* (Chicago: University of Chicago Press, 1988), p. 73.

Myth 15

JANE AUSTEN NEVER MENTIONS THE WAR

One vital fact about Jane Austen is that almost all her novels were drafted, revised, and published in the 22 long years that Britain was at war with France, first with Revolutionary France (1793–1799) and then with Napoleonic France after Napoleon Bonaparte became the nation's de facto ruler (1799–1804) and then emperor (1804–1814, 1815). These were global wars extending from Europe and the Mediterranean to the West Indies, the Caribbean, South Asia, and the Americas. The wars form a backdrop to most of Austen's writing. As Gillian Russell observes, "The hum of wartime, if not the blast or cry of battle, pervades her fiction."[1]

The Marxist literary and cultural critic Raymond Williams, a great admirer of Jane Austen and "the intricacy of her social observation," tackled the myth when he wrote:

> It is a truth universally acknowledged, that Jane Austen chose to ignore the decisive historical events of her time. Where, it is still asked, are the Napoleonic wars: the real current of history? But history has many currents, and the social history of the landed families, at that time in England, was among the most important.[2]

We could take Williams's point further: the Napoleonic Wars themselves play a vital role in Austen's world, in the social history of landed families and their making and remaking. Austen doesn't come out with all guns blazing, but she keeps the Napoleonic Wars in her sights.

30 Great Myths About Jane Austen, First Edition. Claudia L. Johnson and Clara Tuite.
© 2020 John Wiley & Sons, Inc. Published 2020 by John Wiley & Sons, Inc.

Indeed, as Mary Favret details, the Napoleonic Wars are significant as the first instance of what she calls "war at a distance." Until the battle of Culloden in 1745, Britain experienced "a century of almost constant military action" on home soil, but thereafter "distance – either geophysical or temporal – was increasingly built into the British nation's understanding of war."[3] Most people experienced war in the background, *not* in the foreground. This distance is partly an effect of the scale of war. The Napoleonic Wars are the first to have a global reach. They included the Peninsular War (1808–1814), Britain's main contribution to the war against Napoleon, fought in the Iberian peninsula, and the first guerrilla war in modern history ("guerrilla" being a diminutive of *guerra*, war). In opposing Napoleon's invasion of Spain, ordinary Spanish civilians defeated the standing French army, killing many more French troops than their British supporters did, through an ingenious resistance based on mobility, secrecy, and surprise, including ambushes and camouflage, against a larger, more visible, but less mobile army.[4]

Austen's novels register the wars' impact on the England of her time. Unprecedentedly high proportions of the male population were mobilized for military or naval service, including the Austen family, who had not been involved with the army in peacetime. In the first years of the war, trained citizens were formed into militias in the southern counties to meet the perceived threat of invasion by France and to free up the regular army for overseas wars. Jane Austen's brother Henry joined the Oxfordshire militia in 1793, serving as a lieutenant, captain, paymaster, and adjutant, and later becoming an army agent. James Austen had a regimental chaplaincy purchased for him by his father-in-law, while Francis (Frank) and Charles both went to sea at an early age and had distinguished careers in the Royal Navy. Frank eventually became an Admiral of the Fleet after leaving home at 13 to train in the Royal Naval Academy at Portsmouth.

Frank's letters home and Jane's conversations with Frank and Charles when they were ashore provided her with first-hand accounts of war. The details of war, in effect commemorating her brothers' careers, are inscribed into Austen's fictions in subtle, often intricate ways.

While marriage was the sole source of social advancement for women of Austen's time, advancement for men occurred predominantly through the armed services, the church, and the professions. Austen's novels register the dramatic increase in military numbers during the Napoleonic Wars, exploring its increasing importance in the history of the landed families. The novels engage contemporary debates about social advancement and military behavior. The militia were politically contentious, particularly in areas where they were billeted by locals, as *Pride and Prejudice* registers; Catherine and Lydia "were well supplied," Austen's narrator tells us, "both with news and happiness by the recent arrival of a militia regiment in the neighbourhood." The novel adverts to the soldiers' misbehavior when the women discuss delicious scandals such as how "a private had been flogged" (*PP*, 31, 67).

Austen's novels portray a social milieu animated by shifting power relations across and within classes, the increased social and sexual power of officers, and the experience of wartime culture, not on the battlefield but in the social spaces where young gentry women circulated. The novels often portray the army satirically, while representing the navy more sympathetically. In *Pride and Prejudice*'s George Wickham, Austen recycles the figure of the rakish seducer from eighteenth-century fiction; and it is significant that she chooses the militia as the habitat of this refashioned specimen of fatal masculinity. In contrast to Wickham's "affectation" and "frivolous gallantry" (*PP*, 259), Captain Wentworth's repeated bows are not swaggering flourishes but gentle displays of courtesy (seemingly addressed only to Anne), combining intimacy and politeness. In each case, Austen uses a military milieu to show social customs and rituals as registers of historical change.

Pride and Prejudice offers a detailed representation of the military, exploring its social power through the craze for men in uniform, or "regimentals" (*PP*, 32, 80):

> In Lydia's imagination, a visit to Brighton comprised every possibility of earthly happiness. She saw with the creative eye of fancy, the streets of that gay bathing place covered with officers. She saw herself the object of attention, to tens and to scores of them at present unknown. She saw all the glories of the camp; its tents stretched forth in beauteous uniformity of lines, crowded with the young and the gay, and dazzling with scarlet; and to complete the view, she saw herself seated beneath a tent, tenderly flirting with at least six officers at once. (*PP*, 258)

The tents were sites of assignation; a fashionable accessory for ladies in 1794 was a fan decorated with a map of the Brighton militia camp, guiding ladies ("camp followers") to their *reconnoitres* without being seen, as the map on the fan was only visible to its owner. (See Figure 4.)

Everyone was fascinated by regimentals during the Napoleonic Wars. Social historian Linda Colley points out, "Never before or since have British military uniforms been so impractically gorgeous, so brilliant in colour, so richly ornamented or so closely and cunningly tailored. And the more exclusive a regiment an officer belonged to, and the higher his rank, the more dazzling his uniform was likely to be. In every sense he was dressed to kill."[5] British soldiers during the Napoleonic Wars were masters of self-fashioning, and did it with a

Figure 4 Fan decorated with the layout of the Brighton militia camp (1794). Costume collection, Worthing Museum and Art Gallery.

vengeance. Austen is fascinated by these young men's social and sexual power, as the services become a primary avenue of social advancement for men without property or wealth.

The service uniform returns in *Mansfield Park* when Fanny Price's brother William parades before his family, all decked out in his new "Lieutenant's uniform, looking and moving all the taller, firmer, and more graceful for it" (*MP*, 444). William is a new kind of hero, at the lower end of the social scale, the talented young midshipman who is promoted to lieutenant. Austen intriguingly plots the machinations involved in that process of promotion – and its interrelations with the romance plot of Henry Crawford's untoward affections for Fanny. As Brian Southam notes, Henry Crawford completes another chain in the novel's "overarching drama of obligation" when he assists William Price to gain promotion by securing the "interest" of his uncle Admiral Crawford, and then tells Fanny he has done it all for her.[6]

The Napoleonic Wars were also partly colonial wars between Britain and France. Britain blockaded the Continent, cutting Napoleon off from French islands in the Caribbean, and in 1813 he banned the importation of sugar in the lands he controlled. This rivalry informs *Mansfield Park*'s representation of the relationship between the estates in England and the estate in Antigua, where the sugar plantations used slave labor. *Mansfield Park* registers the "dead silence" with which Sir Thomas greets Fanny's awkward question about the slave trade (*MP*, 231). The Austens had a connection to Antigua, where in 1760 George Austen had become a trustee of a plantation belonging to an Oxford contemporary, James Nibbs.[7] Depending on money from plantations while also expressing their horror of slavery, they lived with the contradictions shared by many of their class and religious outlook in the period.

When the slave trade was abolished in 1807, the navy was called upon to intercept slaving ships at sea, just as they had been charged with protecting the trade before it was outlawed. "Slavery," Frank Austen had written, "however it is modified is still slavery." He denounced the "harshness and despotism" of the "land-holders or their managers in the West India Islands."[8] Charles Austen, too, was a man of principle, known for promoting the welfare of his soldiers. In 1827, he received an inscribed sword from the Venezuelan Simón Bolívar "as a mark of his esteem."[9] Bolívar fought against Spanish rule in America after the French invasion of Spain, and proclaimed the independence of the former Spanish colonies of Colombia, Ecuador, Panama, and Venezuela.

In *Persuasion*, the hero Captain Wentworth is a young man who is originally thought unworthy of the heroine but redeems himself (and becomes wealthy) through service to his country. Austen's novel is set in 1814, during the period known as the "false peace," when Napoleon was imprisoned on the island of Elba before his triumphant return to Paris. *Persuasion* explores Anne's feelings for Wentworth while providing insights into the lives of England's sailors. It is Austen's most sustained account of war as an emotional experience, of living through war and, indeed, not quite being able to live out of it – Anne offers the civilian perspective of the "sailor's wife" during the false peace, when "the dread of a future war [was] all that could dim her sunshine" (*P*, 275).

Persuasion illuminates this experience of contemporary war, while locating that experience as an age-old one for women – overlaying Anne's experiences with those of Dido and Cleopatra, the characters of Ovid's *Heroides*, archetypal figures of women at home separated from their lovers by war. The poignancy of *Persuasion* is that Wentworth is at first so distant and then so close – but still apparently unattainable for Anne.

This point brings us back to a central claim in addressing our myth. War for Jane Austen is not in the foreground, as it is with Walter Scott, who goes back to the battle of 1745 in *Waverley* (1814) and puts the traditional mode of warfare front and center. Contemporary war was different because of its remoteness. Favret suggests that "the experience of war at a distance prompts a move toward abstraction,"[10] but there is more than this in Austen's case, for her style is far from abstract.

Mary Poovey suggests that indirection is a key feature of Austen's fictional world: Austen "carefully managed the historical traces her novels contain" in order "simultaneously to register and to deflect attention away from historical realities."[11] This sheds new light on Richard Simpson's observation in 1870 that Austen "lived and wrote through the period of the French Revolution and the European war without referring to them once."[12] Poovey's insight suggests that this observation is correct, but also complicates it by demonstrating that Austen's texts are not about reference but about indirection, allusion, the subtle encoding of historical reference. We might think of Austen's representational tactics, with their asymmetrical, irregular forms, as being like those of guerrilla warfare.

War has also been an important part of the context for the reception of Austen's fiction: how it was read and by whom. For readers during the two world wars of the twentieth century, it was the apparent avoidance of war that made Austen's fiction so welcome as a kind of retreat or refuge. And with this our focus shifts to the emotional experience Austen's fiction provides as an antidote to war. Writing in the wake of World War I (the so-called Great War), the critic A.C. Bradley observed that "her novels make exceptionally peaceful reading. She troubles us neither with problems nor with painful emotions, and if there is a wound in our minds she is not likely to probe it."[13]

Kathryn Sutherland emphasizes Austen's reception during World War I, particularly by soldiers in the trenches, and notes that the first scholarly texts of Austen, the five-volume 1923 Clarendon Press edition of *The Novels of Jane Austen*, was edited by R.W. Chapman on his return from fighting in Macedonia.[14]

In a blog post on Austen's "wartime packaging," Janine Barchas notes that the American Library Association's War Service Library program distributed "over 100 million books and magazines to hospitals and encampments. ... Presumably Austen was deemed wholesome and entertaining reading as well as a fitting reminder of the traditions the military fought to protect."[15] Later, in World War II, when soldiers were provided with "lightweight paperbacks designed to fit in the pocket of a uniform, Jane was part of Penguin's 'Forces Book Club' series for British servicemen."[16] Similarly, D.W. Harding, the psychology lecturer and war psychologist, terms Austen "a formidable ally who stands with you against the things *you hate*."[17]

Also during World War II, Virginia Woolf writes of Austen and Scott: "Wars were then remote. ... Today we hear the gunfire in the Channel. We turn on the wireless. ... Jane Austen never heard the cannon roar at Waterloo." But, as Favret observes, "Woolf herself loses sight of the distinction between war and war mediated. Her war is brought to her by the wireless radio, by disembodied voices in the air."[18] Yet this is how war comes to many of us all over the world. Indeed, it is increasingly how Austen comes to us too, first experienced through movies and television and then through the books.

The Syrian war that commenced in 2011 has been one of the longest and deadliest wars of the twenty-first century so far. The Jane Austen Literacy Foundation has been working to counter the normalization of an enduring state of war. Established in 2014 by Caroline Knight, Jane Austen's fifth great-niece, the foundation seeks "to harness the global passion for Jane Austen to support literacy through volunteer programs and fund literacy libraries for communities in need across the world." This includes funding libraries for temporary schools in Syria so that schoolchildren can access the education interrupted by war.[19]

Notes

1 Gillian Russell, "The Army, the Navy, and the Napoleonic Wars," *A Companion to Jane Austen*, ed. Claudia L. Johnson and Clara Tuite (Chichester: Wiley Blackwell, 2009), p. 262.

2 Raymond Williams, *The Country and the City* (London: Hogarth Press, 1993), p. 117, 113.

3 Mary Favret, *War at a Distance: Romanticism and the Making of Modern Wartime* (Princeton, NJ: Princeton University Press, 2010), p. 10.

4 Andrew Roberts, *Napoleon & Wellington* (London: Phoenix, 2003), p. 114.

5 Linda Colley, *Britons: Forging the Nation 1707–1837* (New Haven, CT: Yale University Press, 1992), p. 19.

6 Brian Southam, *Jane Austen and the Navy* (London: National Maritime Museum, 2005), p. 205.

7 See Frank Gibbon, "The Antiguan connection: Some new light on *Mansfield Park*," *The Cambridge Quarterly*, 11, (1982), pp. 298–305.

8 Honan: Frank Austen quoted in Park Honan, *Jane Austen: Her Life* (New York: Fawcett Columbine, 1989), p. 422.

9 Southam, *Jane Austen and the Navy*, p. 176.

10 Favret, *War at a Distance*, p. 10.

11 Mary Poovey, "From politics to silence: Jane Austen's nonreferential aesthetic," *A Companion to Jane Austen*, ed. Claudia L. Johnson and Clara Tuite (Chichester: Wiley Blackwell, 2009), pp. 251–252.

12 Richard Simpson, quoted in *Jane Austen: The Critical Heritage*, ed. B.C. Southam, vol. 1 (London: Routledge & Kegan Paul, 1987), p. 242.

13 A.C. Bradley, English Association lecture, 1911.

14 See Kathryn Sutherland, *Jane Austen's Textual Lives* (Oxford: Oxford University Press, 2005), pp. 16–17, 23–24.

15 Janine Barchas, "G.I. Jane: Austen goes to war," https://jhupress.wordpress.com/2014/04/23/g-i-jane-austen-goes-to-war/, accessed 17 February 2019.

16 Ibid.
17 See Wendy Lee, "Resituating 'regulated hatred': D.W. Harding's Jane Austen," *ELH* 77, (2010), pp. 995–1014.
18 Favret, *War at a Distance*, p. 46.
19 https://janeaustenlf.org/about-us, accessed 30 June 2019.

Myth
16 SOMETHING HAPPENED TO JANE AUSTEN WHEN SHE WROTE MANSFIELD PARK

"What became of Jane Austen?"[1] That's the question Kingsley Amis famously asked when considering the peculiarity of *Mansfield Park*. What happened, he wondered, to make the author who had just penned the famously light, bright, and sparkling *Pride and Prejudice* produce the dark, dense, and dour *Mansfield Park*? What happened to the clever dialogue, the lively heroine, the attractive gents, the hilarious fools and knaves? Perhaps unconsciously echoing the discourse of pathology, disease, and vitiation that runs through this novel, many readers have asked the same questions. Did Jane Austen undergo a conversion to evangelicalism, and thus on the grounds of religious principle dramatize the triumph of seriousness over liberty, duty over desire? Or, framing the question psychologically, did she suffer some sort of moral crisis, compelling her to revenge herself upon her own imagination, to scourge her wit, to punish the sassy Elizabeth Bennet by recasting her as the shallow worldling Mary Crawford?

These actually aren't bad questions in themselves. After all, though Mary Crawford mentions evangelicalism sarcastically when mocking Edmund's seriousness, other religious matters – prayer, the reading of sermons, clerical duties – indeed do make up the dialogue in *Mansfield Park* far more conspicuously than in any other novel. And it is likewise extremely important to think about Austen's attitude to wit and liveliness of mind, qualities that are close to damned in this novel, and that arouse

30 Great Myths About Jane Austen, First Edition. Claudia L. Johnson and Clara Tuite.
© 2020 John Wiley & Sons, Inc. Published 2020 by John Wiley & Sons, Inc.

discernible anxiousness in characters like Henry Tilney, Elizabeth Bennet, and Emma Woodhouse as well. What makes these questions wide of the mark is the assumption that something must have been or gone wrong for Austen to take them up in the first place.

When Austen undertook *Mansfield Park*, she was anything but distressed or distraught. Indeed, she was chuffed with the achievement of *Pride and Prejudice*, while at the same time thinking about taking another direction. A letter to Cassandra gives us a clue as to what she was thinking about when she undertook it:

> The work [*Pride and Prejudice*] is rather too light & bright & sparkling; it wants [i.e. needs] shade; – it wants to be stretched out here & there with a long Chapter – of sense, if it could be had; if not, of solemn specious nonsense … anything that would form a contrast & bring the reader with increased delight to the playfulness and general Epigrammatism of the general style.[2]

We don't know exactly how serious or long lasting Austen's (slight, possibly joking) misgivings about *Pride and Prejudice* were. What we *do* know is that Austen clearly wanted her next novel – *Mansfield Park* – to be altogether different: "Now I will try to write of something else; – it shall be a complete change of subject – Ordination."[3] Whether *Mansfield Park* is really about ordination is a matter of debate. But that it is "a complete change of subject" is not. *Mansfield Park* is, after all, the first novel that Austen composed and published entirely in her adulthood and in it we can see her flex her authorial muscle. It is altogether a bigger novel, and its ambition is apparent in the scope and sometimes symbolic resonance of its scenes (e.g. the wilderness, the theatricals, and the debates about acting, the game of Speculation) and in the public importance of issues it raises (e.g. about the role of the clergy in national life, the importance of education, about female manners, about slavery). Austen quite purposefully sought to write "something else" – and that *something* is in pointed contrast to *Pride and Prejudice*.

The first and most startling departure in *Mansfield Park* is its shy, inhibited heroine, Fanny Price. We see Elizabeth Bennet muddying her petticoats by running energetically to Netherfield, her complexion flushed with the exercise, but Fanny tires easily and needs an arm for support. Strolling around a large room, Elizabeth Bennet pays no mind when Darcy says he can better admire her figure from where he is seated, but Fanny cringes with embarrassment when she learns that Edmund and her uncle commented with approval upon her figure. Compliments never take Elizabeth Bennet by surprise, but Mrs. Norris's nasty admonition – "Remember, wherever you are, you must be the lowest and last" (*MP*, 258) – fails to arouse anyone's indignation, much less Fanny's, because Fanny already regards herself as the lowest and the last. Not simply ingenuous, like Catherine Morland, Fanny is seriously damaged by what we today call "low self-esteem," and this sets her apart from Austen's other heroines, even the quietest of whom (such as Anne Elliot) possess a firm sense of self-consequence. Painfully self-conscious, abashed, even abject, Fanny is certainly Austen's most controversial character, sometimes loved as a gentle dutiful Christian girl, sometimes deplored as a passive aggressive killjoy, and sometimes loved and hated alike as a sort of perversely powerful vampire. But regardless of whether we like Fanny or not, the important thing is that she is Austen's most original, most experimental creation, a heroine who has clearly been injured not only by the neglect and scorn of her rich relations but also by the imperative that she must always be grateful for the neglect and scorn she is told to receive as kindness and attention. Never before had a novelist placed so injured a heroine at the center of a novel. To underscore the audacity of Austen's achievement here, consider for a moment what it would be like if the young heroine of *Jane Eyre* thought Mrs. Reed and her horrid son were somehow justified in regarding her as a nuisance, and if she submitted to rather than rebelled against their persecution.

The originality of *Mansfield Park* isn't a matter of the meek heroine alone, but also (inevitably) of the entire context in which she is placed: Mansfield Park itself. Banished from this great house and sent back to the squalid clatter of her birth-home in Portsmouth in order to learn a lesson about the importance of an eligible marriage offer, Fanny fondly thinks back upon Mansfield Park:

> At Mansfield, no sounds of contention, no raised voice, no abrupt bursts, no tread of violence, was ever heard; all proceeded in a regular course of cheerful orderliness; everybody had their due importance; everybody's feelings were consulted. If tenderness could be ever supposed wanting, good sense and good breeding supplied its place. (*MP*, 453)

Not so long ago, this passage was read as Jane Austen's credo, an affirmation of the ideology of the Great House. But the free indirect discourse gives us Fanny's thoughts, not those of Austen or her narrator. To be sure, Fanny thinks of Mansfield Park as a Great Good Place, where everyone and everything is harmoniously and responsibly ordered, where all the contention and conflict that inevitably arise in family life are, if not excluded, at least minimized by fairness and politeness, by benevolent, caring, and effectual authority. In short, Fanny sees Mansfield Park as another Pemberley. But, ever since the first chapter of this novel, we have been shown that this is emphatically not the case. Sir Thomas authorizes Mrs. Norris's nastiness; the Bertram sisters fight as intensely over Henry

Crawford as Fanny's Portsmouth sisters fight over a knife; Sir Thomas approves Maria's loveless marriage to a rich and well-connected dolt; Tom Bertram has depleted Mansfield Park's coffers with his gambling debts. Indeed, the "tread of violence" and the "sounds of contention" – all loud and clear at Portsmouth – are not heard, but that's only because no one – least of all Sir Thomas – is listening. There is a class difference between Portsmouth and Mansfield Park, to be sure, and this is nothing to sneeze at, but there is not really a moral difference. And then, of course, there is the issue of Antigua, where Sir Thomas must repair to fill the coffers his son has drained, and of the slavery on which it subsists. If nothing else, Pemberley shows us that Jane Austen knew how to make the great estate look good, and *Pride and Prejudice* comedically fosters and indulges this effort of idealization. Fanny's idealization, by contrast, is so wishful as to verge on delusional, as her own presence in Portsmouth proves.

Mansfield Park explores not only failures of authority but also, relatedly, failures of basic lucidity. While Austen's other novels prize discernment and contrive scenes of enlightenment or self-understanding, in *Mansfield Park* the language of pathological intellection seems to jump out of every page. Characters are always pronouncing *other* people's minds as "diseased," as "vitiated," as "disordered," or "tainted;" Mansfield is supposed to act as "a cure," much as Fanny's exile to Portsmouth is a "medicinal project" upon Fanny's "understanding" designed to heal her "powers of comparing and judging." Indeed, all of the characters in this novel, Fanny not excepted, seem to shut their eyes while they look, or their understandings while they reason, as the narrator says specifically of Julia Bertram. The kinds of figures in whom we are accustomed to repose trust are in this novel all worrisomely benighted. On whom can we rely? Not the dignified paternal figure, who while always making a pompous pose of rectitude is really interested in money and influence. Not the serious young clergyman who, befuddled by his own desires, is seduced by Mary Crawford's dodginess and blind to his own inconstancy. Not the lively heroine, who is always calculating and blundering. Not the good girl who, struggling (alas not always successfully) with feelings of jealousy, resentment, and neglect, misrecognizes abuse as love and rhapsodizes over some of the novel's weakest and most feckless characters.

To appreciate the singularity of Austen's project here, consider for a moment the very different state of affairs in *Pride and Prejudice*, when Elizabeth Bennet utters the following to her sister Jane:

> "Mr. Collins is a conceited, pompous, narrow-minded, silly man; you know he is, as well as I do; and you must feel, as well as I do, that the woman who marries him, cannot have a proper way of thinking" (*PP*, 153–154).

These words are thrilling because they mark a moment of full disclosure. No need for politeness or equivocation or candid allowances. Elizabeth and Jane are alone – and the simple truth can be uttered confidently. And the reason this can happen, the reason this is alluring, is because there are others in the novel – other sane persons with insight, authority, or both – who do agree or surely would agree with Elizabeth's vigorously uttered truth: characters like Mr. Bennet for one, who will not force Elizabeth to marry Collins, or like Darcy, or Bingley, or the Gardiners, or even mild Jane, characters whose intelligence is both a guide and a comfort. All of this demonstrates the tendency of Austen's novels – inside them, and outside them – to perform the work of distinction, to create a community of insiders, characters who are good guys because they are discerning, because they have (as Elizabeth Bennet puts it) "a proper way of thinking." This discernment holds at bay the fools, knaves, and wannabees outside their charmed circle. Such distinction can itself be invidious or benighting, to be sure, but within the novel it can also feel sheltering.

This is of course one of the most cherished "myths" about or of Jane Austen: that her novels provide and create an effectual community of moral intelligence, but this is precisely the myth *Mansfield Park* does not indulge, instead placing Fanny in a world where no one seems to have an entirely "proper way of thinking," to recollect Elizabeth Bennet's phrase. This void places an uncommon burden of discernment on the reader. Students encountering the novel for the first time tend to ask with puzzlement what they are *supposed* to think, as if searching for a guiding hermeneutic polestar the novel is determined not to provide. On the contrary, the novel seems bent on challenging and developing our "powers of comparing and judging" by staging the differences between the worlds of Mansfield Park and the worlds of the Crawfords as a series of morally loaded oppositions – country/city, gravity/levity, truthfulness/gamesmanship, plain-speaking/punning, lawfulness/lawlessness, constancy/changefulness, sincerity/theatricality, in short good/bad – only to collapse them and in the process baffle our too-easy judgments. Sir Thomas "speculates" just as much as Mary Crawford does, and he "acts" a part as persuasively as Henry Crawford. Edmund talks a good game about moral conduct, but he is as equivocating as any wit. Fanny may not be a bad girl to the same degree as Maria is, but in having formed a powerful romantic attachment secretly and without license she too has shown an erotic independence that is the very essence of bad-girl-itude as imagined in this novel.

The final chapter of *Mansfield Park* famously announces, "Let other pens dwell on guilt and misery. I quit such odious subjects as soon as I can, impatient to restore everybody, not greatly in fault themselves, to tolerable comfort, and to have done with all the rest" (*MP*, 533). Up until this point, *Mansfield Park* has dramatized guilt and misery, and the final chapter continues to do so. Still, in the interests of pulling a happy ending out of her hat much as she had done in *Northanger Abbey*, where the "tell-tale compression of pages" tells us we are hurdling forward to "perfect felicity," Austen makes a feint at separating the good guys (those "not greatly in fault themselves") from the bad guys ("the rest"), allowing some modicum of happiness to the former and consigning the latter to narrative hell. But this act of separation, of distinction, is very much against the grain of the novel itself, which has consistently invited us to observe failures of rule and containment – the ha-ha can be breached, lover's vows can be broken, even the incest taboo itself can't perform its task of fencing off erotic desires.

So: what happened to Jane Austen when she wrote this novel? Nothing and everything. She simply sought to defy our expectations of finding a charming rather than inhibited heroine, a reliable rather than unsteady hero, a judicious rather than mercenary paternal figure, and an euphorically expansive and benign rather than dysphorically occluded and menacing sense of sexuality, and a credibly happy ending rather than an eleventh-hour patch-up job. In the process, Austen pushed against the boundaries of her own novelistic practice and brought us closer to the world of Victorian fiction.

Notes

1 Kingsley Amis, "What became of Jane Austen?" *Spectator* (4 October 1959), pp. 339–340.
2 Jane Austen to Cassandra Austen, 4 February 1813, *Jane Austen's Letters*, ed. Deirdre Le Faye, third edition (Oxford: Oxford University Press, 1995), p. 203.
3 Jane Austen to Cassandra Austen, 29 January 1813, *Letters*, p. 202.

Myth
17
JANE AUSTEN DISAPPROVED OF THE THEATER

"Shameful! Shameful! But the world is so censorious, no character escapes."
(Richard Brinsley Sheridan, *The School for Scandal*)

In 1809, Jane Austen spoke these words while playing the part of Mrs. Candour in Sheridan's *The School for Scandal* (1777), which was privately performed at a Twelfth Night party. William Heathcote, son of her friend Elizabeth Bigg, remembered Austen playing the part with "great spirit."[1] She knew the play well, having alluded to it in one of her early playlets, "The Visit," which she wrote when she was 13 years old and dedicated to her brother James, who had directed home theatricals for her family between 1782 and 1789. One version of our myth has it that Austen enjoyed private theatricals when she was young but turned against them as she grew older. But her spirited performance as the duplicitous rumor-monger in Sheridan's satirical comedy suggests Austen was enjoying home theatricals well into her thirties. (Sheridan himself regarded *Pride and Prejudice* as "one of the cleverest things" he had read.)[2] Coincidentally, six months earlier in June/July 1808, Austen had visited her brother Henry and his wife Eliza at 16 Michael Place in Brompton, near London, for a month. Living next door to them at No. 17 with her unmarried sister was the actress Miss Jane Pope, who had been the original Mrs. Candour in 1777, and who had just retired, giving her farewell performance at Drury Lane on 26 May 1808.

In fact, Jane Austen's letters show she was an avid and knowledgeable theatergoer throughout her life. She used theatrical techniques in her novels; the mature novels and early writings amply evidence theater's

30 Great Myths About Jane Austen, First Edition. Claudia L. Johnson and Clara Tuite.
© 2020 John Wiley & Sons, Inc. Published 2020 by John Wiley & Sons, Inc.

vivid influence. Given her lifelong interest, how did the rumor arise that Austen disapproved of theater?

This myth is founded upon a reading of *Mansfield Park* (1814), the Austen novel that deals most explicitly with theater. In its central episode, the Bertram children rehearse a production of the racy play *Lovers' Vows*, Elizabeth Inchbald's translation of *Das Kind der Liebe* (Love Child), by August von Kotzebue. The children use the license of "playing" to conduct romantic experiments and flirtations, taking their assigned roles as chances to act out of character. But Sir Thomas returns unannounced from his estate in Antigua and promptly forbids the rehearsals, commands that the sets be torn down, and burns every copy of the play. In the anti-theatrical reading, Austen's attitude is identified with that of her disapproving heroine, Fanny Price, who sees acting as a form of duplicity, disguise, and self-deception.

To be sure, the narrator's sympathies often lie with Fanny, but she is more an object of psychological interest (and a figure of pathos) than a conventional heroine. Fanny is the meek one who inherits, but she is also a study of vulnerability, repression, and subtle familial oppression – someone "totally unused to have her pleasure consulted, or to have any thing take place at all in the way she could desire" (*MP*, 326). Is Austen really asking us to take Fanny's views as the author's commands? Rather, Fanny's circumspection about the theatricals is another sign of her inability to feel comfortable in her own skin, much less in any other that might be foisted on her.

Theater historian Jonas Barish offers a sophisticated version of our myth, analyzing *Mansfield Park* as an updated version of the "antitheatrical prejudice" that emerged during the Protestant Reformation, when playgoing ranked as a sin.[3] This reading assumes the home theatricals episode is intended didactically, as a parable about the dangers of theater, which figures duplicity and insincerity. On the contrary, however, the role of Edmund/Anhalt shows that theater's powers are, if anything, too truthful: "Austen and Mary Crawford recognize that casting Edmund in the role of Anhalt is not a distortion of his character, but a revelation that Edmund and Fanny cannot bear."[4] Austen's novelistic practice does not emphasize disguise or concealment but the illuminating, truth-telling power of theater.

When Austen was in London in March 1814 arranging the publication of *Mansfield Park*, she had a busy schedule of theater-going. At Drury Lane, she saw Edmund Kean ("so great is the rage for seeing Keen") – a new sensation who would become one of the greatest Shakespearean actors – playing one of his most famous roles, Shylock (a role that Henry Crawford wants to play): "I cannot imagine better acting. … I shall like to see Kean again excessively, & to see him with You too; – it appeared to me as if there were no fault in him anywhere; & in his scene with Tubal there was exquisite acting."[5]

The Merchant of Venice was followed by another play, *Illusion, or The Trances of Nourjahad*, which was billed as "a melodramatic spectacle."[6] It featured her favorite actor, Robert Elliston, but she was "too much tired to stay" for all three acts. She observed, "there is a great deal of finery & dancing in it, but I think little merit. Elliston was Nourjahad, but it is a solemn sort of part, not at all calculated for his powers."[7] Far from suggesting anti-theatrical suspicion, Austen's judgment that she is just "too tired" to stay might suggest a slightly jaded overfamiliarity. She is a discriminating theatergoer, practiced in evaluation, and one of her pleasures is articulating what she likes and doesn't like.

Elliston was intended for the church, but ran away to tread the boards at the Theatre Royal in Bath.[8] During Austen's years in Bath from May 1801 until July 1806, *Lovers' Vows* was performed there no fewer than 17 times, with Elliston often playing the part of Frederick. Clearly, the play was an old acquaintance of Austen's by the time she introduced it to Fanny Price in 1814.

We should also appraise Austen's alleged anti-theatrical prejudice in light of both the content of her novels (*what* they represent) and their form (*how* they represent it). In fact, theater informs her entire *oeuvre*. Part of Austen's innovation lies in how she subtly incorporates theatrical methods into the design and practice of her novel-making.

Contrary to the assumption that Austen rigidly identified theater with artifice and insincerity, there is abundant evidence that she used theatrical devices in her novels in ways that emphasized both the everyday and the artificial – secrecy and revelation. John Wiltshire describes Austen as having "naturalized the stage convention of overhearing, making it seem an incidental and common event of ordinary communal life;" he also observes that the "carefully particularized positioning of the various players" in *Persuasion*'s ending "carries a trace of the theatre" and combines "with the near-rhetoric of her principals" to give the scene an "almost operatic grandeur."[9]

A marvelous example of Austen's complex and multi-vocal use of theatricality occurs when Sir Thomas catches the children in the act of rehearsal. Even Fanny has now relented sufficiently "to *read* the part" (if not act it) so the others can begin:

> They *did* begin – and being too much engaged in their own noise, to be struck by unusual noise in the other part of the house, and had proceeded some way, when the door of the room was thrown open, and Julia appearing at it, with a face all aghast, exclaimed, "My father is come! He is in the hall at the moment."

END OF VOLUME I

VOLUME II

CHAPTER I

How is the consternation of the party to be described? To the greater number it was a moment of absolute horror ... [N]ot a word was spoken for
half a minute; each with an altered countenance was looking at some other
... It was a terrible pause; and terrible to every ear were the corroborating
sounds of opening doors and passing footsteps. (*MP*, 201, 202–205)

What stands out here is how Austen's division of volumes and chapters
mimics the layout of scenes in a play. The dramatic suspense is heightened
by her mastery of timing – by the "terrible pause" corroborated by the
father's "opening doors and passing footsteps." Austen's text brings the
curtain down on this heightened *dénouement* in a consummately theatrical way.

This theatricality draws attention to stage conventions, reminding
readers that they are watching a scene. For all the terror associated with
Sir Thomas's entrance, and all the "iniquity" Austen associates with the
young people's theatrical activities, according to Barish, the tonal register
here is one of comedy, melodrama, and farce. The return of the father is
presented farcically. His footsteps inspire terror in his children, but in the
reader they inspire laughter. It is a pantomime of patriarchal authority
under threat.

This episode has been read as an allegory of political rebellion, informed
by the counter-revolutionary 1790s, where the paternal figure is associated with the survival of the monarchy. The radical political philosopher
Tom Paine saw the French Revolution as unmasking a monarchy "kept
behind a curtain" and cultivating "a wonderful air of seeming solemnity;
but when, by any accident, the curtain happens to be open, and the company see what it is, they burst into laughter."[10] Austen, too, gets a laugh
out of patriarchal solemnity. The Bertram children are terrified, but we
read with gleeful delight. This is not to suggest that Austen shares Tom
Paine's radical politics, but the two writers do share a sense of irony
and a gift for comedy. In this classic moment of dramatic irony – when
the audience is given a different perspective on the events being
staged – Austen is having too much fun to be disapproving.

Barish argues that the theatricals in *Mansfield Park* are "charged with
a mysterious iniquity that defies explanation."[11] This speaks to the
novel's dark tone, but it is too literal a reading. The novel represents
theatricality in a slyly ironic way, giving it a range of meanings. It is
promiscuous in its use of theatrical devices – and in its range of tones

(including "iniquity," delight, suspense, and joyful parody). This creation of tone and atmosphere is one of the tasks of theatrical staging. Austen creates atmosphere by layering different tones and perspectives. For Fanny, theater has a mysterious iniquity, but there is also delight, suspense, and a gentle parody of her censorious view. Austen's staging balances all these tones and presents a range of perspectives to the reader. Far from being anti-theatrical, *Mansfield Park* is arguably the most theatrical novel Austen wrote.

Where does Austen go with the subversion of paternal authority? For Fanny, "all her former habitual dread of her uncle was returning, and with it compassion for him" (*MP*, 206–207). Suddenly, Sir Thomas is an object of sympathy. This perverse mix of dread and compassion is appropriate for a traumatized child who now feels sorry for her oppressor. But her sympathy extends to "almost every one of the party before him." Austen shows Fanny as an engaged and sympathetic spectator – "feeling" for others, becoming part of something shared and not standing apart. Through theater, by the end of this episode, Austen has coaxed her heroine into being an active, responsive spectator of all those around her.

Another vital domain of theatricality in Austen is musical performance, particularly piano playing. This is perhaps more fraught than theater, and a more neglected topic in Austen studies, because of the conflicted culture of "accomplishment" that informed female education and bourgeois sociability. Performance was at odds with ideals of feminine modesty, but domestic piano playing was almost compulsory for young women. Sheridan's *School for Scandal* itself parodies the rage for accomplishment as a sign of bourgeois aspiration by recalling Lady Teazle's origins as "the Daughter of a plain country Squire," whose "evening amusement" was "to be stuck down to an old Spinnet" (Act II, Scene 1, lines 30, 41, 43–44).

Austen was a life-long piano player who practiced daily from the age of 12 and performed for her family in the evenings. Yet, as Gillen D'Arcy Wood observes, her novels convey an "ambivalent image of music."[12] They include a range of negative images – Marianne Dashwood's "misery" at the keyboard; the secret gift of the Broadwood piano that indexes Jane Fairfax's own secrecy; Mary Crawford's siren-call on the harp; and Mary Bennet's anxious displays of unremarkable pianistic accomplishment – all of which seem to prosecute a case against what the Tory feminist Hannah More called the "frenzy for accomplishment,"[13] a case also supported by the radical Enlightenment feminist Mary Wollstonecraft. As Wood suggests, "Austen's disapproval of musical accomplishment appears to contradict her own personal commitment to the piano,"[14] but her representation of the culture of the piano is much more complex.

Intriguingly and counter-intuitively, Austen associates music, in its most profound and resonant sense, with interiority rather than theatricality. Both the vogue for public recitals and the more intimate mode of domestic performance entail a form of audience-oriented interiority, much like Austen's free indirect discourse, which gives the reader access to her protagonist's inner life. What Wood identifies as the "lyric interiority that Austen's fiction shares with the Viennese music she knew so intimately" is also a mode of ironic sensibility; "in Austen and late Beethoven," irony is "directed toward essentially the same historical object: the parlor-room culture of the 1790s."[15]

Anne Elliot embodies this irony and interiority, trained upon her family through Austen's free indirect discourse: "her performance was little thought of, only out of civility, or to refresh the others, as she was well aware. She knew that when she played she was giving pleasure only to herself; ... she had never ... since the loss of her dear mother, known the happiness of being listened to. In music she had been always used to feel alone in the world" (*P*, 50). Musical performance is associated with Austen's most original and accomplished contributions to the novel form, particularly the technique of free indirect discourse, which maintains the ironic distance *and* sympathy Austen extends to all her heroines.

Austen's world is perhaps not so censorious after all.

Notes

1 See Paula Byrne, *The Real Jane Austen: A Life in Small Things* (New York: Harper Perennial, 2014), p. 139, 142.
2 Quoted in Claire Harman, *Jane's Fame* (Melbourne: Text Publishing, 2009), p. 60.
3 Jonas Barish, *The Antitheatrical Prejudice* (Berkeley, CA: University of California Press, 1981), p. xx.
4 Daniel O'Quinn, "Jane Austen and performance: Theatre, memory, and enculturation," Claudia L. Johnson and Clara Tuite (eds.), *A Companion to Jane Austen* (Chichester: Wiley, 2009), p. 382.
5 Jane Austen to Cassandra Austen, 2–3 and 5–8 March 1814, *Jane Austen's Letters*, ed. Deirdre Le Faye, third edition (Oxford: Oxford University Press, 1995), pp. 256, 257–258.
6 See Le Faye, *Letters*, p. 430, n. 6.
7 Jane Austen to Cassandra Austen, 5–8 March 1814, *Letters*, pp. 257–258.
8 See Byrne, *Real Jane Austen*, p. 146. Byrne also discusses Elliston in *Jane Austen and the Theatre*, pp. 39–41. See also Belville S. Penley, *The Bath Stage* (London, 1892), pp. 75–80.

9 John Wiltshire, *The Hidden Jane Austen* (Cambridge: Cambridge University Press, 2014), p. 166.

10 Tom Paine, "Rights of Man," *Burke, Paine, Godwin, and the Revolution Controversy*, ed. Marilyn Butler (Cambridge: Cambridge University Press, 1984), p. 110.

11 Barish, *Antitheatrical Prejudice*, p. 301.

12 Gillen D'Arcy Wood, *Romanticism and Music Culture in Britain, 1770–1840* (Cambridge: Cambridge University Press, 2010), p. 155.

13 Quoted in Wood, *Romanticism and Music Culture*, p. 155.

14 Wood, *Romanticism and Music Culture*, p. 155.

15 Ibid, pp. 152–153, 167.

Myth

18

JANE AUSTEN WAS A CHRISTIAN MORALIST

This is a complex and delicate subject. That Jane Austen was a sincere and practicing Christian is certainly no myth. Her father was a priest in the Church of England, as were her brothers James and (after failing in his career as a banker) Henry. Regular church attendance and daily prayer were part of her life. The diction and rhythms of *The Book of Common Prayer* animate Austen's prose, but there are only a few references to it in her novels. This sparseness certainly does not indicate indifference. Probably just the opposite, an appropriate reticence. Mr. Collins's declaration that he is "ever ready to perform those rites and ceremonies which are instituted by the Church of England" is absurd not because there is anything risible in the performance of these rites and ceremonies but rather because making an announcement about it is unnecessary and unseemly – hence Elizabeth's bemusement over his "kind intention of christening, marrying, and burying his parishioners whenever it were required" (*PP*, 71). The Church of England is a pervasive, matter-of-fact frame of reference in Austen's novels, requiring little in the way of particular pronouncements or reference.

The givenness of Anglicanism for Austen means that religious subjects appear as a matter of course. Though religious subjects appear markedly in *Mansfield Park*, there is disagreement about how they add up; in other novels, religious resonances can often pass by unnoticed. When Emma finds herself *in charity* or *out of charity* with others or with herself, readers might not feel the full weight of the term *charity*, signifying the duty of neighborly love and active good will. Similarly, readers might not apprehend that when Anne Elliot withdraws to her room for an "interval of meditation" in order to grow "steadfast and fearless in the thankfulness of

30 Great Myths About Jane Austen, First Edition. Claudia L. Johnson and Clara Tuite.
© 2020 John Wiley & Sons, Inc. Published 2020 by John Wiley & Sons, Inc.

her enjoyment" (*P*, 266), she is praying. But if the givenness of Christian teaching and practice appears throughout Austen's novels without any fanfare or emphasis, satire does as well. We all know that Mr. Collins and Mr. Elton, among Austen's most ridiculous and reprehensible characters, are clergymen, and their profession plays no small part in their social climbing and their sense of self-importance. Minor figures such as James Morland and Dr. Grant do not bode much better. If Edmund Bertram is correct in asserting the central role of the clergy in forming the manners and mores of the country – "It will, I believe, be everywhere found, that as the clergy are, or are not what they ought to be, so are the rest of the nation" (*MP*, 109) – then England would appear to be in serious trouble.[1]

Austen is both unobtrusive and undefensive in her representations of and allusions to the Christian religion, but after her death her family felt the need to underscore Austen's piety over and above her genius. In his "Biographical Notice," Henry Austen has nothing to say about Austen's literary character, representing her as modestly retiring. But he has a lot to say about the strenuousness of her piety: "She was thoroughly religious and devout; fearful of giving offence to God, and incapable of feeling it towards any fellow creature … her opinions accorded strictly with those of our Established Church" (*P*, 331). As if anxious that the novels might convey the opposite impression, Henry Austen (like J.E. Austen-Leigh after him) stresses Austen's loving kindness: "She never uttered either a hasty, a silly, or a severe expression" (*P*, 329). Any reader of Austen's letters and novels might well suspect there is some mythologizing going on here. Henry's "Biographical Notice," doubtless heartfelt, has the effect of blandly sanctifying Jane Austen, as if the price for bringing her into public view as writer – "outing" her officially as the author of *Northanger Abbey* and *Persuasion* and the four previous novels – were obscuring her in another way. Henry insists that Austen was never satiric, never barbed, never unusual, funny, or even individuated in any way, but was rather generically sweet, mild, and gentle in word and deed – precisely the kind of "picture of perfection" that Austen once described as making her "sick and wicked."[2]

Whatever the efforts of Austen's family in managing Austen's posthumous reputation for piety, most readers are ready to agree that Austen, as Archbishop Whately observed in 1821, "is evidently a Christian writer."[3] But Whately's use of "evidently" here deserves much closer attention than we have customarily given it. Whately insists – with enthusiastic approval – that Austen is not a didactic writer, and he takes pains to stress Austen's artistry over moralism. Her *evident* Christianity contrasts sharply with the blatant Christian teaching of Hannah More's *Coelebs in*

Search of a Wife, a novel Austen did not enjoy. The "moral instruction" we receive from her novels is not obtrusive and is observable instead only by inference. But the content of these "moral lessons" turns out to be unhelpfully bland and nonspecific. Whately cites a very long passage from Chapter 2 of *Mansfield Park*, where the Bertram girls are fondly indulged as they marvel at their "prodigiously stupid" little cousin's ignorance of watercolors, geography, and "all the metals, semi-metals, planets, and distinguished philosophers" (*MP*, 20). Thus, as Whately would have it, we "learn" that "selfishness, self-importance, and a want of moral training" can lead to bad ends. This is the lesson Sir Thomas draws from the catastrophe of Mansfield Park as well, but it is a lesson hardly commensurate to the complexity of this very searching novel.

Some readers find Austen's "evident" groundedness in Anglicanism the very bedrock of her practice as a novelist, or as C.S. Lewis phrases it, "the religious background of the author's ethical position." C.S. Lewis emphasizes "the hardness – at least the firmness – of Jane Austen's thought," by which he meant the unequivocal, uncompromising certainty with which Austen deploys the "great abstract nouns of classical English" – e.g. good sense, courage, contentment, fortitude, impropriety, indelicacy, vanity, folly, ignorance, and reason. The supposedly tidy clarity of these concepts is, further, what makes Austen's comedy possible, for they constitute the bedrock of norms against which departures from norms can be found laughable. Lewis thus points to Catherine Morland's shame at suspecting General Tilney of murder, and Elizabeth Bennet's humbled realization that she has been vulnerable to flattery and blinded by her own prejudice, as if the disillusioning of her heroines were the essence of Austen's moral project, and as if the novels stopped right there.[4] But Catherine Morland comes back to and reaffirms her Gothic suspicions about the General. And Elizabeth may have been wrong about Wickham, but she was not wrong in judging Darcy to have been insolent and high-handed. Darcy himself registers this by changing his behavior for her sake. While we agree that Austen's lexicon is grounded in the "great abstract nouns of classical English," we do not find these sufficient to account for the dramas of her novels. Moralized readings of Austen tend to fix judgments of and on characters who are themselves always in dramatic motion, who always find themselves reassessing, and sometimes reversing, their judgments that first seemed so conclusive.

The vexing element in this myth, then, is not the "evident" normativeness of Christian mores for Austen, but rather her classification as a "moralist" and with that the character of her writing. If we define *moralist* in this case as someone whose writing explores moral issues, then we could only find a very few novelists who are *not* moralists. But if we define *moralist* more specifically as someone whose writing recommends specific moral behaviors or teachings, the case for Austen is hard to make. Consider, for example, the fate of Lydia in *Pride and Prejudice*. In any conventional novel of the period, she would have returned to Longbourn shame-faced and broken, and she might have even taken to her bed and died, as Marianne Dashwood almost did. Instead, we behold Lydia's full-bodied presence: "Lydia was Lydia still; untamed, unabashed, wild, noisy, and fearless" (*PP*, 348). Without a doubt, there is something shocking about Lydia's impermeability to shame and about her concomitant self-ishness, but there is also something unnerving and rather fascinating about her robustness that Austen – pointedly – refuses to moralize about. The moralizing is left to Mr. Collins, in a scolding letter addressed to Mr. Bennet:

> I must not ... neglect the duties of my station, or refrain from declaring my amazement, at hearing that you received the young couple into your house as soon as they were married. It was an encouragement of vice; and had I been the rector of Longbourn, I should very strenuously have opposed it. You ought certainly to forgive them, as a Christian, but never to admit them in your sight, or allow their names to be mentioned in your hearing. (*PP*, 403)

Austen adduces this judgment to refuse it – "That is his notion of Christian forgiveness!" Mr. Bennet laughs. Manifestly, Austen is not recommending Lydia's behavior: Elizabeth is shocked by her sister's coarseness and audacity. But the point is that Austen does not punish or censure her. Lydia is not to be tidily disposed of and her presence – her very survival in other words – is itself intriguing, if also irritating.

Austen's disinterest in pronouncing moral judgments is even more evident in *Mansfield Park*, sometimes considered her most moralizing novel. Here the high crime that constitutes the dénouement of the novel is adultery: Maria (Bertram) Rushworth runs off with Henry Crawford, who at the time is engaged to Fanny Price. Austen presents a wide range of responses to this catastrophe as Fanny comes to learn about it. Mary Crawford describes it as "a moment's *étourderie*" (*MP*, 506). The newspaper describes it as "a matrimonial *fracas*" (*MP*, 509); Fanny's father suggests "a little flogging" (*MP*, 509) by way of punishment and preventative. Mrs. Price calls it "shocking" (*MP*, 510) and then lapses back into complete indifference. Finally, it is Fanny who, inwardly, pronounces moral judgment:

> The horror of a mind like Fanny's, as it received the conviction of such guilt, and began to take in some part of the misery that must ensue, can hardly be described. At first, it was a sort of stupefaction... The event was so shocking,

that there were moments even when her heart revolted from it as impossible – when she thought it could not be. A woman married only six months ago – a man professing himself devoted, even *engaged* to another; that other her near relation – the whole family, both families connected as they were by tie upon tie; all friends, all intimate together! It was too horrible a confusion of guilt, too gross a complication of evil, for human nature, not in a state of utter barbarism, to be capable of! (*MP*, 510–511)

For "a mind such as Fanny's," adultery arouses a degree of abhorrence more often associated with violations of the incest taboo, a confusion, a co-mingling of entities that ought to be distinct. Clearly, Fanny's response is excessive, revealing not only a vehemence and fervor often contained in the apparent placidity of her temper but also a naivete about "human nature, not in a state of barbarism." Whatever else it may be, Maria's adultery is at least exogamous. And isn't the co-mingling of ties, friends, and families something Fanny dearly wishes? She registers no uneasiness when her cousin Edmund later greets her with the statement, "My Fanny, my only sister; my only comfort now!" As Fanny pronounces on the others' evil, she shows confusion herself. The authority of her moral judgment here is undercut by her *schadenfreude*. Much as her sister Susan's broad smiles at leaving Portsmouth for Mansfield Park are concealed by her bonnet, Fanny's heart also swells with secret joy as she realizes that the scandal has both vindicated her and wrested her beloved Edmund from the grasp of Mary Crawford.

Austen's narrator is fond of Fanny – "My Fanny" (*MP*, 533) – but her attitude to adultery contrasts quite pointedly with Fanny's:

> Mr. Rushworth had no difficulty in procuring a divorce; and so ended a marriage contracted under such circumstances as to make any better end the effect of good luck not to be reckoned on. She had despised him, and loved another – and he had been very much aware that it was so. The indignities of stupidity, and the disappointments of selfish passion, can excite little pity. His punishment followed his conduct, as did a deeper punishment, the deeper guilt of his wife. *He* was released from the engagement to be mortified and unhappy, till some other pretty girl could attract him into matrimony again, and he might set forward on a second, and, it is to be hoped, more prosperous trial of the state – if duped, to be duped at least with good humour and good luck; while *she* must withdraw with infinitely stronger feelings to a retirement and reproach which could allow no second spring of hope or character. (*MP*, 537)

Far from describing Maria's crime as surprising or unthinkable, the narrator finds it was all too predictable. Any "better end" could not "be reckoned on" given that Maria "despised" Rushworth from the start and that he actually knew it from the start, as did everyone else who cared to notice. Fanny dwells with horror on the "complication of evil," while the narrator dwells on the "indignities of stupidity, and the disappointments of selfish passion." To be sure, the narrator is not condoning adultery: guilt and selfishness are called by their names. But she dials down the moralizing language and replaces it with a noticeably worldlier, even slightly jaded, discourse about folly, and the "punishment" meted out here is social: humiliation for him, and banishment from polite society for her.

As Whately winds down his discussion of *Persuasion*, he pauses over its seemingly equivocal moral conclusion: does it recommend prudence in marriage (certainly a risky thing), or does it advocate trust in the impulses of a loving heart (also a risky thing)? To his credit, Whately seems entirely to enjoy the indeterminacy of this lesson and in so doing shows himself to be a splendid reader of Austen's novels, which work not to fix and foreclose judgments but rather to suspend them with alertness and pleasure.

Notes

1 See Irene Collins's excellent *Jane Austen and the Clergy* (London: Bloomsbury Academic Press, 2002).

2 Jane Austen to Fanny Knight, 23–25 March 1817, *Jane Austen's Letters*, ed. Deirdre Le Faye, third edition (Oxford: Oxford University Press, 1995), p. 335.

3 *Jane Austen: The Critical Heritage*, vol. 1, ed. B.C. Southam (London: Routledge & Kegan Paul, 1987), p. 95.

4 C.S. Lewis, "A note on Jane Austen," *Essays in Criticism*, 4(4), (1954), pp. 361, 363.

Myth 19

IN *EMMA*, JANE AUSTEN CREATED A HEROINE NO ONE BUT AN AUTHOR WOULD LOVE

This myth originated from Jane Austen herself, who apparently remarked of her creation: "I am going to take a heroine whom no one but myself will much like."[1] This piece of family folklore was recounted by her nephew James Edward Austen-Leigh in his *Memoir* (1870). Austen's playful malediction has become a self-fulfilling prophecy, and its ironic challenge to *Emma*'s readers has been all but ignored. Instead, a curious consensus has prevailed to "take" Emma Woodhouse as a paragon of bad behavior and ugly feelings: "patronizing and a little presumptuous," snobbish and vain, she is narcissistic, "without tenderness" and with an "urge to dominate."[2]

Despite its heroine's bad social form, *Emma* is celebrated for "the infinite delights and subtleties of its workmanship."[3] In this novel, Austen masters her most sophisticated techniques and innovations in aesthetic form. The early-twentieth-century Austen critic R.W. Chapman exemplifies this disconnect between dislike of the heroine and praise of the novel: "Emma herself, I suppose, is no one's favorite [but] I find the supremacy of *Emma* in the matchless symmetry of its design, in the endless fascination of its technique."[4] Nevertheless, Emma has had her champions, like Cardinal Newman: "I feel kind to her whenever I think of her."[5] How

30 Great Myths About Jane Austen, First Edition. Claudia L. Johnson and Clara Tuite.
© 2020 John Wiley & Sons, Inc. Published 2020 by John Wiley & Sons, Inc.

odd it is, then, that, while *Emma* is Austen's "kindliest" novel,[6] readers have been so mean to its protagonist.

The mid-century critic Marvin Mudrick, possibly Emma's most unkind reader, attacked what he saw as an unseemly proximity between Harriet and Emma, a certain "tendency" on Emma's part: "Emma is in love with her … Emma prefers the company of women, more particularly of women whom she can master and direct."[7] Whatever the relationship between Emma and Harriet, possibly more scandalous is the intimacy between Emma and her narrator. It explains the novel's paradoxical conjunction of bad behavior and dazzling style. This scandalous intimacy is the effect of Austen's most mature novelistic technique: free indirect discourse. *Emma* is widely regarded as Austen's most accomplished achievement in this form.

Emma marked a turning point in Austen's career. The first of Austen's postwar novels, it was also the first published by John Murray, the prestigious publisher of Lord Byron and Sir Walter Scott, who wrote Austen's first major review. Appearing under Murray's imprint in late December 1815, *Emma* represents the beginning of Austen's public success.

Austen's fourth-published novel has a new technical assurance that matches its protagonist's confidence. A propertied heiress with £30 000 (and no brothers to stand in the way), Emma Woodhouse is Austen's most economically advantaged and socially powerful heroine. The heroines of her other novels are dispossessed (Elinor and Marianne Dashwood), displaced (Fanny Price), explicitly disinherited (Elizabeth Bennet and Anne Elliot), or simply poor (Catherine Morland).[8] Emma's father is lower on the social scale than Knightley, her eventual husband; so, when Emma marries, she marries up. Significantly, though, she does not *have* to marry. In fact, her father, rather perversely, does not want her to marry. Unlike Austen's other heroines, Emma Woodhouse is in no danger of being thrown into poverty; she can afford to wait.

Much of the traditional ambivalence toward Emma relates to her extraordinary social power, which is announced in the novel's opening sentence:

> Emma Woodhouse, handsome, clever, and rich, with a comfortable home and happy disposition, seemed to unite some of the best blessings of existence; and had lived nearly twenty-one years in the world with very little to distress or vex her. (*E*, 3)

To have endured very little distress or vexation emphasizes the "blessings" of Emma's "existence," where her worst misfortunes are being aggrieved by something petty or having to be polite to people who vex her.

The novel's innovation lies in its anatomy of privilege and politeness. Many moments feature Emma striving to be polite, as at the Westons' dinner party: "For her own sake she could not be rude; and for Harriet's … she was even positively civil; but it was an effort." When Emma starts to suspect that Mr. Elton is "beginning to transfer his affections from Harriet to me," the narrator presents this reflection as "an internal suggestion," then comments in indirect discourse ("she was even positively civil"), before shifting to free indirect discourse ("it was an effort"), mimicking Emma's voice and embodying the intimacy between narrator and protagonist that is the hallmark of the free indirect style (*E*, 127). This subtle movement between indirect and free indirect – moving in and out of the deep imbrication between narrator and character – characterizes the sophistication and subtlety of Austen's mature style.

The novel might be said to aid and abet Emma's privilege, the opening sentence seeming to endorse a particularly female kind of power. At the same time, it ironizes Emma, showing us how she misuses her power in her matchmaking, her condescension to the poor, her graceless teasing of Miss Bates at Box Hill, and her interactions with the denizens of Highbury who make Emma their "Queen."[9] The combination of sympathy and critique marks the free indirect style. Despite the narrator's complicity with Emma's bad behavior, the narrative subjects Emma nevertheless to subtle critique; this occurs as moments of startling self-revelation, so that the critique is softened by its almost instantaneous – luminous – transfiguration into self-revelation. Two moments stand out in this regard: Knightley's reprimand for Emma's shabby treatment of Miss Bates, which Chapman refers to as "the agony of Box Hill – the climax of [which] is to me, after a score of readings, almost intolerable," and the climax of the romance plot, "when Emma learns, in two blinding flashes, that she has always been wrong and that she has never been wrong" about Knightley.[10]

A brilliant example of the novel's conjunction of complicity and critique occurs with the visit to Miss Bates. When Emma and Harriet are taking a walk, they pass Miss Bates's house and Emma feels obliged to drop in, having told Harriet they were "just now quite safe from any letter from Jane Fairfax." With her "politeness at hand," Emma disingenuously asks Miss Bates whether she has heard from Miss Fairfax lately (*E*, 166, 167). But they are far from safe, as it transpires. Miss Bates begins "eagerly hunting for the letter" and regaling them with its contents. The rest of the chapter becomes a farcical account of Emma's attempt "without seeming very rude, of making her escape from Jane Fairfax's letter": "'I am afraid we must be running away,'" said Emma, glancing at Harriet, and beginning to rise–" (*E*, 168–169). Miss Bates, of course, protests in vain:

And not all that could be urged to detain [Emma] succeeded. She regained the street – happy in this, that though much had been forced on her against her will, though she had in fact heard the whole substance of Jane Fairfax's letter, she had been able to escape the letter itself. (*E*, 173)

Austen's narrator is complicit with Emma in the humor at Miss Bates's expense, in the passing over of Miss Bates's protests, and in the deadpan reference to "the letter itself."

Here, Emma the character's drama of bad social form is intimately connected to *Emma* the novel's drama of high aesthetic form. The distinction between content ("substance") and form ("the letter itself") mirrors the novel's wider distinction between content (or story) and form, between *what* is narrated and *how*. The novel's subtle maneuvers draw attention to its own modes of narration, inviting the reader to appreciate the how as well as the what.

Emma also has an abiding preoccupation with forms of letter writing, exploring the epistolary style associated with the novels of Austen's beloved predecessor, Samuel Richardson. Jane Fairfax's letter offers one example of the aesthetic mastery with which Austen conducts this exploration. Another is Robert Martin's proposal letter – living for a few minutes on Harriet's pleasure only to die "twisted" in her hand after Emma's faint praise (*E*, 55).

The episode of Jane Fairfax's letter offers Emma herself as an object of comedy, in her determination not to listen to any more about Jane Fairfax: "she tires me to death" (*E*, 192). Here, we see Austen liking her character in different ways. She can like Emma but be able to laugh at her, as the novelist Elizabeth Bowen noted in 1936: "Emma is seen, and felt, as divinely unconsciously funny throughout."[11]

Why is Emma so sensitive about Jane, the vulnerable young woman on the verge of governessing ("the sale – not quite of human flesh – but of human intellect"; *E*, 325)? What is it about Jane that so provokes Emma? The novel's very next gesture, in an implicit rebuke to Emma, is to acknowledge Jane Fairfax's autonomy as a character and source of interest for others. It does this by opening the next chapter (Volume II, Chapter II) with the name of Jane Fairfax, the name Emma cannot bear to hear ("One is sick of the very name of Jane Fairfax"; *E*, 92), and then devoting that chapter to Jane's history: "Jane Fairfax was an orphan, the only child of Mrs. Bates's youngest daughter." These bare facts alone explain Jane Fairfax and her social position, making an immediate claim upon the reader's sympathy (*E*, 174).

Austen encourages our questioning by taking us into Emma's ambivalent feelings for and critical judgments of Jane: "She was, besides, which was worst of all, so cold, so cautious!" (*E*, 180). The exclamation mark emphatically registers the embeddedness of free indirect style, underscoring the narrator's mimicry of Emma's voice, and thereby seeming to endorse her point of view. But this embeddedness is double-edged: sympathetic but also ironic, mimicking but mocking, so close but also so far. This moment displays the free indirect style's prerogative to mimic the protagonist in order to critique. This critique continues in the final line of the chapter: "Emma could not forgive her," and runs on in Chapter III, which opens, with an elegant formality, like a corona sonnet, by repeating this line (*E*, 181, and see 182). This re-statement of Emma's inability to forgive is a pointed indictment, further complicating our myth by demonstrating that Austen too – like the rest of us – is capable of being critical of Emma (and *not* liking her) as occasion demands.

Emma is rightly celebrated in the history of the novel for developing this sophisticated technique with which to present its protagonist's interior life – as though to bear out Emma's claim that

> It is very unfair to judge of any body's conduct, without an intimate knowledge of their situation. Nobody, who has not been in the interior of a family, can say what the difficulties of any individual of that family may be. (*E*, 157)

Emma's statement of self-defense to Knightley could serve as a manifesto for the free indirect style that her author perfects not only to bear out this claim but also to enable her readers "to judge" Emma by giving them the goods ("the interior") to do so. Emma's narrator has an "intimate knowledge" of Emma's situation, and she has "been in the interior" of her family. But this very intimacy raises the possibility of confusion – indeed exploits opportunities for confusion. Who, exactly, is speaking? This brings us to a central paradox of Austen's novel: that its aesthetic complexity – the intimacy between narrator and protagonist – is also a source of readerly confusion.

The complicity and scandalous intimacy between Emma and her narrator-author is comically rendered; hence the pleasurable confusion that greets *Emma*'s readers. Yet this veers at times into darkness – "vexation," "hate," and "a black morning's work" (*E*, 38, 20, 4) – as well as the tangles of romantic plotting that bemuse Austen's characters in "the thickets she weaves about their heads," as Brigid Brophy memorably puts it.[12] The novel is energized by the speed with which pleasure can turn into fear, as when the prospect of meeting Emma inspires "as much panic as pleasure" in Harriet (*E*, 24). Social discomfort is compounded by high emotion, as when Emma rebuffs Mr. Elton's sudden proposal during an unwanted "tête-a-tête drive" back from the Westons. In "swelling resentment, and mutually deep mortification, they had to continue for a few minutes longer," trapped in a shared carriage: "If there had not been so much anger, there would have been desperate awkwardness; but their straight-forward emotions left no room for the little zigzags of embarrassment" (*E*, 143). In this crazy world, it's hard to tell what is worse: "desperate awkwardness" or "straight-forward emotions." On one reading, they might pine for the zigzags, but then on another raw emotions are a refuge from social awkwardness. This novel is preoccupied with the dark emotions inspired by social obligations – emotions that are always on the verge of taking "a perverse turn" (*E*, 135).

Setting the tone is *Emma*'s keenly honed Shakespearean intertext, *A Midsummer Night's Dream* – exuberant, zany and dark by turns.[13] Unlike *Mansfield Park*, with its censorious heroine, Fanny Price, and her un-fun-loving, anti-theatrical ways, *Emma* features a daring "imaginist" as its heroine, "on fire with speculation," a playful narrator, and a dynamic theatrical intertext in Shakespeare's romance: "There does seem to be a something in the air," chirps the merry matchmaker Emma: "'The course of true love never did run smooth' – A Hartfield edition of Shakespeare would have a long note on that passage" (*E*, 362, 79–80). Nevertheless, other people's ideas of midsummer fun can make Emma anxious; so when Frank Churchill proposes that she revive the Crown Inn as a neighborhood ball-room for public dances, she imperiously reminds him of the "difficulty in every body's returning into their proper place the next morning" (*E*, 213).

Austen's narrator (like Emma herself) plays tricks on her readers, inviting them to mistake illusion for reality, as in Shakespeare's *Dream*, where magic and illusion are central. Another shared feature is the piquancy of ambivalent emotion, as when the servants rejoice in "the happiness of frightful news" about Harriet's encounter with the gypsies (*E*, 363). *Emma*'s readers need to keep their wits about them, so they don't mistake appearance for reality, or confuse the character's point of view with that of the author. A large source of *Emma*'s mischief is the narrator's readiness to keep readers on their toes lest they be deceived or caught unawares, as Harriet is by the gypsies.

An audacious instance of the narrator's readiness to deceive us is when Emma observes Harriet and Mr. Elton as "lovers": "The lovers were standing together at one of the windows. It had a most favourable aspect" (*E*, 96). Yet, for all Emma's machinations, Elton and Harriet are not lovers. Elton wants Emma herself as his lover (and will soon become her rejected suitor). Emma's matchmaking "glory" is short-lived; her scheme soon turns back upon herself with triangulated *Midsummer* perversity.

The "favourable aspect" is an illusion, as its delivery in free indirect mode slyly suggests. Austen lets the illusion stand, as a trap for the unwary or inattentive reader, coaxing us to test our preconceptions by showing us that what we see is often merely what we *wish* to see. For the morning after the ball, Emma's "eyes were suddenly opened" about Mr. Elton; "The fever was over" (*E*, 359).

Consider another group setting with lovers that dramatizes the distinction between appearance and reality:

> The appearance of the little sitting-room as they entered, was tranquillity itself; Mrs. Bates, deprived of her usual employment, slumbering on one side of the fire, Frank Churchill, at a table near her, most deedily occupied about her spectacles, and Jane Fairfax, standing with her back to them, intent on her pianoforté. (*E*, 259)

In fact, Frank Churchill and Jane Fairfax are anything but tranquil, and are, on the contrary, absorbed in staging the appearance of being engrossed in anything and everything but one another. In an inversion of the Harriet and Elton scene, the lovers are there, but hiding in the group, not standing together but seated apart. The figure of the spectacles cunningly draws attention to the – reader's – act of seeing. This scene anticipates *Persuasion*'s climactic scene, where characters who seem to be otherwise engaged (not even within earshot of one another) are revealed to be deeply involved, acutely aware, steadily listening, and hanging on every word. The striking figure of the mysterious woman at the pianoforte, with her back to the visitor whose arrival is seemingly unperceived, is one that Henry James would later use in *The Portrait of a Lady* (1881): so Madame Merle seduces the ingénue Isabel Archer through her performance of absorption at the piano, staged for the benefit of the new arrival at Gardencourt, before turning to greet her "as if but just aware of her presence."[14]

And if the artfully laid appearances of Austen's novel invite the reader *not* to take the intimacy between its heroine and narrator at face value, we may be sure that Austen's deedily droll deprecation of her heroine was offered in a similar spirit.

Notes

1 J.E. Austen-Leigh, *A Memoir of Jane Austen and Other Family Recollections*, ed. Kathryn Sutherland (Oxford: Oxford University Press, 2008), p. 119.
2 William Dean Howells (p. 63); Anthony Trollope on vanity (p. 51); Marvin Mudrick (p. 107, 114); in *Jane Austen: Emma: A Casebook*, ed. David Lodge (London: Macmillan, 1991).
3 Reginald Farrer, 1917, in Lodge, *Jane Austen: Emma*, p. 65.

4 R.W. Chapman, *Jane Austen: Facts and Problems* (Oxford: Clarendon Press, 1948), p. 202.

5 John Henry Newman, in Lodge, *Jane Austen:* Emma, p. 50.

6 Farrer, in Lodge, *Jane Austen:* Emma, p. xx.

7 Mudrick, in Lodge, *Jane Austen:* Emma, p. 115.

8 See Ruth Perry, "Family matters," *A Companion to Jane Austen*, ed. Claudia L. Johnson and Clara Tuite (Oxford: Wiley Blackwell, 2009), p. 323.

9 Farrer, in Lodge, *Jane Austen:* Emma, p. xx

10 Chapman, *Facts and Problems*, p. 210.

11 Ian Littlewood, *Jane Austen: Critical Assessments* (London: Routledge, 1999), pp. 252–259.

12 Brigid Brophy, Introduction to *Pride and Prejudice* (London: Pan, 1967), p. xii.

13 Sianne Ngai describes the zany as a "seemingly lighthearted but strikingly vehement aesthetic, in which the potential for injury always seems right around the corner." See her *Our Aesthetic Categories: Zany, Cute, Interesting* (Cambridge, MA: Harvard University Press, 2012), p. 7.

14 Henry James, *The Portrait of a Lady* (Harmondsworth: Penguin, 1963), p. 172.

Myth
20
JANE AUSTEN AND THE AMOROUS EFFECTS OF BRASS

Today readers and moviegoers in the general public think of Austen's novels as love stories. But oddly enough, historically many readers have also believed not merely that there is no sex in the novels but also that there is no real love either. In Austen's novels, it is claimed, so far as matters of the heart are concerned, what we find instead is prudence, practicality, even a degree of mercenariness. Some readers, such as Ralph Waldo Emerson, despise Austen on this account:

> The one problem in the mind of the writer in both the stories I have read, "Persuasion", and "Pride & Prejudice", is marriageableness; all that interests any character introduced is still this one, has he or she money to marry with, & conditions conforming?[1]

For Emerson the question of whether a character has "money to marry with" is not merely unromantic but deadly dreary: "Suicide is more respectable," he quips. But others have praised Austen's treatment of "marriageableness" as stunningly lucid. As W.H. Auden puts it in "Letter to Lord Byron,"

> You could not shock her more than she shocks me;
> Beside her Joyce seems innocent as grass.
> It makes me most uncomfortable to see
> An English spinster of the middle-class
> Describe the amorous effects of "brass",
> Reveal so frankly and with such sobriety
> The economic basis of society.

30 Great Myths About Jane Austen, First Edition. Claudia L. Johnson and Clara Tuite.
© 2020 John Wiley & Sons, Inc. Published 2020 by John Wiley & Sons, Inc.

For Auden, Austen's novels lend themselves to Marxist analysis. Her novels are brilliantly shocking because her treatment of "the amorous effects of 'brass'" reveals something more truly obscene than the merely sexy passages in Joyce: "the economic basis of society," which we cover up and mystify with notions such as love or taste or romance.

Both assessments are responding to the same truth about Jane Austen's novels. Rarely are major characters – and many minor ones as well – introduced without very specific information about their fortunes. This is worth noticing. Jane Austen is so sparing with physical descriptions that G.H. Lewes imagined her to be near-sighted: "The absence of all sense of the outward world – either scenery or personal appearance – is more remarkable in her than in any writer we remember."[2] But regarding incomes and fortunes, Austen provides very specific information, in which everyone takes an interest. Income figures make up the gossip of neighborhoods and the converse of friends and family. The range of annual incomes for gentlemen is wide. Austen's richest man is her stupidest: Mr. Rushworth, whose annual income is £12 000. Darcy follows with £10 000 a year, John Dashwood with £6000, Mr. Bingley with £4000–£5000, Mr. Bennet with £2000 – to name only a few. These gentlemen are "marriageable," because they have, to recur to Emerson's phrase, "money to marry with & conditions conforming" – that is, an income sufficient not merely to live but to possess and sustain the accoutrements of their rank. These would include several female servants, a coachman or a footman, a carriage of suitable style, and horses, requiring an annual income of at least £1000. No wonder Mrs. Bennet is thrilled for her daughters' sakes when she learns that "A single man of large fortune" has just settled in the neighborhood.

But of course it is not merely women who assess the marriagebleness of suitors by ascertaining their fortunes. Unmarried men are also eager to assess the fortunes of prospective wives. Leading the pack is Miss Grey of *Sense and Sensibility*, whose fortune of a whopping £50 000 is the allurement for her good-for-nothing husband, Willoughby. Mr. Elton aspires to Emma Woodhouse's inheritance of £30 000, but after he is summarily rebuffed, he settles on Miss Hawkins, believing (as everyone in the village avers) her fortune to be £20 000, only later to learn that it is £10 000 or "thereabouts," a qualification that has prompted many readers to suspect that Mrs. Elton's actual fortune might dwindle even further. (*E*, 195) General Tilney eagerly courts Catherine Morland on behalf of his son Henry after he is misinformed that her fortune is £10 000–£15 000; he rudely banishes her from his home when he is later misinformed that she is virtually penniless; and he finally consents to her marriage when he learns that her fortune is £3000, a figure that actually seems implausibly high given that her father is a country clergyman with a family of 10. While proposing to Elizabeth Bennet, Mr. Collins promises never to reproach her for bringing no more than a mere £1000 to her marriage, and when she declines his proposal he replies, "it is by no means certain that another offer of marriage may ever be made you. Your portion is unhappily so small that it will in all likelihood undo the effects of your loveliness and amiable qualifications" (*PP*, 122). We may deplore Mr. Collins for saying so, but he is right. As Colonel Fitzwilliam tells Elizabeth, younger brothers without fortunes cannot afford to follow their hearts alone, which is, among other things, a tactful announcement that his interest in her can be no more than a polite flirtation.

The few characters in Austen's novels who claim to be indifferent to wealth in matters of love are either silly, crafty, or naive. Thus we find the sentimental heroines of *Love and Freindship* announcing their noble determination to subsist on love alone, disdaining the "mean and indelicate employment of Eating and Drinking" (*J*, 111) only later to hallucinate food. And Isabella Thorpe professes an indifference to wealth, but she ditches her fiancé when she learns he has no fortune and instead pursues Captain Tilney and his money. Marianne Dashwood loftily declares, "What have wealth or grandeur to do with happiness," but when it comes actually to specifying what she requires for subsistence – "A proper establishment of servants, a carriage, perhaps two, and hunters" – we realize that her needs are grand indeed, requiring around £2000 a year (*SS*, 105). Marianne's romantic notions about wealth having nothing to do with happy marriages, we gather, are claptrap.

The connection between money and marriage is particularly urgent for single women without fortunes, because, as the narrator observes in *Mansfield Park*, "there certainly are not so many men of large fortune in the world, as there are pretty women to deserve them" (*MP*, 3). Men without income can go off and make their fortunes in business, as Mr. Weston in *Emma* does, eventually returning home, buying land, and setting himself up as a marriageable gentleman. Or, like Captain Wentworth in *Persuasion*, they might join the Navy and make their fortunes in prize money. Women obviously cannot do this. Lacking fortunes of their own, their options are few: like Mrs. and Miss Bates in *Emma*, they can eke out a frugal life in Highbury on £100 a year; or like Jane Fairfax, they can consider becoming governesses, earning £30 a year.[3] Or they can get married.

The necessity of marriage to the subsistence of women without fortunes is the very premise of *Pride and Prejudice*. Intelligent but unlovely, Charlotte Lucas unlike Elizabeth is not destined to be a heroine: her Prince will not come and propose not once but twice, and she knows it.

At 27 she takes control of her future and in the process brings about a rupture from which the novel does not recover: she encourages and accepts Mr. Collins's proposal of marriage and in the process loses the good opinion of her friend Elizabeth. Charlotte has no illusions. She sees as effortlessly as Elizabeth does that Mr. Collins is "neither sensible nor agreeable," that "his society was irksome" and that his feelings for her are "imaginary." For her, marriage is not a matter of love or an avenue towards happiness. Rather it is "the only honourable provision for well-educated young women of small fortune" (*PP*, 138). Charlotte's example obliges us to ask how far Austen is willing to go in exploring the relation between marriage and money for sympathetic characters. The answer is both very far and not far enough. We are invited to scorn cads like Willoughby or fortune-hunting females like Lucy Steele. The case gets more complex in *Mansfield Park*, where Sir Thomas urges Fanny Price to accept a man she does not love in order to be grateful to himself, where Lady Bertram declares: "it is every young woman's duty to accept such a very unexceptionable offer as this" (*MP*, 384) and where even her beloved Edmund assures her that love will come later. Fanny holds out against Crawford for a long while, but she shows signs of weakening before the novel's final crises place her beyond danger.

Charlotte's case is yet more equivocal. Elizabeth's response to Charlotte's engagement is unsettling. We can understand the rude, almost Lydia-like incredulity with which she bursts out, "Engaged to Mr. Collins! my dear Charlotte, impossible!" (*PP*, 140). But her private reflections, which the narrator neither endorses nor refutes, are curiously extreme:

> She had always felt that Charlotte's opinion of matrimony was not exactly like her own, but she had not supposed it to be possible that when called into action, she would have sacrificed every better feeling to worldly advantage. (*PP*, 141)

Marriage to Mr. Collins a "worldly advantage"? When Charlotte says, "I am not romantic ... I ask only a comfortable home" (*PP*, 140) she is stressing her need for a decent roof over her head, a "preservative from want" (*PP*, 140), hardly worldly advantage. Charlotte's engagement not merely shocks Elizabeth, it mortifies her: "Charlotte the wife of Mr. Collins, was a most humiliating picture!" (*PP*, 141). The nature of Elizabeth's sense of personal humiliation is puzzling. The Bennet sisters, after all, need the same "preservative" Charlotte does. Despite the sparkle of *Pride and Prejudice*, the five Bennet daughters are very perilously situated. Because there is no Bennet son to inherit Netherfield upon Mr. Bennet's death, their home and all its furnishings devolve to the next closest male relative – Mr. Collins – and the displaced daughters will have nothing more to subsist on than the £40 annual income each from their mother's side. The likelihood of this outcome should make us have a bit more compassion for Mrs. Bennet's "nerves" than her husband has. But much to Mrs. Bennet's indignation, Mr. Bennet seems unconcerned, and Elizabeth declines two marriage proposals without a second thought for the future of herself or her family. Does Elizabeth's sense of humiliation show that she is a heroine above worldly considerations?

Concerning the "amorous effects of brass," Austen seems to have her cake and eat it too. Having shown her superiority of character in declining two marriage proposals despite the uncertain future of her family and herself, Elizabeth is more than a little susceptible to "worldly advantage." Beholding the grounds at Pemberley for the first time, Elizabeth muses: "to be mistress of Pemberley might be something!" (*PP*, 271). When she enters the house and beholds the paintings, the furniture, the portraits within, Elizabeth indulges a moment's fantasy of personal possession: "'And of this place,' thought she, 'I might have been mistress! With these rooms I might now have been familiarly acquainted!'" (*PP*, 272). Elizabeth's response here calls Mr. Collin's behavior at Longbourn to mind, when he examines and praises the "hall, the dining-room, and all its furniture" so vigorously that Mrs. Bennet cannot suppress the "mortifying supposition of his viewing it all as his own future property" (*PP*, 73). Starting with Sir Walter Scott, many readers have believed that the splendor of Pemberley brings Elizabeth to her senses at last: she "does not perceive that she has done a foolish thing [in refusing Darcy's hand] until she accidentally visits a very handsome seat and grounds belonging to her admirer."[4] Yet it is not wealth – as reflected in the building and grounds – that moves her, but rather the harmonious, well-regulated state of relations they signify, ordered as they are by a man whose virtues are conceived relationally: "As a brother, a landlord, a master, she considered how many people's happiness were in his guardianship!" (*PP*, 277). Elizabeth does not mistake the furniture for the owner whose good polity in the regulation of relations are what makes it desirable in the first place. Is it possible by this account, then, that Elizabeth cools towards her friend Charlotte not because she married for money but rather because to be mistress of Hunsford, unlike Pemberley, is if not exactly *nothing* still definitely not "something" enough. Elizabeth's heart is changed by Pemberley, and Darcy's personal worth and social worth are not fully separable. His subsequent actions seal the deal: he buys Wickham off in order to save Lydia's reputation, paying his debts of more than £1000 pounds, purchasing a commission for him of about £400–£600, and providing a settlement of £1000 for Lydia herself.

So, where does Austen stand on the amorous effects of brass? On both sides. Austen's heroines do not marry for money alone, but they are not obliged to go without it either, though Elinor comes the closest, with £850 year, hardly poverty but on the edges of gentility. In the world of Austen's novels and Austen's time, marital love seems both distinct from and entangled with the prestige of wealth and class.

Notes

1 *Journals of Ralph Waldo Emerson: 1856–1863* (1913), vol. 9, pp. 336–337. Reprinted in *Jane Austen: The Critical Heritage*, vol. 1, ed. B.C. Southam (London: Routledge & Kegan Paul, 1987), p. 28. This volume collects and introduces major assessments of Jane Austen from 1811–1870.
2 Ibid, p. 159.
3 My discussion of the relative values of incomes is much indebted to Edward Copeland, "Money," in *The Cambridge Companion to Jane Austen*, Edward Copeland and Juliet McMaster eds. (New York: Cambridge University Press, 1997), pp. 131–148; and to Katherine Toran, "The economics of Jane Austen's world," http: //www.jasna.org/publications/persuasions-online/vol36no1/, accessed 17 November 2019.
4 Southam, *Critical Heritage*, p. 65.

Myth 21

PERSUASION IS AN AUTUMNAL NOVEL

"*Persuasion* has a charm that is traditionally, and accurately, called 'autumnal'."

(Lionel Trilling, *Beyond Culture*)

Persuasion is routinely labelled "autumnal," but we may doubt if this traditional term does justice to its many charms. It certainly offers a gateway to the novel's mood, but elsewhere *Persuasion* has been read as celebrating a "second spring" and as "Austen's *Winter's Tale*."[1] The novel has so many moods and tones that "the autumnal paradigm" makes us somewhat deaf and blind to their range.[2]

Persuasion's seasons are out of order. The autumnal reading assumes that Austen is endorsing the natural order of things, correcting aberrations and righting wrongs: "she learned romance as she grew older – the natural sequel of an unnatural beginning" (*P*, 32). But if the novel is driven toward a restoration of the natural order, its greatest interest lies in its deviations from that order. This is a novel of disjunctive temporality and "disordered feelings" (*P*, 87). It also engages the bodily world of "sensations" that resist processing into feelings. The term "autumnal" fails to capture the complex drama and region of disturbance where the novel spends most of its time. Besides, in the politics of Austen's day, the restoration of the Bourbon monarchy after Napoleon's defeat had shown that the project of restoration is a fraught one that can never fully bring back the past. Is Captain Wentworth's bitterness over the broken engagement ever fully repaired?

However well intentioned, a preoccupation with the novel's autumnal qualities has tended to circumscribe our reading of *Persuasion*. The reading comes with various assumptions about the novel, its author, her

30 Great Myths About Jane Austen, First Edition. Claudia L. Johnson and Clara Tuite.
© 2020 John Wiley & Sons, Inc. Published 2020 by John Wiley & Sons, Inc.

oeuvre, and the novel form generally. But the "autumnal paradigm" is too restrictive to be an accurate guide to the novel's complex emotional land-scape and the curious spatiotemporal order it installs, not to mention its extraordinary achievement as an event in literary history. Through this novel, as Virginia Woolf observes, Austen was "beginning to discover that the world is larger, more mysterious, and more romantic than she had supposed."[3] Nevertheless, it is a strange and rather perverse romanticism that Austen discovers in this novel.

The assumption that *Persuasion* was written under the shade of a benign autumnal mood makes us less responsive to the novel's wider palette of tones and emotions, including the complexity of the pain Anne endures. It misconstrues the novel's anxious scheme of things, which Marilyn Butler refers to as "the novelist's distortion of the two 'normal' outward dimensions: time is recklessly speeded up, space grotesquely contracted." This distortion produces "the effect of high-wrought nerv-ous tension."[4] Anne's keyword is "nervous"; she is nervous and "quite ashamed of being so nervous" (*P*, 87). "Awkward" is another keyword.

The autumnal reading is frankly too cheerful; it does not do justice to the intensity of the protagonist's emotions or the dark powers of the nov-elist's practice. It has the same "plainly overcompensating cheerfulness" as Mrs. Smith, whose happy face often counters Anne's sad one.[5] And it underplays the fact that some of the novel's highlights are moments of outright darkness. The novel's tone is sometimes elegiac, but its comedy often has what Woolf calls "asperity" or harshness.[6] The autumnal para-digm tends to regard the comedy – a mixed mode of social comedy and elegy – as a flaw in the novel's design. But the integration of Anne's social and interior lives is central to the novel's effect. Primary among the social formalities that sweep across Anne's field of vision are Wentworth's wordless, poignant bows ("Her eye half met Captain Wentworth's; a bow, a curtsey passed" and then "their visitor had bowed and was gone"; she later sees him "making a distant bow" to her father) (*P*, 64, 197). These fleeting bows appear almost subliminally as flickering images that register these awkwardly related worlds – of the shared family and social gathering and of Anne's interior pain.

The autumnal reading emphasizes a mood of quiet melancholy, when in fact all the action – or rather inaction – stirs up some rather ugly feelings. *Persuasion*'s plot is one of waiting, as Anne famously elaborates in her speech about women's "nature" and constancy: "We live at home, quiet, confined, and our feelings prey upon us" (*P*, 253). But within that confined space, there is action and strife enough. The autumnal reading assumes passivity and resignation, which the novel is at pains to argue against, and which Anne belies by being highly active in all her suffering.

The moment when Anne and Wentworth meet again after eight long years is fraught with this suffering:

> a thousand feelings rushed on Anne, of which this was the most consoling, that it would soon be over. And it was soon over ... [T]he room was cleared, and Anne might finish her breakfast as she could.
>
> "It is over! it is over!" she repeated to herself again and again, in nervous gratitude. "The worst is over!" (*P*, 64).

But of course it has only begun. (Even so, Austen tinges this suffering with stage-comic pathos when Wentworth's long-anticipated re-appearance interrupts Anne's breakfast.) The novel picks up an ancient poetic rhythm that makes of the end a new beginning, as, recently, in Carol Ann Duffy's poem "Over," where *over* means the end of the affair, but also repetition – not an end but a beginning – cued by the quotation of Robert Browning's thrush that "sings each song twice over" to "recapture / The first fine careless rapture!"[7] This is surely the point of any quotation: to sing the song over, yet to repeat with difference.

The ambivalent figure of "nervous gratitude" develops the complex *pas de deux* between pleasure and pain that is Anne's primary state of emotional commotion. Always communicating through indirection, she remarks to Wentworth of Louisa Musgrove's fall at Lyme: "but when pain is over, the remembrance of it often becomes a pleasure. One does not love a place the less for having suffered in it, unless it has all been suffering, nothing but suffering" (*P*, 200). When Anne exclaims in her giddy, nervous abjection that "The worst is over!" she is anticipating that moment when pain will be converted to pleasure. Or is she already in the throes of conversion? It's hard to tell. Austen infuses Anne's anxious desire for Wentworth with a particular experience of time: these are "disordered feelings," after all.

It is hard to tell when pain stops and pleasure begins. And we are not the only ones. After Wentworth has "placed her" in the carriage, as if by magic though "his will and his hands had done it," Anne is convinced in equal measure of his "unjust resentment" and his "warm and amiable heart," which, the narrator tells us, "she could not contemplate without emotions so compounded of pleasure and pain, that she knew not which prevailed" (*P*, 98). The startling proximity of pleasure and pain has an edge of masochism.

Indeed, Anne's suffering enacts a form of active resistance that speaks to Leo Bersani's eloquent theorization of masochism and the birth of human subjectivity: "How could we be merely receptive to the massive influx of stimuli that would ... destroy us if we failed to take pleasure in being nearly overwhelmed by them?"; like that exemplary subject, Anne is able to "survive by masochistically receiving a mass of stimuli," inhabiting a form of "pleasure in pain" that can "also be thought of as ... active *resistance* to the world."[8] To be used and abused is Anne's way of showing her strength: "as our bodies are the strongest, so are our feelings; capable of bearing most rough usage, and riding out the heaviest weather," she says to Captain Harville, all the while speaking back to the "tough nut" analogy she has overheard Wentworth fashion for Louisa, as he celebrates the nut for having "outlived all the storms of autumn" as a pretext for praising Louisa's "firmness" (*P*, 253, 94).

Anne is actively resistant through the drama of listening to Wentworth's conversation with Louisa. She is quiet, confined, and overhearing: "she feared to move, lest she should be seen." "Her own emotions still kept her fixed." She "had heard no evil of herself, but she had heard a great deal of very painful import" (*P*, 86, 87, 95). With pleasure and pain so mixed up, Austen's prose reaches out for different words to describe these emotional and bodily states: "extreme agitation." These are not feelings but "sensations" (*P*, 96). With Anne thus pinioned in overhearing absorption, they are all prey to Anne's feelings and voyeuristic anxiety.

As many critics have noted, there is far less dialogue in *Persuasion* than in Austen's other novels. In the most revelatory scenes, Anne communicates with the reader through free indirect discourse. Characters communicate with one another just as indirectly through overhearing and reported conversation, as when Mary reports to Anne a conversation between Wentworth and Henrietta Musgrove that she has overheard:

> Henrietta asked him what he thought of you, when they went away; and he said, "You were so altered he should not have known you again." (*P*, 85)

Anne's response, presented in free indirect discourse, stages another moment of active submission: "'Altered beyond his knowledge!' Anne fully submitted, in silent, deep mortification" (*P*, 65). What she submits to is the mortifying indignity of overhearing Wentworth's bitter, resentful words echo the myth of vanished bloom that is continually rehearsed by her father (yet more of the autumnal myth's baggage). Compounding the sting is Mary's insensitive handling of this intelligence, "perfectly unsuspicious of inflicting any peculiar wound." Even here, Anne perversely "soon began to rejoice" in these words. They "allayed agitation; they composed, and consequently must make her happier" (*P*, 61, 65)

The agitation and nervousness in *Persuasion* is not confined to Anne, but is also social and political. The novel is set during the Napoleonic Wars, from the summer of 1814 to the spring of 1815, when the end was in sight. In 1814 there was national rejoicing after Napoleon was forced to abdicate and went into exile in Elba. But then he came back. Austen began the novel on 8 August 1815, the day it was generally known that Napoleon had gone into permanent exile, after the second abdication and the Bourbon restoration (*P*, xxx). By the end of the novel, once Anne is married, "the dread of a future war [was] all that could dim her sunshine" and "she must pay the tax of quick alarm" (*P*, 275).

Status anxiety is a different kind of nervousness again, staged in the novel's satirical opening tableau of the baronet in search of an heir, as Sir Walter Elliot alternately preens and frets over the mirror of the *Baronetage*. From the outset, Austen's narrator subtly distinguishes her own point of view, and that of Lady Russell, from Sir Walter's, while nevertheless focalizing in free indirect discourse:

> His two other children were of very inferior value. Mary had acquired a little artificial importance, by becoming Mrs. Charles Musgrove; but Anne, with an elegance of mind and sweetness of character, which must have placed her high with any people of real understanding, was nobody with either father or sister: her word had no weight; her convenience was always to give way – she was only Anne. (*P*, 5–6)

The qualifier "but Anne" flicks the switch, as the narrator moves to pay tribute to Anne against "either father or sister" for whom Anne was "nobody;" and by the end of the passage the narrator has distinguished her own reading of Anne from that designated with the pointed irony "– she was only Anne."

After presenting Lady Russell's loving attitude toward her "highly valued god-daughter," the narrative moves back more incriminatingly within Sir Walter's point of view:

> A few years before, Anne Elliot had been a very pretty girl, but her bloom had vanished early; and as even in its height, her father had found little to admire in her. (*P*, 6)

Here we have a complex dovetailing of social satire with the emotional drama of Anne's interior life. In its focus on the novel's interior dimension, the autumnal reading doesn't properly account for its satire. Another limitation of the autumnal reading, then, is that it over-determines *Persuasion* as a drama of vanished bloom; this in turn identifies the novel too closely with Sir Walter's impoverished perspective. As we have seen, Wentworth, too, views Anne from within the paradigm of feminine beauty; for much of the novel, he carries around this conception of the woman he loved eight years ago.

Anne's faded "bloom" and its revival are a key part of the novel's drama. But the novel is equally writing back to that myth and its distorting gendered discourse. By the end of the novel, the "sweet scenes of autumn" are indeed "put by" (*P*, 91), rendered a kind of cliché, once Anne commences her second spring (which may well be another cliché). As Anne says to Harville, "if you please, no reference to examples in books" (*P*, 255). These books might include the classical genre of the heroic epistle, initiated by Ovid's *Heroides* ("Letters of Heroines"), featuring the elegiac love letters of Sappho, Hero, Dido, Ariadne, and Hermione. Austen reworks and rewrites the tradition of the deserted woman, with the return of the lost male lover and a kind of role reversal. By having Wentworth write and declare his love at the very moment that Anne is identifying this gender difference, Austen transforms the genre, placing the man in the traditionally female position of importunate, deserted lover. Wentworth has the pen, but he is also putting himself on the line by declaring his love.

In the spring of 1816, Austen became ill with what is thought to be the Addison's disease that killed her the following year, complaining of a variety of symptoms such as nausea, muscle weakness, and fatigue. The autumnal myth conflates content and form – reading *Persuasion* as a novel both *about* and *of* vanished bloom. It also confuses author and text, reading *Persuasion* as an index of Austen's waning physical powers. But *Persuasion*, like *Sanditon* after it, embodies radical modes of aesthetic vitality and style. Autumnal suggests "mature," and conveys conventional expectations of what a mature novel (and mature novelist) should be. *Persuasion* and Austen's next novel, *Sanditon*, both frustrate these expectations.

Contrary to the autumnal reading, *Persuasion* is a novel that looks forward – not back. Far from being immersed in retrospective nostalgia, *Persuasion* looks forward to new possibilities of novelistic form by finding ways to bring the past into the present. Its supreme innovation lies in registering the experience of time and showing the workings of memory as both remembering and forgetting. *Persuasion* is not just about wistful, melancholy recall; it also involves the distortions of forgetting: "the general air of oblivion" and "apparent unconsciousness" of Anne's family and friends that mark their conspiracy of silence (*P*, 33, 32).

Virginia Woolf is surely right when she asserts that if Austen had lived longer "she would have been the forerunner of Henry James and of Proust,"[9] Woolf's contemporaries. What Woolf means is that Austen is already their forerunner – and her own.

Notes

1 Claire Tomalin, *Jane Austen: A Life* (London: Viking, 1997), p. 259; Kathryn Sutherland, *Jane Austen's Textual Lives: From Aeschylus to Bollywood* (Oxford: Oxford University Press, 2005), p. 165. See also Jocelyn Harris, *A Revolution Almost Beyond Expression: Jane Austen's Persuasion* (Newark, DE: University of Delaware Press, 2007), pp. 118–190.

2 Claudia L. Johnson, *Jane Austen: Women, Politics, and the Novel* (Chicago: Chicago University Press, 1988), p. 145.

3 Virginia Woolf, "Jane Austen" (1925), *Collected Essays*, vol. 1 (London: The Hogarth Press, 1980), p. 152.

4 Marilyn Butler, *Jane Austen and the War of Ideas* (Oxford: Oxford University Press, 1989), p. 277.

5 D.A. Miller, *Jane Austen, or The Secret of Style* (Princeton, NJ: Princeton University Press, 2003), p. 74.

6 Woolf, *Collected Essays*, p. 152.

7 Carol Ann Duffy, *Rapture* (London: Picador, 2005), p. 62.

8 Leo Bersani, *Receptive Bodies* (Chicago: University of Chicago Press, 2018), p. x.

9 Woolf, *Collected Essays*, p. 153.

Myth
22

JANE AUSTEN WAS A FEMINIST/JANE AUSTEN WAS NOT A FEMINIST

Any subject we raise about Jane Austen is soon likely to become rather tangled. Because Austen herself is such a mythic, beloved figure, many readers have tended to align her with their own yearnings, social outlooks, and dispositions. And regarding the subject of feminism, those yearnings, outlooks, and dispositions have been – and still are – polarizing (hence the title of our chapter). Even when the matter of feminism is not, one way or another, personally fraught, readers have tended to bring to the table their own ideas about what feminism is, when feminism "started," and what spectrums of other social or political positions feminism is imagined to be aligned with.[1] Not surprisingly, both elements of this myth are true and untrue.

How did the myth that Jane Austen was not a feminist begin? James Edward Austen-Leigh's biography of his aunt, *Memoir of Jane Austen* (1869/1870), both emerges from and contributes to a particular view of Austen herself and of a woman's proper place. That place is squarely within the home. Foregrounding Austen's affection for children, Austen-Leigh domesticates his illustrious aunt, foreclosing any suspicion that she might have thought of herself as an author, that her temper was anything other than gracious and gentle. Delightedly putting away her writing papers and pens whenever her nieces and nephews ran into the room, Austen to her nephew is not a novelist of stunning detachment but a modest spinster-spinner of delightfully, innocuously trifling little stories. Of course Austen had no ambition of literary fame or fortune! Of course she preferred playing with her nephew to writing *Emma*! An angel of the

30 Great Myths About Jane Austen, First Edition. Claudia L. Johnson and Clara Tuite.
© 2020 John Wiley & Sons, Inc. Published 2020 by John Wiley & Sons, Inc.

house of sorts, Austen, according to this reading, is a benign and reassuring figure, who, as Alice King wrote in 1882, is "a picture of what a female author and artist should be: true to home duties,"[2] much as Saintsbury in 1894 praised Austen's Elizabeth Bennet for having nothing "offensive, nothing *viraginous*, nothing for the 'New Woman.'"[3] Arguments against Austen's non-feminism were often, clearly, linked implicitly or explicitly to a determination to resist the stirrings of feminism during the Victorian – or any – period by opposing Austen to them.

Proponents of this view of Austen certainly did not consider themselves hostile to women – indeed, the domestic woman was ostensibly a celebrated ideal – but they did dismiss any notion that Austen or her novels engaged in any favorable, conscious reflection upon women's rights or duties. Sensible and unassuming, she was not anti-feminist as much unfeminist. Any notion that Austen might have been a feminist must be absurd not simply because Austen was imagined to be contented with a life of modest, feminine domesticity but also on the grounds that concepts and arguments about the structure of society in general or rights in particular were imagined to be as much beyond her ken as they were beyond her inclination. This was the dominant Victorian view of Austen. As G.H. Lewes put it in 1852, "There is nothing *doctrinaire* in Jane Austen; not a trace of woman's 'mission,'" by which he means that Austen has no views on or notions about the position or role of women in her novels.[4] Richard Simpson elaborated on this in 1870, when he wrote that Austen had no "conception of society itself."[5] This view is echoed by Leslie Stephen, who writes that "she is absolutely at peace with her most comfortable world. She never even hints at a suspicion that squires and parsons of the English type are not an essential part of the order of things."[6] This sense that Austen, in effect, had no ideas, and especially no ideas about women's place in society, proved remarkably durable throughout much of the twentieth century. At mid-century, Lionel Trilling echoes this, with a twist, when he observes that Emma Woodhouse is remarkable for having "a moral life as a man has a moral life," a statement that still strikes us as brilliant and productive, and possibly suggestive of a feminist or even proto-feminist agenda. But before we can develop possibility, Trilling shuts it down, insisting that Austen has no doctrinaire intent to cast Emma as a "new woman" but merely happens to create a character untrammeled by feminine modesty.[7] Austen, in other words, is not so uppity as to create a heroine with such an unapologetic sense of self-consequence. Trilling thus removes Austen from any access to feminist ideas, whether, anachronistically, to late-Victorian ones (the "new woman") or late-eighteenth-century ones (e.g. Mary Wollstonecraft) that were available to her in her own times. On the grounds of temperament, orientation, and imaginative capacity, then, many of Austen's readers place her outside the very possibility of social critique, especially any social critique of women's place in society.

This *almost* changed with the seminal work of Marilyn Butler's *Jane Austen and the War of Ideas* (1975). Butler brilliantly shows that Austen's contemporaries were absorbed in the revolutionary and counter-revolutionary debates that shook English culture in the wake of the French Revolution. This meant precisely that highly contested "ideas" – about liberty, authority, social structure, manners, marriage, primogeniture, and, not least, the rights of women – were everywhere in public discourse, and especially in the novels Austen certainly read by men and women alike. It would now appear impossible to assume that Jane Austen had no access to social criticism. Curiously enough, however, Butler still places Austen outside these debates, contending at last not that Austen herself was engaged in the "war of ideas" but rather that she had simply inherited old-fashioned notions that were imparted to her by the sermons and conduct books that formed her mind. Butler classes Austen as a Tory conservative because she imbibed tendentious, reactionary propaganda she is imagined to have been indoctrinated with since childhood, without being able or inclined to consider or discern the interests served by its representations. Assuming that both conservatism rejected feminism and feminism had nothing in common with conservatism, a view very much typical of the 1970s, when *The War of Ideas* was written, Butler maintains that a strong streak of anti-feminism – in reaction against the radical Mary Wollstonecraft – informs Austen's outlook, leading her to chide the assertive Emma Woodhouse and Elizabeth Bennet and to celebrate the meek Fanny Price and Anne Elliot. Butler thus made it possible to conceive of Austen as doctrinaire. A political orientation could now be attributed to Austen, but still not a political intelligence as such.

Interestingly enough, Butler came to reverse this position in her second edition of *Jane Austen and the War of Ideas*, with a new preface allowing that "Tory feminist" existed. But Butler's admission was somewhat belated and somewhat misleading because the "feminism" of Austen's time was often not contested, not at "war." What did that feminism look like? Of course, the word did not exist, but a very lively and well-developed discourse about women and their place in society certainly did. This "feminism" was not about women's right to work, or women's right to vote, or women's right to reproductive freedom. Rather, it was about the moral equality of the sexes, and with that the duty to educate women rationally so that they could makes responsible choices and be better able to execute their social and religious duties. On the very first page of her Introduction to the *Vindication of the Rights of Woman* (1792),

Wollstonecraft describes the present problem with female education in a way few could reasonably quarrel with:

> I attribute [these problems] to a false system of education, gathered from the books written on this subject by men, who, considering females rather as women than human creatures, have been more anxious to make them alluring mistresses than affectionate wives and rational mothers.

Reviewers, far from attacking Wollstonecraft's *Vindication of the Rights of Woman* when it was first published, treated it as yet another, largely commendable, critique of the kinds of female education that promoted superficial accomplishments – accomplishments which served male vanity or male sensuality but excluded the cultivation of rationality, reflection, and usefulness in women, and thus unfitted them for responsible moral agency. It is instructive to remember that, so far from it being the case that feminism was the property of radicals in the war of ideas, Wollstonecraft wrote the *Vindication* precisely because her progressive political allies failed to recognize that women required the same sort of moral independence that men did. The *Vindication* is addressed to her political allies, to men who touted the rights of man while still adoring docile, infantine women.

Jane Austen undoubtedly favored the principles of the rational, moral cultivation of women and of the exercise of sound judgment in conducting their lives in such a way as to minimize the nature of sexual difference. These principles motivate Mrs. Croft (whom we see take reins from her husband, the Admiral, when his management of the carriage falters!) to scoff at Captain Wentworth's high-toned notions about female delicacy: "I hate to hear you talking so like a fine gentleman, and as if women were all fine ladies, instead of rational creatures" (*P*, 75). These are the principles that Elizabeth Bennet asserts when she tells Lady Catherine, "I am only resolved to act in that manner, which will, in my own opinion, constitute my happiness, without reference to *you*, or to any person so wholly unconnected with me" (*PP*, 396). And because we know that Elizabeth is an educated "rational creature" she, unlike (say) Lydia, can be relied on to choose her happiness wisely. These are the principles Fanny Price herself must observe by, in effect, rebelling against her uncle when he tries to coerce her into accepting Henry Crawford, scolding: "But you have now shewn me that you can be wilful and perverse; that you can and will decide for yourself" (*MP*, 367). At the conclusion of *Mansfield Park* we learn that almost all of the disasters narrated in this novel can be chalked up to Sir Thomas's failure to educate his daughters into the sort of self-responsibility that

Wollstonecraft recommends and that he himself decries as "disgusting" when he scolds Fanny.

The moral equality of the sexes does not mean in Austen that the manners governing male and female behavior are identical in her novels. The respective prerogatives governing male and female autonomy are set forth clearly in a scene in *Northanger Abbey*, where, comparing marriage and dancing, Henry Tilney explains that "man has the advantage of choice, and women only the power of refusal" (*NA*, 74). Here is quite an asymmetry, which gives men an "advantage." But the power of refusal is still a power, and not an inconsiderable one. Yet Austen's novels very often present us with situations where women's "power of refusal" is denied. In *Pride and Prejudice*, memorably, Mr. Collins simply cannot hear, cannot conceive of, cannot allow for Elizabeth Bennet's "no" to his marriage proposal, and he persists in assuming her "yes" without any sense that he is being obnoxious, offensive, or, in a different generic mood, sinister. *Mansfield Park*, which glances at the subject of slavery – a condition where "no" is impossible, everywhere shows Fanny's power-lessness to say "no." Sir Thomas, for example, "advises" Fanny to go to sleep after the ball, but "advice" is a term that gives Sir Thomas and Fanny alike a false sense of her autonomy and his benevolence, because the "refusal" of his "advice" is not conceivable. As the narrator tells us, Sir Thomas's "advice" is actually "absolute power," so it is not surprising that he is stunned by Fanny's refusal to marry Mr. Crawford and deter-mined to oblige her to do so, all while claiming solely to "advise" her (*MP*, 326). And in *Persuasion*, Captain Wentworth spends years feeling ill used by Anne's "no," casting it as an act of pusillanimity rather than accepting it as her rational prerogative. In none of these instances does Austen frame her position as a "feminist" one – the word did not yet exist – but they still demonstrate an awareness of a social issue of urgent importance. In all these instances, and more, we see Austen assum-ing – and defending – the necessity of women's autonomy in making choices about their lives, and showing that a proper education is neces-sary so that the choices women do make are more like Elizabeth's and Fanny's rather than Lydia's and Maria Rushworth's.

As we have seen, many Victorians cherished Austen as a woman author who knew her place and who would have nothing to do with feminism of any sort. Devoney Looser has lately shown, quite on the contrary, that in 1908 marchers sponsored by the Women Writers' Suffrage League took to the streets during the "Great Procession," a march of some 10,000 people across London to the Royal Albert Hall, holding on high banners of celebrated women, among whom was Jane Austen herself.[8]

We cannot infer from this that all or most of these marchers necessarily regarded Austen as an ally in women's quest for the vote. But Looser's discussion helps us realize that it is certainly not a mistake to imagine early feminists of all periods recognized Austen's commitment to exploring the moral dignity of women and her novels' commitment to representing the challenges and choices of women's lives as true adventures.

Notes

1 For a review of feminist criticism of Austen, see Devoney Looser, *Jane Austen and Discourses of Feminism* (Palgrave, 1995).
2 Quoted in *Jane Austen: The Critical Heritage 1870–1940*, vol. 2, ed. B.C. Southam (London: Routledge & Kegan Paul, 1987), p. 38.
3 Ibid, p. 218.
4 *Jane Austen: The Critical Heritage*, vol. 1, ed. B.C. Southam (London: Routledge & Kegan Paul: 1968), p. 141.
5 Southam, *Critical Heritage*, vol. 2, p. 250.
6 Ibid, pp. 174–175.
7 Lionel Trilling, "The legend of Jane Austen" first published as the "Introduction to the Riverside Edition" of *Emma* (Boston: Houghton Mifflin, 1957), and widely reprinted thereafter.
8 Devoney Looser, *Making of Jane Austen* (Baltimore: Johns Hopkins University Press, 2017), Ch. 9.

Myth
23

JANE AUSTEN'S LETTERS ARE MEAN AND TRIVIAL

"Little Embryo is troublesome I suppose."

Jane Austen, *Letters*

Jane Austen's letters have never been popular. In his anti-Austen tract, "Jane Austen: A Depreciation" (1928), H.W. Garrod spoke for many when he described the letters as "a desert of trivialities punctuated by occasional oases of clever malice."[1] (E.M. Forster later referred to the letters' "triviality, varied by touches of ill breeding and sententiousness."[2]) Garrod's critique makes sense coming from a self-styled "depreciator" of Austen, but this doesn't explain why so many Austen fans have found the letters so unlovable.

By the time the first collected edition of the letters appeared in 1932, their unpopularity was so entrenched that R.W. Chapman felt compelled to acknowledge in his preface that they had "received little whole-hearted praise from the 'idolaters' of the novels."[3] Indeed, they have received more blame than praise from Austen idolaters. Even Sheila Kaye-Smith and G.B. Stern, who belong to Austen idolatry's golden age, refer to the letters as "at times wearisome," giving the example of Austen's letter to Cassandra on a sponge-cake: "'You know how interesting the purchase of a sponge-cake is to me'," "Yes, but of her power to make the purchase of a sponge-cake interesting to immortality, she will never know."[4] Ouch.

Chapman is at pains to demur: "But I would not seem to be apologetic where I see no need for apology. Are these letters in fact uninteresting? I have not found them so."[5] Yet this is hardly a ringing endorsement. The main issue of contention concerns the gulf between the letters and the

30 Great Myths About Jane Austen, First Edition. Claudia L. Johnson and Clara Tuite.
© 2020 John Wiley & Sons, Inc. Published 2020 by John Wiley & Sons, Inc.

novels: stylistic finish, perfection, and thematic plenitude on the one hand, and spareness and lack of "incident" on the other.

Basically, the letters were everything they could have been expected *not* to be, especially since Henry Austen had attested to the continuity between the novels and the letters: "The style of her familiar correspondence was in all respects the same as that of her novels ... she never dispatched a note or letter unworthy of publication."[6] But they are not the same at all. The trouble starts with Henry, then. As Marilyn Butler writes, Henry's claim in the 1818 preface to *Northanger Abbey* and *Persuasion* had unintended consequences that "embarrassed the next generation of the family."[7] It set up an inappropriate set of expectations; and the letters' inability to meet them goes some way to explaining the origins of our myth.

Everything in the novels finds its opposite in the letters: a "desert" rather than a garden of delights; "sententiousness" instead of subtlety; scratchy "banality" instead of finish; "ill breeding" instead of good; "vulgarity" instead of style. And where are all the picnics? (Anne Thackeray Ritchie, daughter of William Thackeray, the novelist and famed Victorian host, writes: "her picnics are models for all future and past picnics" – but only in the novels, not in real life.[8])

Puzzling over the problem, Kaye-Smith and Stern claim that there is more "real feeling" and "naturalness" in the novels: "Rarely ... does real feeling break through the light froth, the comic detail of her own letters; when it does ... it is curious to note how naturalness forsakes her."[9] It gets worse. Even Austen's legendary satirical wit deserts her in the letters:

> Jane Austen's letters show ... her excessive delight in the small, odd, senseless behavior of all those who come and go within her range of vision. Perhaps this is what makes them at times wearisome reading; they arrive, they stay five minutes, and they depart again, yet within that five minutes Miss Austen has run a sharp little instrument, like a pastry-cutter, around their chief absurdity, so that she may serve it up for the delectation of her sister, Cassandra, next time she writes.[10]

Austen's wit is painful, and only Cassandra enjoys the astringent delicacy it serves up. Too many people come and go too soon. In the novels, people stay, and "we grow to know a small community," and "we have a lust to know them better and better." But in the letters, we are "spattered" with the names of people we do not know.

The letters' earliest critique is Mrs. Humphry Ward's scathing review of Lord Brabourne's 1884 edition of his great-aunt's letters. Ward complains about "the ponderous effect of the earlier chapters, with their endless string of names," ruing the fact that "the name of one of the nimblest, quickest, and least tiresome of mortals" has been "associated with ... family pedigrees of which she would have been the first person to feel the boredom and the incongruity."[11] For, as Sylvia Townsend Warner notes: "There is no trace in Jane Austen's letters of snobbishness or social anxiety. Her outward gaze on the world was alert, but cool," unlike many of her relatives.[12]

Hence Chapman's dilemma in editing the letters and deciding where and for how long to introduce all these folks. With scrupulous care, he explains that his notes "give summary identifications of any persons who are *ambiguously* mentioned in the text." Armed with the plan only to explain when ambiguity demands, Chapman is nevertheless aware of the awkwardness of his task: "There is an element of solemn absurdity in any commentary on familiar letters such as these."[13] By "familiar letters," Chapman means what he elsewhere calls "family correspondence."[14] But we can also take him to mean that he does not wish to overwhelm commonplace letters with hifalutin footnotes.

Stylistic comparisons between the two genres aside, the first thing we note is that the letters (unlike the novels) were never intended to be published. Jane Austen's letters were not "finished" but were intended as part of an intimate ongoing conversation. Though they lived together for all of their lives, Jane and Cassandra wrote to one another when they were away on holidays or visiting friends and family. One thing that strikes the reader of the letters is the possibility that Jane is the receiver in this relationship, and Cassandra the giver: "I am sure nobody can desire your letters so [much as I do]," Jane wrote to Cassandra.[15] Was it the same for Cassandra? Maybe not: "I am not surprised my dear Cassandra, that you did not find my last Letter very full of Matter, & I wish this may not have the same deficiency; – but we are doing nothing ourselves to write about, & I am therefore quite dependant upon the Communications of our friends, or my own Wit."[16] Indeed, Chapman believed Cassandra did not bring out the best in Jane as a correspondent. There was too much news to convey (and all those names). But conveying news was a job, even when there was none to convey. "Epistolary production," Carol Flynn notes, was "one of [Austen's] domestic duties, what women do for free."[17]

Cassandra is the central protagonist in the letters' story, not only as their main addressee but also as compiler of the posthumous archive that was edited and published. Caroline Austen tells us that Cassandra destroyed many letters and decided which would be published.

The letters between Jane and Cassandra provided ways of connecting two branches of a large family, which eventually inherited the letters after Jane Austen's death and took control over how they would be published, with the growing public interest in Austen's writing. Most of the letters come from these two sides of the family. James Edward Austen-Leigh had access to the Austen side's letters in compiling his *Memoir* of his aunt (in 1870 and 1871); then in 1884 the first Lord Brabourne published letters he inherited from his mother, Jane Austen's niece, Fanny Knight. A third group of letters are those to Francis Austen, published in *Jane Austen and her Sailor Brothers* (1906). In 1913, William Austen-Leigh and R.A. Austen-Leigh published some in their *Life and Letters of Jane Austen* (1913).

But let's return to the expectation that the letters should be novelistic, which is the basis of our myth. Responding to Garrod's critique, Chapman offers an account of what makes them letters and not excerpts from a novel. The letters, he writes:

> straggle over twenty years, and lack a plot. Their details, therefore, unlike the details of *Emma*, are not the ingredients or embellishments of a rounded composition. If they can be called works of art, they are so only because, as their writer reminds us, "an artist cannot do anything slovenly". But as fragments – fragments of observation, of characterization, of criticism – they are in the same class as the material of the novels; and in some respects they have a wider range.[18]

So the letters, as "fragments of observation," are like the novel but also unlike. Kathryn Sutherland writes that "Jane Austen's letters are ... the contested place where the ordinary becomes extraordinary ... The letters are the raw data for the life and the untransformed banalities which, magically transmuted, become the precious trivia of the novels."[19] Similarly, Carol Flynn reads Austen's letters as a "painfully calibrated understanding of the disappointments and adjustments which mark the feminine experience," and notes that "Austen's awareness of the texture of domestic life ... generates her densely realized novels."[20]

That's the triviality. What about the meanness? For D.W. Harding, the transmutation of the stuff of everyday life involves a kind of psychic alchemy of hatred, taking the dross from the mouths of her "associates of everyday life," the neighbors she apparently hated, and turning it into comedy they would enjoy because they would not recognize themselves in the portraits she drew. It is "part of her complex intention as a writer" to satirize the witless people around her, on whom she depended for emotional (and economic) support; "the first necessity was to keep on reasonably good terms with the associates of everyday life."' We might think of this kind of transmutation as a calculated invitation to misread: "she took good care (not wittingly perhaps) that the misreading should be the easiest thing in the world."[21]

Chapman too puts the alleged malice into context:

> The question is ... whether she ... reveals a cold heart, a meagre intelli- gence, and a petty spirit. We know that Jane Austen the novelist had ... a zest for the small concerns or belongings of her creatures, which her genius made communicable ... The letters abound in gentle or playful malice; and sharper strokes are frequent.[22]

"Playful malice"? The plot thickens. Elsewhere, he observes that the let- ters are "not spiteful" but "exquisitely wicked."[23]

As Garrod's negative reading suggests, the letters are sometimes loved *for* their malice, which is the source of their "oases." Marilyn Butler refers to Austen's letters as "hardly those of a nice woman" and writes (seem- ingly approvingly) that Harding and Marvin Mudrick "have both noted a vein in Austen that is less than enthusiastic about humanity, even actively inhumane."[24] What was Austen nasty about? Her critics seem to have fastened on to certain topics. The accusation of malice may have more to do with her failure to find news of births and deaths momentous: "poor Woman! How can she honestly be breeding again?" she writes of a new acquaintance; and to Cassandra, complaining of a dearth of news: "I treat you with a *dead Baronet* in almost every letter."[25]

Her letters make many disparaging comments about the effects of child- bearing on the women she knows (most particularly her sisters-in-law, two of whom died in childbirth). And, as Roger Sales notes, "The dishevelled state of a sister-in-law, Mary, after giving birth in 1798, discouraged her from wanting 'to lay in myself'."[26] She writes to her niece, Fanny Knight: "I wd. recommend to her & Mr. D the simple regimen of separate rooms."[27] Austen writes to Fanny about her niece, Anna: "Poor Animal, she will be worn out before she is thirty. – I am very sorry for her ... I am quite tired of so many Children."[28] Elsewhere, she observes: "The house seemed to have all the comforts of little Children, dirt & litter. Mr. Dyson as usual looked wild, & Mrs. Dyson as usual looked big."[29] For all their scandalous- ness, the letters' anti-breeder comments are in fact compatible with the tenor of the novels, which coolly terminate at the happy ending, avoiding the messy afterlives of marriage involving childbirth and raising children.

That said, Austen's letters make it clear that she adored her nieces and nephews and spent a lot of time with them. Take this early letter about her nephew George (the second son of Edward Austen Knight):

> My dear itty Dordy's remembrance of me is very pleasing to me; foolishly pleasing, because I know it will be over so soon. My attachment to him will be more durable; I shall think with tenderness & delight on his beautiful & smiling Countenance & interesting Manners, till a few years have turned him into an ungovernable, ungracious fellow.[30]

Fondly mimicking George's baby talk, Austen anticipates how the sweet child will grow into a bumptious boy.

Much of what seems mean in Austen's letters is her resistance to the expectation that she should "keep [her] countenance."[31] In the letters to Cassandra she says what she thinks. Take her intriguing comment about her brother Frank's wife, Mary: "Mrs. F.A. seldom either looks or appears quite well. – Little Embryo is troublesome I suppose."[32] This child, "Little Embryo," was Mary's seventh, Elizabeth, born in early 1817. Is this letter tender or cold? The tone is undeniably complex, hovering between sympathy and detachment. Austen liked Mary and had written a poem to celebrate her marriage. If the letter's directness makes it "exquisitely wicked," it is also deeply empathetic toward Mary and her unborn child. The use of the diminutive in "Little Embryo" reflects tenderness and recognizes its precarious state and the fact that its birth is by no means assured (hence "troublesome" for the mother). Lying-in could result in death for the baby or mother, as it did in fact for Mary when she gave birth to her eleventh child.

So birth is closely related to death, the other topic that brings out the mean streak in Austen's letters. Austen's most notorious transgression of the code of politeness around childbearing and death is a letter that combines both these freighted topics. She told Cassandra: "Mrs. Hall of Sherborne was brought to bed yesterday of a dead child, some weeks before she expected, owing to a fright. I suppose she happened unawares to look at her husband."[33] Then there's the reference to Mrs. Bromley, the landlady at Bath, "a fat woman in mourning,"[34] which is unnervingly close to the narrator's comment in *Persuasion* about Mrs. Musgrove's "large fat sighings over the destiny of a son, whom alive nobody had cared for" (*P*, 73). But that is a novel, which raises a different set of questions. As Carol Flynn astutely observes, "The very style of her novels, tersely and laconically epigrammatic, insists upon a graceful inevitability of social forms that must triumph over individual acts of rebellion and desire. Nothing is ever so inevitable in Austen's own letters, however."[35] But even so, every now and again, as in this moment, the narrator of Austen's novels seems to cross over from the letters, as though having eluded the novelistic finish customarily applied to the raw fragments of observation that is the stuff of Austen's world.

Notes

1 H.W. Garrod, "Jane Austen: A depreciation," *Transactions of the Royal Society of Literature*, new series, 8 (1928), p. 23.
2 E.M. Forster, *Abinger Harvest* (London: Edward Arnold, 1936), p. 156.
3 R.W. Chapman, *Jane Austen's Letters to her Sister Cassandra and Others*, second edition (London: Oxford University Press, 1952), p. xxxix.
4 Sheila Kaye-Smith and G.B. Stern, *Talking of Jane Austen* (London: Cassell, 1943), pp. 119, 120.
5 Chapman, *Letters*, Preface, p. xl.
6 J.E. Austen-Leigh, *A Memoir of Jane Austen and Other Family Recollections*, ed. Kathryn Sutherland (Oxford: Oxford University Press, 2008), p. 141.
7 Marilyn Butler, *Jane Austen* (Oxford: Oxford University Press, 2007), p. 96.
8 Anne Thackeray Ritchie, *A Book of Sibyls: Mrs Barbauld, Miss Edgeworth, Mrs Opie, Miss Austen* (London: Smith, Elder & Co., 1883), p. 201.
9 Kaye-Smith and Stern, *Talking*, p. 119.
10 Ibid, p. 119.
11 Mrs. Humphry Ward, "Style and Miss Austen," *Macmillan's Magazine* (1885), *Jane Austen: The Critical Heritage 1870–1940*, vol. 2, ed. B.C. Southam (London: Routledge & Kegan Paul, 1987), pp. 182–183.
12 Sylvia Townsend Warner, *Jane Austen* (London: Longman's, Green & Co, 1964), p. 9.
13 Chapman, *Letters*, Preface, p. vii.
14 Ibid, p. xxxix.
15 Jane Austen to Cassandra Austen, 25 November 1798, *Jane Austen's Letters*, ed. Deirdre Le Faye, 3rd edition (Oxford: Oxford University Press, 1995), p. 21.
16 Jane Austen to Cassandra Austen, 10–11 January 1809, *Letters*, p. 162.
17 Carol Houlihan Flynn, "The letters," *The Cambridge Companion to Jane Austen*, ed. Edward Copeland (Cambridge: Cambridge University Press, 1997), p. 106.
18 Chapman, *Letters*, Preface, p. xlii.
19 Kathryn Sutherland, "Jane Austen's life and letters," *A Companion to Jane Austen*, ed. Claudia L. Johnson and Clara Tuite (Chichester: Wiley Blackwell, 2009), p. 18.
20 Flynn, "The letters," p. 101.
21 D.W. Harding, "Regulated hatred" (1940), reprinted in *20th Century Literary Criticism: A Reader*, ed. David Lodge (London: Longman, 1984), p. 263, 264.
22 Chapman, *Letters*, Preface, p. xliii.
23 Ibid, pp. xliv, xlv.
24 Butler, *Jane Austen*, pp. x, 297.
25 Jane Austen to Cassandra Austen, 2 October 1808, *Letters*, p. 140; Jane Austen to Cassandra Austen, 8 September 1816, *Letters*, pp. 320–321.
26 Roger Sales, *Austen and Representations of Regency England* (London: Routledge, 1994), p. 50.

27 Jane Austen to Fanny Knight, 20–21 February 1817, *Letters*, p. 330.
28 Jane Austen to Fanny Knight, 23–25 March 1817, *Letters*, p. 336.
29 Jane Austen to Cassandra Austen, 11 February 1801, *Letters*, p. 81.
30 Jane Austen to Cassandra Austen, 27–28 October 1798, *Letters*, p. 17.
31 Jane Austen to Cassandra Austen, 26 October 1813, *Letters*, p. 245.
32 Jane Austen to Cassandra Austen, 8–9 September 1816, *Letters*, p. 320.
33 Jane Austen to Cassandra Austen, 27–28 October 1798, *Letters*, p. 17.
34 Jane Austen to Cassandra Austen, 17 May 1799, *Letters*, p. 40.
35 Flynn, "The letters," p. 101.

Myth
24

JANE AUSTEN WAS ANONYMOUS

It is commonly assumed that women novelists always published anony-mously during Jane Austen's time. This was very often the case. Though men could and did sometimes write anonymously as well, publicity was a distinctively risky business for women. Given prevalent standards of female respectability and modesty, fame could easily slide into infamy, and being a woman in public could slide very easily to being seen, in some sense, as a public woman. Austen's contemporary Mary Brunton (1778–1818) regarded the disclosure of her authorship as tantamount to the worst sort of self-exposure:

> To be pointed at – to be noticed & commented upon – to be suspected of literary airs – to be shunned, as literary women are, by the more unpretending of my own sex; & abhorred, as literary women are, by the more pretending of the other! I would sooner exhibit as a rope dancer.[1]

As Brunton explains for women authors, at least, there was no such thing as positive celebrity. To be "noticed & commented upon" was a disgrace regardless of what that notice and comment might be. Still, there were several immensely popular and highly esteemed women novelists who took precisely this risk. Indeed, Austen's favorite novelists, Frances Burney, Ann Radcliffe, and Maria Edgeworth, published many of their novels using their own names, particularly after their success was established, and they clearly survived this ordeal. Jane Austen did not take this risk. Unlike these three sister novelists she admired, Jane Austen was a respected but not popular author, and she chose not to have her name appear on the title page of the novels. When *Sense and Sensibility* (1813) was first pub-lished, the title page informs us that it was written "By a Lady." This was the first and last time this locution would appear on Austen's title pages.

30 Great Myths About Jane Austen, First Edition. Claudia L. Johnson and Clara Tuite.
© 2020 John Wiley & Sons, Inc. Published 2020 by John Wiley & Sons, Inc.

Her subsequent novels identify her as the author of her previous novels. Thus *Pride and Prejudice* is "by the author of *Sense and Sensibility*;" *Mansfield Park* is "by the author of *Sense and Sensibility* and *Pride and Prejudice*" (the second edition drops the former); and *Emma* is "by the author of *Pride and Prejudice* &c."; and *Persuasion and Northanger Abbey* (published posthumously) "by the author of *Pride and Prejudice, Mansfield Park.* &c.". *Sense and Sensibility*, it would appear, gets dropped out as an Austenian signifier, presumably because it was felt not to have much value as advertisement. In any case, though Austen's name did not appear on her title pages during her lifetime, her corpus was identified, her sales boosted, and her identity shielded all at once.

At the outset of her career, Austen clearly went out of her way to conceal her identity, not anonymously but pseudonymously. When Austen sold *Susan* (later *Northanger Abbey*) to publisher Richard Cosby and Son in 1803 for £10, she used the pseudonym Ashton Dennis, a pen name every bit as gender-neutral as Currer Bell. But concealing her gender could not have been Austen's primary aim, since she used the honorific "Mrs" in 1809, when she wrote Crosby and Son to request the return of this manuscript, which, to her clear irritation, was advertised but never published. (Austen perhaps enjoyed the bitter little joke of signing herself "M.A.D."[2]) How could Austen have been anything other than *mad* that the manuscript of what would become *Northanger Abbey* was still unpublished after six years?[3] At the time, Austen could not spare the £10 to buy the manuscript back. Perhaps this is why she abandoned the pseudonym when she started publishing with *Sense and Sensibility* (1811). With the manuscript of *Susan* still out there as the property of a publisher under the name of Ashton Dennis, Austen could not very well use this pseudonym for *Sense and Sensibility*, and so she evidently chose the anonymity of "By a Lady" as her byline instead.

Elena Ferrante, surely the best living practitioner of anonymity, has considered Austen's decision freeing rather than repressive, as an active and empowering authorial choice. Ferrante sees the character of Elinor Dashwood as emblematic of Austen's practice of anonymity, observing: "What makes her different is not coldness but an attention to others that allows her to reduce to the minimum her own need to be central." For Elinor, this self-erasure is the means of achieving equilibrium in a very trying world. For an author like Austen, *lady*-like self-erasure provides a space for expansive freedom:

> It seems to me that Austen, by not putting her name on the books she published, did the same thing as Elinor, and in an extremely radical way. She uses neither her own name nor one that she has chosen. Her stories are

not reducible to her; rather, they are written from within a tradition that encompasses her and at the same time allows her to express herself. In this sense they are indeed written by a lady, the lady who does not fully coincide with everyday life .... The lady-who-writes can set aside dissatisfaction and bitterness, spread a light, ironic glaze over the old world that, with its wrongs, is collapsing and the new world that is emerging, with its abundance of new wrongs. But pay attention, for the lightness conceals pitiless depths – it's a glaze that, miraculously, doesn't sweeten anything.[4]

Ferrante's remarks are a powerful counterbalance to the assumption that writing anonymously is a constraint, much less a reflex of immodesty. Signing her novels "By a Lady" by this account makes it possible for Austen to emancipate herself from the "natural resentments towards daily life" that she must inevitably have felt, especially as a woman author, much as Elinor Dashwood overcomes "the dissatisfaction and bitterness" of her life through her comparably impersonal, anonymizing practice of politeness. Indeed, as Ferrante would have it, lady-like anonymity made everything we think of as distinctively Austenian – impersonality, critical distance, irony, and "pitiless depth" – possible, for "the lady-who-writes" exposes the wrongs of the old world and the new one without being injured from them. From Austen as "a Lady" to the grandeur of Reginald Farrer's Divine Jane there is only a small step. Curiously enough, however, "By a Lady" didn't quite stick. Later newspaper advertisements (in a perhaps intentional reversal) printed instead that *Sense and Sensibility* was "By Lady A," which probably had the effect of further obscuring Austen's identity, creating an air of mystery perhaps by attributing a higher class position to her.

Clearly, at the earliest stages of her career, Austen was serious about concealing her identity from all except a very small circle. Among friends and family members not in the know, this secrecy might call to mind the dodginess of the secret that Jane Fairfax and Frank Churchill have in *Emma*, where secrecy has the status of espionage, of putting everyone not in the know at a social and epistemological disadvantage. To start with, at least, Austen hid her authorship so well that when her niece Anna saw a copy of *Sense and Sensibility* at the local circulating library, Anna brushed it away, saying that it must be rubbish. Anonymity must have made comments like this deliciously amusing, and Austen did not let Anna in on the secret until several years later.

This was not to last long, however. When *Pride and Prejudice* (1813) appeared it became almost instantly popular among elite readers in high-society and among the literati. In a letter of May 1813, Annabella Milbanke, Lord Byron's future wife, observed, "I have finished the Novel called *Pride and Prejudice*, which I think a very superior work... it is the *most probable* I have ever read," and she predicted further that it would be "the fashionable novel" of the season. She was right. The reviews were glowing, and the literary world was charmed. Richard Sheridan declared: "It was one of the cleverest things he ever read";[5] and Susan Ferrier longed "to see that same *Pride and Prejudice* which every body dins my ears with."[6] With this critical acclaim the concealment of Austen's identity could not last long. Delighted by this success and, no doubt, not unwilling to put himself forward in the process, Henry Austen could not resist telling his well-connected friends and associates that his sister was the author. Austen well knew "what I shd be laying myself open to" by entrusting her literary affairs to her brother Henry, who could not be counted on for reserve. "Henry heard P. & P. warmly praised in Scotland, by Lady Robt Kerr & another Lady, & what does he do in the warmth of his Brotherly vanity & Love but immediately tell them who wrote it!" Austen surely knew that this was not the only time Henry blabbed: "the secret has been spread so far that it is scarcely the Shadow of a secret now... I beleive whenever the 3rd [novel] appears I shall not even attempt to tell Lies about it."[7] Insofar as she continued to withhold her name from her title pages, Austen did continue "to tell Lies" about her authorship, but she also realized that, for a sizeable portion of her readership, anonymity was a fiction, an open secret.

Was Austen angered by Henry's indiscretion? Was she amused by it? Resigned? Gratified? She declined the invitation to be introduced to admirers through Henry, and she decided not to meet fellow novelist Madame de Staël. Austen could have many reasons for declining her company, or for entering into the company of strangers with only Henry's presence to buffer her. Would Austen have declined the chance to meet Ann Radcliffe or Frances Burney?[8] All this is speculation. But one matter is clear: writing anonymously did not mean that one was anonymous, and this is why Austen's anonymity is finally something of a myth. Sir Walter Scott wrote his novels anonymously as well, and Austen, for one, obviously knew that he wrote *Waverley*. In much the same way, Austen enjoyed the benefits of having it both ways. She had the protections of anonymity, and the satisfactions of success and recognition. She may not have approved of the Prince Regent – and she certainly thought his librarian was absurd – but she did not decline, when requested (i.e. commanded), to dedicate *Emma* to him, and she could not have been anything but pleased with the respect she earned among the highest echelons of English literary society.

Henry Austen managed the posthumous publication of *Northanger Abbey and Persuasion*, and though he did not place his sister's name on the title page, his biographical notice identifies her as his sister, much as the obituary notices he composed for her also named her as an author. Clearly, he had it both ways as well, for he both formulated the myth of Austen's serenely ladylike anonymity – "in public she turned away from any allusion to the character of an authoress" – even as he flagrantly violated that apparent wish to tout her celebrity and perhaps garner some for himself as well.

Notes

1 Quoted in Claire Tomalin, *Jane Austen: A Life* (New York: Vintage Books, 1999), p. 217. From a letter quoted on p. xxxvi of Brunton's *Emmeline* (1819).

2 Jane Austen to Crosby & Co., 5 April 1809, *Jane Austen's Letters*, ed. Deirdre Le Faye, third edition (Oxford: Oxford University Press, 1995), p. 174.

3 Park Honan speculates that Crosby sat on the manuscript and eventually declined to publish because the firm had a financial interest in Ann Radcliffe, whose work was parodied in *Susan*. See *Jane Austen: Her Life* (New York: Fawcett Columbine, 1987), p. 384.

4 Elena Ferrante on *Sense and Sensibility*: "I was passionate about Austen's anonymity," *Guardian* (16 October 2015).

5 Quoted in Claire Harman, *Jane's Fame* (Melbourne: Text Publishing, 2009), p. 60.

6 Deirdre Le Faye, *Jane Austen: A Family Record*, second edition (Cambridge: Cambridge University Press, 2003), pp. 196–197.

7 Jane Austen to Francis Austen, 18 February 1812, *Letters*, p. 231.

8 Jeffry Nigro, "Jane Austen, Madame de Staël, and the seductiveness of conversation," *Persuasions On-Line*, 33(1), (Winter 2012).

Myth
25
JANE AUSTEN'S NOVELS DEPICT THE TRADITIONAL WORLD OF THE ARISTOCRACY

In Francis Grose's *Dictionary of the Vulgar Tongue* (1811), a "nob" is a member of the nobility, while a gentleman is a "gentry cove."[1] The relative amiability of "gentry cove" is telling; "cove" is almost a term of endearment, far from the unflattering "nob." While genteel usage repudiates the vulgar tongue, Grose distinguishes between the nobility and the gentry as clearly as better-bred reference works such as *Debrett's Peerage*. In Grose's work, as in Austen's novels, there is a profound difference between titled aristocracy and gentry. Austen's world is that of the gentry.

There aren't many nobs with hereditary titles in Austen's novels, and these rare aristocrats often have a sting in their tail. So the poisonous Lady Catherine de Bourgh, appalled by the prospect of a familial alliance with Elizabeth Bennet, exclaims: "Heaven and earth! ... Are the shades of Pemberley to be thus polluted?" (*PP*, 396). The effect is just as callous in *The Watsons* when the aristocrat Miss Osborne passes over little Charles Blake, to whom she has promised a dance, in favor of a lord. The insult or gesture of indifference resonates beyond the moment to establish an enduring undertone of menace.

From the seventeenth century, an aristocrat was defined by his ability to sit in the House of Lords. The order of precedence was detailed in *Debrett's Peerage*, Sir Walter Elliot's book of books. Sir Walter himself was not a peer but a baron, and hence was addressed as "Sir." A baronetage was hereditary, but it did not entitle the holder to sit in the House of

30 Great Myths About Jane Austen, First Edition. Claudia L. Johnson and Clara Tuite.
© 2020 John Wiley & Sons, Inc. Published 2020 by John Wiley & Sons, Inc.

Lords. Baronets occupied the top rung of gentry society, and many sat in the House of Commons.

While there were powerful forces policing the boundaries between aristocracy and gentry, those boundaries are somewhat permeable during Austen's period. The term "gentleman," in particular, is increasingly imprecise. It is at once a social position – someone with no regular trade or occupation – and an aspirational position conferred by social recognition of the value of one's conduct. In Austen's fiction we see the beginnings of the nuanced elaboration of gentility as an evaluative category separable from fixed social status.

The most esteemed gentleman in Austen's novels, Mr. Darcy of Pemberley, doesn't have a title at all, though he is from a landed family. His titled aunt, Lady Catherine de Bourgh, describes his paternal line as "respectable, honourable, and ancient, though untitled" (*PP*, 394). This is a vital point of cleavage in Austen's world: between titled aristocrats and members of the gentry. She is intent not only on discriminating between ranks and titles but also on analyzing how they are perceived. These social forms were nevertheless highly imbricated; and to make matters even more complex gentility can also be an evaluative category that often trumps title.

This complexity is a primary focus of Austen's novels. As Thomas Keymer argues, "it is hard to think of a contemporary or precursor in whose fiction there is quite so thorough an immersion in, and calibration of, the minutiae of the system."[2] Raymond Williams observes that "estates, incomes and social position … are seen as indispensable elements of all the [personal and psychological] relationships that are projected and formed."[3] But Austen's fictions do not simply track the fortunes of the great landed families; they are actively engaged in conferring status through recognition while self-reflexively drawing the reader into that process of recognition and evaluation.

John Habakkuk describes Austen as belonging to "a junior branch of a landed family."[4] As Linda Bree and Janet Todd note, both her parents were from respected clergy families. "George Austen, Jane's father, was the rector of two small Hampshire country parishes, at Steventon and Deane, and her mother, Cassandra (nee Leigh) came from the academic clergy of Oxford." Her extended family was spread across various social ranks. "They included the rich landowners, the Leighs of Stoneleigh Abbey and the Knights of Godmersham, as well as men and women lower in the social scale such as poorer clergy and even a milliner's apprentice."[5]

Of all the characters in Austen's completed fictions, it is the Dashwood women in *Sense and Sensibility* whose unremarkable social condition comes closest to her own: they embody the everyday social indignities of women on the margins of good society. Edward Copeland observes that the Dashwood women's inheritance of £500 matched what George Austen left at his death. "Austen speaks from experience on this one."[6] Far from the world of the aristocracy, Austen's world of the cultivated rural gentry is far more diffuse and intriguing. Hence why Austen's nuanced acts of discrimination are so important in catching those moments of recognition and constitution.

As the conferral of social recognition takes place primarily through language, Austen's preoccupation with social minutiae extends to her characters' speech. As Mary Lascelles memorably observes, Austen

> tends to suggest social variants in speech by syntax and phrasing rather than by vocabulary ... [T]here is such exact keeping of scale that the distinctions remain clearly apparent: no sentence of Elizabeth Watson's could be transferred to her sister Emma, however their opinions may agree, because of their different upbringing; nor could a Steele vulgarism be mistaken for that of a Thorpe. Jane Austen never repeats herself. Each social shelf in her little world has its own slang – Isabella Thorpe's, Tom Bertram's, Mary Crawford's; and so have the professions, when they appear.[7]

In Austen's "little world," subtle social distinctions operate within classes, ranks, and families as well as between them.

Austen's world, though not aristocratic, was nevertheless supported by servants. Indeed, servants and a carriage were almost obligatory signs of gentility. This is evident in one of Austen's earliest letters, reporting to Cassandra about the temporary washer woman, who "undertakes our Purification. She does not look as if anything she touched would ever be clean, but who knows? We do not seem likely to have any other maidservant at present."[8] In her 1929 article "The Servants in Jane Austen," Lady Eve Balfour observes: "Miss Austen's servants are as classic, in their way, as a Greek chorus. There are at least a hundred servants mentioned in the six books."[9] Most of them are named; among the more important are Lady Bertram's lady's maid, Mrs. Chapman, Mrs. Whitaker at Sotherton (who dismisses two maids for wearing white), and Mrs. Reynolds, the Darcys' housekeeper at Pemberley. Mrs. Elton conspicuously forgets the name of hers: "(one of our men – I forget his name)" (*E*, 319).

In *Emma*, the servants are a vital part of the household, forming an alliance against the gypsies, separated from them behind the iron gates that keep the gypsies out. But not all servants in the novels are cozily benign. Mrs. Younge, Georgiana Darcy's former governess, has a malign influence in hatching the elopement of Wickham and Georgiana, and colludes in the elopement of Wickham and Lydia.

The gentry is tricky to pin down – which is part of its point. It is famously reliant on its connections, exploiting the gray area between who is in and out of the family. Some readers are troubled by Austen's precarious positioning, but others take pleasure in the diversity and richness of its "connections." As Austen wrote to Cassandra, "it is pleasant to be among people who know one's connections & care about them."[10] This reference to "connections" is telling. For the historian David Spring, the idea that "Jane Austen's novels deal with little more than an extended family has a bit of plausibility. ... But her families exemplify a variety of social types."[11] More than that, Austen's account of class is relational, as the emphasis on "connections" suggests. Her liminality allows her to draw upon a wide range of social experience, enhancing her novels' edginess and satirical power.

Some, after Spring, have described Austen's class as the "pseudo-gentry"; but this, as Jan Fergus rightly notes, suggests being "on the make," when in fact it was a traditional practice to draw on connections and contacts. Fergus suggests it is more accurate to describe a clerical family like Austen's as being "located on the fringes of the gentry. This marginal position was built into the elite social structure; it was not an arriviste creation."[12]

Readings of Austen's fraught class position often reveal readers' investments. Some read Austen's marginal position as bitter and isolated, cut off from comforts she can only aspire to. For others, it gives her access. For example, it is a point of pride for D.J. Greene that "when [Austen] creates families with any pretensions to gentle birth, she almost always endows them with names belonging to actual British families, sometimes with an extinct title of nobility, sometimes with a living one." This is part of the "ideal of verisimilitude" that Austen's fiction lives by.[13] (See Myth 5.)

Austen's contemporary Sir Walter Scott uses the general term "the middling classes of society" to refer to Austen's social milieu: "her most distinguished characters do not rise greatly above well-bred country gentlemen and ladies; and those which are sketched with most originality and precision, belong to a class rather below that standard."[14] Spring suggestively focuses on the gentry's need for mobility, observing that Austen's class "had a sharp eye for the social escalators, were skilled in getting on them, and (what was more important) no less skilled in staying on them."[15]

When considering Austen's stylistic innovations, we tend to associate free indirect discourse exclusively with interiority, but interiority is focused on – and situated within – an external social world. The technique is trained on both heroine and narrator's discriminations of social rank and conduct. Free indirect discourse is always relational: first in the relation between narrator and heroine, and then in the shuttling between direct and indirect discourse, catching the flow of an inner life as it engages with the wider world, and as its narrator mediates the heroine's point of view. The narratorial eye is engaged in conferring recognition. Through its inherent self-reflexivity, the free indirect style shows the process of conferring recognition as part of the reading of social position, class, and rank. The narrative "technique" and texture is about refining that conjunction between the point of view and voice of the narrator and her protagonist.

What makes Austen's fiction so innovative is not only its immersion in the social system but also its reading of that system through a reflexive practice that embodies the new social reality of relative mobility within fixed boundaries. We tend to focus on the question of social mobility in relation to the novels' endings, but their so-called "marriage plots" are not just events of closure; they are cumulative elements sustained throughout the novels.

Likewise, social mobility does not only happen through marriage. Anne Elliot observes her family's craven attempts to reactivate the dormant connection with their cousin Lady Dalrymple and her daughter after the local press reports that the two have arrived in town (in Bath):

> Anne had never seen her father and sister before in contact with nobility, and she must acknowledge herself disappointed. She had hoped for better things from their high ideas of their own situation in life, and was reduced to form a wish which she had never foreseen – a wish that they had more pride; for "our cousins Lady Dalrymple and Miss Carteret;" "our cousins, the Dalrymples," sounded in her ears all day long. (P, 160–161)

Anne registers (through Austen's free indirect representation) the gaping distance between gentry and nobility, and her family's excruciating "agony" about "how to introduce themselves." The distance is marked by a troubling sense of so-near-and-yet-so-far. Much of the social intrigue of Austen's novels lies in their navigating these murky waters of social liminality.

Once she meets the Dalrymples, after her family has finally secured their acquaintance, Anne feels "ashamed. Had Lady Dalrymple and her daughter even been very agreeable, she would still have been ashamed of the agitation they created, but they were nothing." Even "Lady Russell confessed that she had expected something better; but yet 'it was an acquaintance worth having'" (P, 162). The inverted commas signal that the narrator's assessment differs from Lady Russell's that the "nothing" is a "something ... worth having."

In Austen's novels, "nobody" is a term wielded by a great many somebodies. Radically open, it negotiates the ambiguity between gentry and aristocracy: it may register a (lack of) character or social position. Anne's assessment of the Dalrymples is of the first kind. Of the second is a remark by her father, Sir Walter Elliot, about Frederick Wentworth's brother, the curate of Monkford: "You misled me by the term *gentleman*, I thought you were speaking of some man of property: Mr. Wentworth was nobody" (*P*, 26). Sir Walter delivers this priceless line to the lawyer Mr. Shepherd, who advises on renting out country houses. The effect is to exclude Mr. Wentworth from consideration as a tenant of Kellynch Hall, and by extension to exclude clergymen from claims to gentility. That sly gesture of exclusion, however, rebounds on Sir Walter; in using the term to diminish people by their class status alone, he shows the narrowness of his own conception of what a person of merit might be.

Emma riffs on the ambiguities of gentle status in a different way: "As to the circumstances of her birth," Emma says of Harriet, "though in a legal sense she may be called Nobody, it will not hold in common sense. ... That she is a gentleman's daughter, is indubitable to me" (*E*, 65–66). As an illegitimate child, she was *nullius filius*, "the child of nobody" (*E*, 547, n. 7). Later, we are privy to Emma's assumption that Mr. Elton "must know" that "the Eltons are nobody (*E*, 147).

Gainsaying Lady de Bourgh's snobbery, Elizabeth Bennet says, "He is a gentleman; I am a gentleman's daughter; so far we are equal." Lady Catherine accedes, but then immediately raises the question of Elizabeth's mother: "True. You *are* a gentleman's daughter. But who was your mother? Who are your uncles and aunts? Do not imagine me ignorant of their condition." Elizabeth replies, "Whatever my connections may be, ... if your nephew does not object to them, they can be nothing to *you*" (*PP*, 395). Indeed, they are nothing. Austen draws out the ambiguity. "Connections" can be a blessing and a curse, something to be cultivated or suppressed. Lady de Bourgh trains her beady eyes on them all. She is acutely aware of the merits of her own familial lines, haranguing Elizabeth with the claim that her daughter is the ideal wife for Darcy, that they are "formed for each other": "Hear me in silence. My daughter and my nephew are ... descended on the maternal side, from the same noble line" (*PP*, 394). Elizabeth claim is ultimately vindicated through Darcy's recognition. Her retort to Lady Catherine underscores how this opens the system to upward mobility. It's up to Darcy to decide and evaluate, and he decides in her favor. Such is the intricate balance between realism and wish-fulfillment, or aspiration, in *Pride and Prejudice* and its fairytale machinery.

We tend to focus on marriage and social mobility exclusively in relation to the protagonists of the romance, but marriage endings are a social event. A lot of effort is required, both at the personal level and at the level of an entire family and community, to ensure that the marriage binds existing social connections and offers enhancements for the larger community.

What makes Austen new is her recognition that social rank, income, gender, status, region, age, and even birth order are all significant as part of a complex social hieroglyph to be decoded and interrogated. This made Austen seem "Marxist before Marx."[16] Austen might be considered Marxist because she offers such a terse anatomy of the question of romantic *eligibility*, reading rank and position as some of the qualities that make a person socially and economically eligible. This occurs through a voice and tone that is at once settled and profoundly ironic. As Raymond Williams observes, Austen's critique takes place from "within" the gentry houses – not "outside the park walls," as it did for William Cobbett or George Eliot.[17] But to scale such ironic heights from the modest territory of the romance novel is a major achievement.

The "Epigrammatism of the general stile," as Austen wrote of *Pride and Prejudice*, but which applies to her whole oeuvre, is an intricately ironic, allegorical sensibility devoted to discriminating the highly calibrated relationships between rank, income, fortune, and region, as well as moral, psychological, and social disposition. Austen's Epigrammatism sets down a kind of heraldic figuring of these qualities as a new social language of the novel. If heraldry is about enabling recognition, Austen's novel system is about this too. It also critiques the absence of recognition, clocking the slights and the rebuffs, the "agony" of trying to bridge the gaps.

Notes

1 Francis Grose, *Dictionary of the Vulgar Tongue* (London, 1811), http://www.gutenberg.org/ebooks/5402, accessed 25 November 2019.

2 Thomas Keymer, "Rank," *Jane Austen in Context*, ed. Janet Todd (Cambridge: Cambridge University Press, 2005), p. 388.

3 Raymond Williams, *The Country and the City* (London: Hogarth Press, 1993), p. 113.

4 John Habakkuk, *Marriage, Debt and the Estates System: English Landownership 1650–1950* (Oxford: Oxford University Press, 1994), p. 239.

5 Linda Bree and Janet Todd, "Introduction," *Later Manuscripts* (Cambridge: Cambridge University Press, 2008), p. xliv.

6 Edward Copeland, *Women Writing about Money: Women's Fiction in England, 1790–1820* (Cambridge: Cambridge University Press, 1995), p. 136.

7 Mary Lascelles, *Jane Austen and Her Art* (London: Oxford, 1939), pp. 95, 96.

8 Jane Austen to Cassandra Austen, 27–28 October 1798, *Jane Austen's Letters*, ed. Deirdre Le Faye, third edition (Oxford: Oxford University Press, 1995), p. 18.

9 Lady Balfour, "The servants in Jane Austen" (1929), reprinted in *Jane Austen: Critical Assessments*, ed. Ian Littlewood, vol. 2 (Mountfield: Helm Information, 1998), p. 10.

10 Jane Austen to Cassandra Austen, 30 June to 1 July 1808, *Letters*, pp. 137–138.

11 David Spring, "Interpreters of Jane Austen's social world: Literary critics and historians," *Jane Austen: New Perspectives, Women and Literature*, vol. 3 (New York: Holmes & Meier, 1983), p. 56.

12 Jan Fergus, *Jane Austen: A Literary Life* (London: Macmillan, 1991), p. 47. The term "pseudo-gentry" that Spring uses for Austen's family was originally coined by Alan Everitt.

13 D.J. Greene, "Jane Austen and the peerage," in Littlewood, *Jane Austen: Critical Assessments*, p. 32.

14 Walter Scott, unsigned review of *Emma*, *Quarterly Review*, dated October 1815, issued March 1916, pp. xiv, 188–201.

15 Spring, "Interpreters of Jane Austen's social world," p. 61.

16 David Daiches, "Jane Austen, Karl Marx, and the aristocratic dance," (1948), in Littlewood, *Jane Austen: Critical Assessments*, p. 25.

17 Williams, *Country*, p. 117.

Myth
26 JANE AUSTEN WAS A COMIC NOVELIST

What do we mean when we say Jane Austen is a comic novelist? We might mean, for starters, that her novels are funny and lighthearted. Or we might mean something more technical: that they are structured around the courtship plot and end with happy marriages. Taken together or separately, these claims comport with just about everyone's impressions of Jane Austen. There is a lot to be said for them.

To aver that Austen is funny is to risk sounding a little like Mary Bennet, witlessly pronouncing threadbare truisms with an air of philosophic gravity, which is in itself pretty funny. Of course Jane Austen is funny. Did she not describe her own performance in *Pride and Prejudice* as "light, and bright, and sparkling"? What may need stressing, however, is the range of that comic sparkle. At times she is gently drôle, as when Emma and Mrs. Weston each press the other's foot under the table while Mr. Knightley is talking about Jane Fairfax; or when Anne Elliot and Wentworth discretely review their long and painful separation, while "each [was] apparently occupied in admiring a fine display of greenhouse plants" (*P*, 267). Though occasionally warm and sunny, Austen's humor is in other places very edgy. Her epigrams are often mordant:

People always live for ever when there is any annuity to be paid them. (*SS*, 12)

Sometimes they turn on reversals that anticipate Oscar Wilde:

"I wonder who first discovered the efficacy of poetry in driving away love!" (*PP*, 49)

"To find a man agreeable whom one is determined to hate! Do not wish me such an evil." (*PP*, 101)

30 Great Myths About Jane Austen, First Edition. Claudia L. Johnson and Clara Tuite.
© 2020 John Wiley & Sons, Inc. Published 2020 by John Wiley & Sons, Inc.

Austen's understatements can be jaw-dropping:

> Mr. Collins was not a sensible man. (*PP*, 8)

Her delight in sheer nonsense looks back to Henry Fielding's farces and forward to the theater of the absurd, as when someone knocks on the door in *Love and Freindship*:

> One evening in December, as my Father, my Mother and myself, were arranged in social converse round our Fireside, we were on a sudden, greatly astonished, by hearing a violent knocking on the outward Door of our rustic Cot.

> My Father started – "What noise is that," (said he.) "It sounds like a loud rapping at the door" – (replied my Mother.) "It does indeed." (cried I.) "I am of your opinion; (said my Father) it certainly does appear to proceed from some uncommon violence exerted against our unoffending Door." "Yes (exclaimed I) I cannot help thinking it must be somebody who knocks for Admittance."

> "That is another point (replied he;) We must not pretend to determine on what motive the person may knock – though that someone *does* rap at the door, I am partly convinced." (*J*, 106)

Sometimes her deadpan takes on the quality of brain-twisters, mimicking the inanity of her characters:

> [Sir Walter Eliot] considered the blessing of beauty as inferior only to the blessing of a baronetcy; and the Sir Walter Elliot, who united these gifts, was the constant object of his warmest respect and devotion. (*P*, 4)

And her puns can surprise with their brilliance and their bawdry:

> "Of *Rears*, and *Vices*, I saw enough. Now, do not be suspecting me of a pun, I entreat." (*MP*, 71)

Though Austen's admirers all have their own lists of favorites, we can all marvel at the variety of her wit. As a satirist, Austen often aims her humor at moral rather than purely intellectual defects. For good reasons, readers typically enjoy – and believe that Austen herself most commonly enjoys – scenes where characters make fools of themselves without knowing it. *Pride and Prejudice* is teeming with such instances. Mr. Collins repeating his marriage proposal to Elizabeth, despite her persistent refusal, is a classic example. Lady Catherine's inane self-praise is another: "There are few people in England, I suppose, who have more true enjoyment of music than myself, or a better natural taste. If I had ever learnt, I should have been a great proficient" (*PP*, 194). We may smile as Catherine Morland shuffles through papers she suspects are a secret manuscript only to find them to be a laundry list. But once she discovers her mistake, she immediately squirms with embarrassment. By contrast, Mr. Collins and Lady Catherine aren't embarrassed at all. They haven't the slightest notion how ridiculous they are, and their failure to perceive this makes them funny and reprehensible at the same time.

Often described as arch, sly, or knowing, Austen's humor in such instances invites us into a shared position of superiority vis-à-vis these blunderers. Some readers have charged Austen with a mean streak on this account, and we all might well wonder if Austen is secretly laughing at us for being ridiculous in ways we don't suspect. Austen's comedy is most brilliant and most biting when it is aimed at those who place themselves above the possibility of error or embarrassment. In their impenetrable vanity, characters like Mr. Collins, Lady Catherine, Mrs. Bennet, John Thorpe, Lydia, Mrs. Elton, or Sir Walter Elliot cannot be injured by our laughter. They are inhumiliable. As such, they are hilarious but also a little unnerving. It's not hard to imagine how Mr. Collins's risible inability to hear Elizabeth's "no" could morph into something like coercion, of the sort we are obliged to recognize in *Mansfield Park*, when neither Sir Thomas, nor Edmund, nor Henry Crawford can actually fathom, much less honor, Fanny's gentle but firm "no." Definitely not funny.

The myth of Austen's funniness is dented not so much by its frequent darkness – lots of comedy is dark after all – as by Austen's determination to put the will to funniness itself under examination, as both a corrective and as a quality that needs correction. Elizabeth tells us that she dearly loves a laugh, and though we find that Darcy is improved by her laughter, we probably do not feel that Mr. Bennet's love of laughter has improved the character or circumstances of his family. "For what do we live, but to make sport for our neighbours, and laugh at them in our turn?" (*PP*, 403), he asks rhetorically, not long before essentially leaving Lydia to her own wayward devices, bringing the Bennet family to disgrace and near ruin. Austen examines the dangers of wit and laughter more thoroughly in *Mansfield Park* and *Emma*. In the former, Austen pits the levity of the Crawfords – with their repartee and puns and double-entendres – against the dullness of the Bertrams. Edmund Bertram brags: "There is not the least wit in my nature. I am a very matter of fact, plain-spoken being" (*MP*, 109). Many readers wish the Bertrams had a little more wit in their natures, but this novel suggests that wit is a dangerous thing. "Your lively mind can hardly be serious even on serious subjects," (*MP*, 102) Edmund tells Mary Crawford, as if liveliness has vitiated her mind rendering her, like her brother, dangerously labile. In *Emma*, wit is not quite so patholo-gized, but Emma's fondness for a joke is still presented as a failure of moral freedom: "Emma could not resist" (*E*, 403) the opening to ridicule Miss Bates's dullness. And Mr. Knightley claims that puzzles, word games, intrigue, and finesse "pervert the understanding," and instead celebrates "the beauty of truth and sincerity in all our dealings with each other" (*E*, 486). In sum, it's important to remember that Austen in fact did *not* describe *Pride and Prejudice* as "light and bright and sparkling," as com-monly believed. Rather, she described it as "*too* light and bright and spar-kling." Austen does not proffer comedy as an end in itself.

But what about that other meaning of comedy, which refers not essen-tially to humor but rather to a specific kind of plot, sometimes baldly described this way: Boy gets girl; boy loses girl, boy gets girl back? In comic plots – from Shakespeare to Jane Austen and beyond – a young couple's romance is blocked, typically by a wrong-headed parental figure, leading to separations and trials that eventually are resolved, permitting the couple to marry happily and in so doing to constitute a new and bet-ter society. Obviously, this very general definition can only get us so far, but it does describe the general plot of novels by Fielding, Richardson, Burney, Austen, and many others. In this sense Austen is without question a comic novelist: all her major novels dramatize courtship and its vicis-situdes and end with marriage. The complication comes when we ask ourselves about the status of the concluding marriage and the happiness it may be supposed to produce.

The conclusion of *Northanger Abbey* demonstrates this problem per-fectly. The heroine and hero have proceeded more or less successfully through their courtship until General Tilney (incensed to learn that Catherine is not as rich as he thought) angrily forbids their marriage, unceremoniously throwing Catherine out of his house and sending her home disgraced. By taking her heroine to the brink of desolation, Austen follows traditional comic practice. But in yanking her back from the brink Austen is anything but traditional. In the final chapter, when things are looking pretty bad for Catherine, Austen's narrator turns directly to her readers, "who will see in the tell-tale compression of the pages before them, that we are all hastening together to perfect felicity" (*NA*, 259). We all know, she seems to be saying, that comic novels have to end happily, so if there are only two pages remaining, the author will have to find a way out of this jam quickly. Austen continues to stress the blatant fiction-ality of comedy's "perfect felicity." Flouting standards of probability and plausibility she has observed elsewhere in the novel, she brazenly invents an entirely new character and relationship to placate the General's fury: a viscount to marry Eleanor Tilney. "The most charming young man in the world is instantly before the imagination of us all" (*NA*, 260), she avers. Austen is winking at us here, suggesting that if we want a conventionally comic happy ending for Henry and Catherine, we're going to have to imagine it for ourselves.

In *Mansfield Park*, where all the characters (except perhaps Fanny and Susan Price) are shattered, disgraced, and depressed, Austen pulls very much the same stunt, breaking the frame in the final chapter to announce her intention to pull a happy ending out of her hat: "Let other pens dwell on guilt and misery. I quit such odious subjects as soon as I can, impatient to restore everybody, not greatly in fault themselves, to tolerable comfort, and to have done with all the rest" (*MP*, 533). So saying, Austen calls our attention to the wretchedness of her characters heretofore and to the arbitrariness of the happy ending she will now compose. The contentment and "comfort" of the good guys will not come about as the probable outcome of the plot's logic up to this point, but rather as a result of this particular novelist's distaste for "odiousness." And again, as in *Northanger Abbey*, she obliges readers who want a happy ending to invent it for themselves:

> I purposely abstain from dates on this occasion, that every one may be at liberty to fix their own, aware that the cure of unconquerable passions, and the transfer of unchanging attachments, must vary much as to time in different people. I only entreat everybody to believe that exactly at the time when it was quite natural that it should be so, and not a week earlier, Edmund did cease to care about Miss Crawford, and became as anxious to marry Fanny as Fanny herself could desire. (*MP*, 544)

Because the myth that Austen's novels give us happy endings – comic endings, joyous marriages – is so stubborn, it's worth pointing out that Austen's novels actually end with a lot of uncertainty. Yes, the sisters pair off at the end of *Sense and Sensibility*, but the felicity is muted, consisting mainly of keeping their respective husbands from fighting with each other. Though everyone except Mrs. Elton is glad that Emma and Knightley marry at the end of *Emma*, many readers are thrown off balance by Emma's failure to come clean to a man who touts truth and sincerity, and many of these same readers claim that nothing is truly resolved, that Emma is still the mistress of her father's houses, that she is insufficiently punished, and that she will continue in her "imagines" ways. And *Persuasion* is so interesting in part because it narrates the long aftermath of an unhappy ending – the happy marriage that never materialized seven years before the novel begins. *Persuasion* convinces us of the love Captain Wentworth and Anne Elliot happily share, but it also underscores the threat to her happiness: "[Anne] gloried in being a sailor's wife, but she must pay the tax of quick alarm for belonging to that profession which is, if possible, more distinguished in its domestic virtues than in its national importance" (*P*, 275). Leaving aside this sentence's referent problems – as written, it is Anne rather than Captain Wentworth who belongs to a profession here, the profession of sailor's wife – Anne is left in a permanent state of alert.

Why does Austen undercut the happy ending that is supposed to signal the successful conclusion of her comic novels? Is she worried that readers might mistake the closural conventionality of comic plots with marriage as a real-life institution? Is she simply more interested in other elements of novel-writing, as if the happy marriage part were a perfunctory and not especially interesting part of the novelist's art? The jury is out on these questions, but one thing is clear: only *Pride and Prejudice* squarely affirms the comic tradition, uniting a hero and heroine of perfectly complementary birth and worth in a felicitous and stable union that seems to emerge inevitably from the plot. Our tendency to forget this may say more about our own wishes than Austen's complex practice.

Myth 27

JANE AUSTEN'S NOVELS ARE ABOUT GOOD MANNERS

This myth takes different forms and serves different purposes. Generally, "good manners" here refers to specific decorums practiced in early-nineteenth-century England. Such are the manners viewers and reviewers of TV and movie productions of Austen's novels invoke when they observe how Austen's characters bow and curtsy upon entering or leaving a room. "Jane Austen's novels are all about good manners" in this case means something like, "Folks were really polite back then." But since this observation is inflected with a semi-wistful implication that we are boorish by comparison, the myth says as much about ourselves, our supposed decline into unmannerliness, as it does about Austen's novels, where there are plenty of boors to go around. But at the same time as we might be inclined to idealize and to exaggerate the importance of manners in her fiction, stressing the prevalence of manners in the novels has often meant trivializing them, as if they were about *mere* good manners, while novels like, say, *Moby Dick* or *War and Peace* are about grander, deeper, and more important things. In this way, the myth of manners takes away with one hand what it seems to give with the other. Having read Jane Austen during World War II, while laid up with pneumonia, Winston Churchill marveled, with a touch of scorn, "What calm lives they had, those people. No worries about the French Revolution, or the crashing struggle of the Napoleonic Wars. Only manners controlling natural passion so far as they could, together with cultured explanations of any mischances."[1] Many readers have mistaken these remarks for praise. But preoccupied with the "crashing struggles" of world war, Churchill underestimates the depth and power of quieter experiences depicted in Austen's novels,

30 Great Myths About Jane Austen, First Edition. Claudia L. Johnson and Clara Tuite.
© 2020 John Wiley & Sons, Inc. Published 2020 by John Wiley & Sons, Inc.

which evidently strike him as rarefied, remote, and strange: "those people" seem like entirely different creatures from himself. The myth of good manners in Austen's novels must be contended with if we are to understand her orientation with respect to the decorums of her time and to assess the magnitude of her achievement.

So, are Austen's novels particularly preoccupied with good manners? Yes and no. All societies generate forms and rituals that structure social behavior. In Austen's novels, as in virtually all nineteenth-century English novels, these forms and rituals are always functioning in the background, regulating the conduct of characters, shaping their expectations of each other, and making their intentions and feelings legible to each other and to us. In the very first chapter of *Pride and Prejudice*, for example, Mrs. Bennet harangues Mr. Bennet about the necessity of visiting Mr. Bingley, a newcomer to the neighborhood, and because tormenting her is one way he consoles himself for having married her in the first place, he declines to assure her that he will do so. But of course, as he had intended all along, Mr. Bennet does indeed call (or "wait") on Mr. Bingley, and in due time Mr. Bingley returns the visit. The mannerly making and returning of calls, sometimes leaving one's calling card, takes place so often in Austen's novels that we rarely even notice, except perhaps when the decorum is stretched. Caroline Bingley waits so long before returning Jane Bennet's visit in London that even mild Jane recognizes it as a snub, a way of letting Jane know that her acquaintance is not valued highly enough to warrant promptness. Similarly, commonly accepted norms regulate forms of address. As first-time readers we learn that only the eldest daughters are called, for example, "Miss Bennet" or "Miss Elliot," while their younger sisters are addressed as "Miss Elizabeth Bennet" or "Miss Anne Elliot." Further, first naming is off-limits to all but intimates. Mr. Knightley can call Emma by her first name because he has known since she was an infant, but when Willoughby calls Marianne by her first name, Elinor notices and plausibly (though wrongly) infers that they are engaged. Ditto nicknaming. Jane Bennet affectionately calls her sister Lizzy, but a keen reader will immediately notice that when Caroline Bingley refers to Elizabeth – whom she obviously despises – as "Miss Eliza Bennet" she is (without resorting to outright rudeness) failing to treat her with due respect. Forms and customs such as these, often footnoted in classroom editions, make up a good deal of the texture of Jane Austen's novels, and the more we know about social practices during Austen's time, the more we're able to register them and attend to the richness and thoroughness of such details.

That said, Austen's novels do not idealize etiquette, and the characters who make a big fuss about it are often presented as silly or contemptible.

Twenty-first-century readers tend to forget that manners in Austen's time do not consist simply of ideal practices that are basically either polite or considerate in some abstract sense. On the contrary, they are enmeshed in specific class positions and relations. Sir William Lucas, a secondary character in *Pride and Prejudice*, is a perfect instance of this. Thoroughly middle-class in origin, Sir William made his fortune in business and received an honorary, non-inheritable knighthood in connection with having been the mayor, hence his title "Sir." This nominal elevation in rank having gone to his head, Sir William quits his business to devote himself entirely to "being civil to all the world" (*PP*, 19). Being a gentleman to Sir William means behaving with good manners, but the oppressive ostentation of his courteous performance shows that he is not to the manner born.

But manners consist of more than politeness, and Austen's novels expose how characters deploy them to announce and maintain distinction and privilege. Take, for example, the practice of precedence. Then – as now, at highly formal dinners – persons entered a dining room hierarchically according to their rank and status, and the seating arrangement relative to the top and bottom of the table in any genteel home reflected the power and prestige of the assemblage. As a baronet's daughter, Mary Musgrove in *Persuasion* is entitled to enter before her mother-in-law Mrs. Musgrove and to be seated higher, but Mary claims this privilege with unseemly insistence, thus showing herself to be at once hoity toity and mean, like her father. With even less legitimacy, in *Pride and Prejudice*, Lydia Bennet Wickham, whose raucous stupidity renders her oblivious to her disgrace at having been just barely rescued from ruin, flaunts the rights of precedence to which etiquette entitles her: "Ah, Jane I take your place now, and you must go lower, because I am a married woman" (*PP*, 350). Less contemptible, perhaps, but no less "nonsensical" (*E*, 231), as Mr. Knightley terms them, are Emma Woodhouse's snobbish ideas about the signs of rank and distinction. She is pleased to see Mr. Knightley arrive at a dance in his carriage: "This is coming as you should do," said she, "like a gentleman" (*E*, 230). Mr. Knightley has no doubt about his social status: he knows that he is a gentleman regardless of how he arrives. Emma's vigilance about manners as signifiers of status betrays her weaker social position and undercuts her posture of village preeminence. Indeed, it places her dangerously close to Mrs. Elton so far as social anxiety is concerned.

If Austen's novels ridicule practitioners of manners, they sometimes also evince sympathy for characters who are indifferent or oblivious to them, particularly with respect to women. Every conduct book about female manners agrees that young ladies must comport themselves with becoming modesty to members of the opposite sex. Catherine Morland is blissfully unaware of this and, having been tricked into a carriage ride with James

Thorpe instead of keeping her date with Henry and Eleanor Tilney, blurts out to Henry: "I begged Mr. Thorpe so earnestly to stop … and if Mr. Thorpe would only have stopped, I would have jumped out and run after you" (*NA*, 93). Needless to say, jumping out of a carriage and running after the gentleman on whom one has a crush is not good manners, conventionally speaking, and divulging a wish to have done so to the gent in question is tantamount to a declaration of love, which conduct books roundly condemn. But Austen's best characters are either oblivious to some social rules or willing to consciously defy some of them. Austen writes of Henry at this moment, "Is there a Henry in the world who could be insensible to such a declaration? Henry Tilney at least was not" (*NA*, 93). In fact, Henry is so endeared by the unguardedness of Catherine's affection that he is moved to return them. Whereas Catherine defies rules about female manners because she is unaware of them, Marianne Dashwood flouts them on principle. In a very different register, we see the same in *Sense and Sensibility*, which is less about the respective merits of sense and sensibility than it is about the authority manners should have in adjudicating behavior in matters of the heart, with Marianne breaking every rule. Defying Elinor's counsel to behave towards Willoughby with mannerly reserve, Marianne appeals to reason: she "abhorred all concealment where no real disgrace could attend unreserve; and to aim at the restraint of sentiments which were not in themselves illaudable, appeared to her not merely an unnecessary effort, but a disgraceful subjection of reason to common-place and mistaken notions" (*SS*, 63). Marianne's unguarded, unmannerly openness and ardor still wins his heart, much as Catherine's wins Henry's. The fact that Willoughby turns out to be a cad who chooses money over love is another matter.

Austen's readiness to value open-heartedness over mannerliness does not mean that she condones rudeness, of course. Darcy's aggressively audible snub of Elizabeth in *Pride and Prejudice*, like Lady Catherine's ludicrous insolence, deserves and receives censure. But Austen's skepticism about the authority of good manners is far more striking. It is important to register this in order to take the full measure of Austen's unconventionality. The unease surrounding the suave, impeccably well-mannered Mr. Elliot – he "was rational, discreet, polished, – but he was not open. There was never any burst of feeling, any warmth of indignation or delight, at the evil or good of others" (*P*, 175) – was not a late-career discovery. All of Austen's novels prize, as Anne Elliot does, "the frank, the open-hearted, the eager character beyond all others," particularly over those "whose presence of mind never varied, whose tongue never slipped" (*P*, 175). Bad manners, ruptures in good form, permit us to glean the real person underneath. That person may be irritable and mean-spirited, like Mr. Elton, but lapses in good manners can also show us something to treasure – for example the warmth of the coarse Mrs. Jennings, who is preferable to the well-bred but cold Lady Middleton. Elizabeth Bennet's energy in walking three miles *alone*, muddying her petticoats in the process, to visit her sick sister shows Caroline Bingley "an abominable sort of conceited independence, a most country town indifference to decorum" (*PP*, 39). But we suspect that Miss Bingley's defense of good manners here is simply a cover for her jealousy of Elizabeth, and we are relieved when Mr. Bingley recognizes that Elizabeth's journey shows "an affection for her sister that is very pleasing" (*PP*, 38). For Austen real warmth outweighs goods manners every time.

If being a novelist of manners means both affirming the forms and rituals of a given society and also representing those forms and rituals as somehow sufficient to account for the experiences of her characters, then Jane Austen is not a novelist of manners. Austen novels represent manners, inevitably, but they do not treat manners as essentially normative or authoritative. The bows and curtsies and decorums that seem so civilized and elegant to twenty-first-century audiences have no role in averting or relieving the crises besetting her heroines – the betrayal of Marianne by Willoughby, the coercion of Fanny Price at the hands of her "friends," the expulsion of Catherine Morland from Northanger Abbey when she is discovered not to be rich, the mortification of Elizabeth Bennet when she discovers herself to have been wrong, the jubilant cruelty of Emma on Box Hill, or the seven-year desolation of Anne Elliot. These may not be "crashing struggles," to recollect Churchill's phrase, but they are momentous. Churchill certainly had his hands full, but manifestly he was no Janeite.

Note

1 Winston Churchill, *The Second World War*, vol. 5: *Closing the Ring* (Boston: Houghton Mifflin, 1951), p. 3.

Myth
28 JANE AUSTEN'S MUSLINS

"Do you understand muslins, sir?"

(Jane Austen, *Northanger Abbey*)

Jane Austen is only half-joking when she hints that Mrs. Allen is an airhead for suggesting that muslins might occupy an epistemological world with its own layers of mystery. Muslin is famously airy and light – so light it required multiple layers to cover the body. But it is weighty matter in Jane Austen's world; like fashion generally, it has significant social, economic, and symbolic import. Just as Mrs. Allen is deadly serious about muslin and its special effects, so is Austen, although, as Clair Hughes notes, "the difference between Austen's own passion and Mrs. Allen's is that nothing else occupies Mrs. Allen's mind."[1]

The myth of Jane Austen's muslins is double-edged: one version holds that Austen satirizes fashion (as she must); the other that she is uncritically preoccupied with this trivial feminine pursuit. The underlying assumption of both is that fashion is petty women's business. But the matter is much more complicated: while Austen satirizes fashion on occasion, it means a lot to her. In Austen's world, fashion assumes a complex symbolic and material role, emblematizing the conjunction of symbolic and economic orders.

The assumption that fashion is trivial is overturned in Austen's fiction, most famously by *Northanger Abbey*'s Henry Tilney, who impresses Mrs. Allen with his understanding of muslins. In *Pride and Prejudice*, too, the narrator shares the younger Bennet sisters' interest in clothing:

Their eyes were immediately wandering up in the street in quest of the officers, and nothing less than a very smart bonnet indeed, or a really new muslin in a shop window, could recal them. (*PP*, 80)

30 Great Myths About Jane Austen, First Edition. Claudia L. Johnson and Clara Tuite.
© 2020 John Wiley & Sons, Inc. Published 2020 by John Wiley & Sons, Inc.

Muslins and bonnets have sufficient power to "recall" the gaze of young women in pursuit of officers and stand as a potent sign of the "new."

So, if Jane Austen's powers of understanding extend to muslins, what is it they comprehend? In an early letter to Cassandra, who had sent Jane on a shopping errand in Bath, Jane outlines her feelings for sprig, "an ornament resembling a small branch or shoot, esp. on fabric" (*OED*):[2]

> Though you have given me unlimited powers concerning Your Sprig, I cannot determine what to do about it … We have been to the cheap Shop, & very cheap we found it, but there are only flowers made there, no fruit – & as I could get 4 or 5 very pretty sprigs of the former for the same money which would procure only one Orleans plumb … Besides, I cannot help thinking that it is more natural to have flowers grow out of the head than fruit.[3]

Jane Austen is acutely aware of the responsibility of being a buyer for someone else. She can't decide on fruit or flowers, not because she doesn't know which is better but because her own preference is not Cassandra's. Jane thinks flowers are best (and they are cheaper and more aesthetically appropriate than fruit), but Cassandra has asked her to purchase fruit.

This decision must factor in economics and aesthetics. Muslin was comparatively cheap, but its trimmings were expensive, so the decision was a weighty one, with a greater likelihood of indecision. Catherine Morland lies awake "debating between her spotted and her tamboured muslin," and Harriet Smith at Ford's is "tempted by every thing and swayed by half a word, … hanging over muslins and changing her mind" (*NA*, 271). Aesthetic choices are also clues to character. Mrs. Elton displays her vulgarity when she parades in her wedding gown while professing to abhor ostentation: "I have the greatest dislike to the idea of being over-trimmed – quite a horror of finery. I must put on a few ornaments *now*, because it is expected of me. A bride, you know, must appear like a bride, but my natural taste is all for simplicity" (*E*, 327).

Austen's treatment of muslins as both clothing and commodity tells us about her social position in the precarious class of the landless gentry. While she mostly lives in the country, her family is not wealthy. When she visits Bath, the fashionable spa city that draws drifters, chancers, and people on the fringes of elite society, she turns that fringe-dwelling into an occasion for irony, trained on herself as much as on others. She is also keenly self-ironizing in reporting her fashion conquests (and wardrobe malfunctions) to Cassandra. As Barbara Hardy observes, Austen's letters "show a constant but constantly self-amused preoccupation with dress."[4]

Fashion is both a pleasure and an occupation Jane shares with her sister. In one letter, she reports with satisfaction that she "saw some Gauzes in a shop in Bath Street yesterday at only 4s a yard, but they were not so good or so pretty as mine."[5] In another, she apologizes to Cassandra for spending too much on muslin: "I am sorry to tell you that I am getting very extravagant & spending all my Money; & what is worse for *you*, I have been spending yours too; for in a Linendraper's shop to which I went for check'd Muslin, ... I was tempted by a pretty coloured muslin, & bought 10 yds of it, on the chance of your liking it."[6]

From Steventon, she reports, "I have got over the dreadful epocha of Mantuamaking much better than I expected." This seems to have been the making of a new gown; many of the Austen women's new clothes were made by altering existing ones. In the same letter, Jane reports that she is to wear "a Mamalouc cap ... which Charles Fowle sent to Mary, & which she lends me. – It is all the fashion now, worn at the Opera."[7] The "Mamalouc cap" commemorated Horatio Nelson's defeat of the French at the Battle of the Nile in August 1798. A month earlier, Napoleon had worn a Mameluke costume to celebrate his defeat of the Mamelukes. English fashion here reappropriates the cap and deploys it against Napoleon, emphasizing fashion's claim to historical significance. As Roland Barthes writes, "Fashion ... does not suppress meaning; it points to it with its finger."[8]

Austen's muslins offer a case study of consumer desire. Muslin is the pre-eminent commodity in Austen's world. It is a powerful exemplar of the commodity form, which Karl Marx described as a "social hieroglyphic," which "men try to decipher ... to get behind the secret of their own social product."[9] Fashion is a sign, then, that requires reading, and muslins, in all their layers, embody secrets of class, rank, income, gender, and age. Deciphering their hieroglyphic presentation of value is an activity in which Austen's writings are acutely involved.

Muslins, which originated in Mosul in Iraq, were initially imported from India; when Henry Tilney refers to a fabric as "a true Indian," it is a mark of quality (*NA*, 20). The importation of muslin was part of an international trade, occasionally disrupted by war; for example, English demand for muslin rose after Napoleon cut off the export of raw silk from France. (Austen herself was fond of silk stockings.[10]) In France, as Daniel Roche shows, there was an "increase in the import of lighter fabrics – cottons, printed muslins and linens," imported from the Levant and the East Indies. Later came "the triumph of England, on which France came to depend for its cottons."[11] The broader point of Roche's discussion is that clothing was a pervasive topic of discussion in a central intellectual enterprise such as Diderot's monumental *Encyclopédie*, which "ratified the new trends in the sartorial spectacle, the taste for cottons, silks, muslins and taffetas, at the expense of wool ... The clothing system it expounded was strongly influenced by its concern to penetrate to the heart of things and reveal the improved appearance within everyone's reach."[12] Austen's muslins register this shift and participate in the activity of revelation.

Austen's understanding of the enigmas of conspicuous consumption, in which less is often more, imbues the satirical vision of her neighbor, Mrs. Powlett, a clergyman's wife, who is "at once expensively & nakedly dress'd; – we have had the satisfaction of estimating her Lace & her Muslin; & she said too little to afford us much other amusement."[13] In the nineteenth century, "women's dress became progressively more 'undress.'"[14] Later in the century, muslin would be replaced by an even more transparent fabric: tulle.

English and French fashion were closely linked. The famous "Empire line" of the first Napoleonic empire was roughly equivalent to the English Regency style. It was typified by the "chemise dress," which had a fitted bodice ending just below the breasts and a loose skirt that skimmed the body rather than being supported by voluminous petticoats. Its English antecedents had "originated as informal or semiprivate dress, but made their way into a more public and formal realm."[15]

The Empire line is now associated with the name of Jane Austen herself – a name to conjure with in the contemporary global fashion industry. According to American *Vogue*, on the bicentenary of Austen's death in 2017, "Austenmania ... infiltrated fashion." It had its "fullest flowering" at Gucci, where "floral-sprigged book clutches stamped with the titles of Jane Austen novels [were] carried by men and women on the Gucci catwalk," some of them "leashed to the wearer in a punk/S&M manner – very *Pride and Prejudice and Zombies*" (Figure 5). The season's offerings also included "Alexander McQueen's Spencer-like bolero, and the empire lines at both Vera Wang and Delpozo," as well as Molly Goddard's chemise dress in ruffles.[16]

But Austen herself was operating in a milieu of scarcity rather than spectacle, where clothing had acute material and symbolic significance. When Lydia writes to tell Harriet about her elopement with Wickham, she refers to her dress in highly symbolic terms: "I wish you would tell Sally to mend a great slit in my worked muslin gown" (*PP*, 321). Clothing also mediates Mrs. Bennet's response to the news of Lydia's impending marriage to Wickham:

> "This is delightful indeed! ... But the clothes, the wedding clothes!" ...
> She was then proceeding to all the particulars of calico, muslin, and cambric, and would shortly have dictated some very plentiful orders, had not

Figure 5 Jane Austen inspired Gucci, 2017 collection
Pocket-sized edition of Jane Austen's *Emma*, designed to fit within Alessandro Michele's Gucci clutch bag. Marcus Tondo / Indigital.tv

> Jane ... persuaded her to wait, till her father was at leisure to be consulted. (*PP*, 337–338)

The "great slit" in Lydia's gown symbolizes her premature deflowering and the rent she has made in the family's social fabric. Proleptically, it anticipates her father's refusal to pay for her wedding clothes. Clothing brings together the economic and socially symbolic orders, as it does in all Austen's fiction.

And then there is the question of white; as Sylvia Townsend Warner observes, "One after another, novelists are subjugated by the sentiment of a white gown." She is inspired – as Austen surely was herself – by a passage from Samuel Richardson's *Clarissa* (1748) depicting its heroine imprisoned on a trumped-up charge of debt, confined to a sponging-house, where she is "the kneeling lady, sunk with majesty … in her white flowing robes (for she had not on a hoop) spreading the dark, though not dirty floor, and illuminating that horrid corner; her linen beyond imagination white, considering that she had not been undressed ever since she had been there."[17] And Richardson's tableau of persecuted virtue influences the consummate Gothic trope of the woman in white that appears in Ann Radcliffe's *The Mysteries of Udolpho* (1794): Emily St. Aubert in a white veil pursued by worthless relatives through crumbling castles.

Another character who understands the significance of white is Mrs. Allen, Catherine Morland's chaperone in Bath:

> "Mrs. Allen," said Catherine the next morning, "will there be any harm in my calling on Miss Tilney to-day? I shall not be easy till I have explained every thing."
>
> "Go by all means, my dear; only put on a white gown; Miss Tilney always wears white." (*NA*, 90)

Miss Tilney wears white not only because she is impeccable but also because it is the color her beloved Emily St. Aubert wears.

White in England was the color of purity and the "hallmark of elegance."[18] As Edmund tells Fanny in *Mansfield Park*:

> A woman can never be too fine while she is all in white. No, I see no finery about you; nothing but what is perfectly proper. Your gown seems very pretty. I like these glossy spots. Has not Miss Crawford a gown something the same? (*MP*, 259)

Edmund's awkward compliment is a telling example of what *Northanger Abbey*'s narrator calls "the insensibility of man towards a new gown" – even when ostensibly admiring one (*NA*, 71). In the throes of his infatuation with Mary Crawford, Edmund can barely see the gown or Fanny in it. So lacking is he in an understanding of muslins – and so desperately preoccupied with Mary Crawford – that all he can offer is that Fanny's outfit is "perfectly proper" and "seems very pretty," before blurting out (slightly improperly) "I like these glossy spots."

Can we really see Fanny in *glossy spots*? Edmund can't either, and that is the point. He is fantasizing some vision of femininity far more extravagant than Fanny can ever give him. It is a vision that contradicts his pious reassurance to Fanny, for the "glossy spots" border indecorously on the "finery" that Fanny's costume is supposedly too proper to have. He doesn't see Fanny clearly because he can only see Mary through her: "Has not Miss Crawford a gown something the same?" Clumsy in his desire, he gives himself away by associating the "gown" with something else, seeing through Fanny's dress to another woman. The glossy spots summon the proverbial leopard, Mary Crawford, who will never change her spots for him.

Despite Edmund's assurances that a woman can never go wrong in white, not all women were permitted to wear it. Colors were classed, and white was emphatically upper-class, its boundaries policed, as when the housekeeper at Sotherton in *Mansfield Park* "turn[s] away two housemaids for wearing white gowns" (*MP*, 123). We learn from Madge Garland, the first Professor of Fashion, that white was only democratized in the mid-twentieth century, when new synthetics replaced "the ancient triumvirate of silk, wool, and cotton."[19] Only then could we see "the astonishing spectacle ... of the London girl going about her business in bus and tube dressed in pale, light colours and in gleaming white, always spotlessly clean and trim."[20] And below the white dress were legs in nylon stockings, giving "the effect of total nudity."[21] This splendid effect was impossible with Austen's beloved silk stockings, but Austen may well have appreciated seeing women inexpensively and nakedly dressed.

Notes

1 Clair Hughes, "Talk about muslin: Jane Austen's *Northanger Abbey*," *Textile: The Journal of Cloth and Culture*, 4(2), (Summer 2006), p. 187.

2 "Sprig." *Oxford English Dictionary* online: www-oed-com.

3 Jane Austen to Cassandra Austen, 11 June 1799, *Jane Austen's Letters*, ed. Deirdre Le Faye, third edition (Oxford: Oxford University Press, 1995), p. 44.

4 Barbara Hardy, "Properties and possessions in Jane Austen's Novels," *Jane Austen's Achievement*, ed. Juliet McMaster (New York: Harper & Row, 1976), p. 89.

5 Jane Austen to Cassandra Austen, 2 June 1799, *Letters*, p. 42. Gauze is "very fine, open-weave silk"; Aileen Ribeiro, *Dress in Eighteenth Century Europe 1715–1789* (London: Batsford, 1984), p. 206.

6 Jane Austen to Cassandra Austen, 18–20 April 1811, *Letters*, p. 179.

7 Jane Austen to Cassandra Austen, 8–9 January 1799, *Letters*, p. 33.

8 Roland Barthes, *The Fashion System*, trans. Matthew Ward and Richard Howard (New York: Hill & Wang, 1983), p. 303.

9 Karl Marx, *Capital: A Critique of Political Economy*, vol. 1 (Penguin, 1990), p. 167.

10 See *Letters*, p. 41. "She seems 'to have had a weakness for stockings' (Byrde 1999: 28), especially silk ones"; Hughes, "Talk about muslin," p. 187.

11 Daniel Roche, *The Culture of Clothing: Dress and Fashion in the "Ancien Regime,"* trans. Jean Birrell (Cambridge: Cambridge University Press, 1999), pp. 446, 447.
12 Ibid, pp. 446–447.
13 Jane Austen to Cassandra Austen, 8–9 January 1801, *Letters*, p. 70.
14 Valerie Steele, *Paris Fashion: A Cultural History* (Oxford: Oxford University Press, 1988), p. 40.
15 Ibid, p. 41.
16 Laird Borrelli-Persson, "Why Jane Austen matters to fashion now," *Vogue* (31 March 2017), https://www.vogue.com/article/fall-2017-ready-to-wear-jane-austen, accessed 6 May 2019.
17 Sylvia Townsend Warner, *Jane Austen* (London: Longman's, Green & Co, 1964), p. 7.
18 Sarah Jane Downing, *Fashion in the Time of Jane Austen* (Oxford: Shire, 2010), p. 26.
19 Madge Garland, *Fashion: A Picture Guide to its Creators and Creations* (Harmondsworth: Penguin, 1962), p.92.
20 Ibid, pp. 94–95.
21 Ibid, p. 94.

Myth 29
JANE AUSTEN WRITES ESCAPE FICTION

J.R.R. Tolkien famously wrote that jailers are the only people who could legitimately object to escape fiction: "Why should a man be scorned if, finding himself in prison, he tries to get out and go home? Or if, when he cannot do so, he thinks and talks about other topics than jailers and prison-walls?"[1] Tolkien's remark seems so obviously true that it shouldn't feel discomfiting to discuss reading Jane Austen for escape, but the subject is so wrapped up in loaded judgments, assumptions, and confusions about classes of literature, kinds of reading, and escape itself that conversations about it can feel booby-trapped. Reading "for escape" can sometimes refer to specific kinds of literature – "genre" fiction and popular fiction, such as harlequin romances, spy novels, or mysteries – that are readily consumable, readily forgettable (despite being momentarily absorbing) and readily wish-fulfilling. The term "escape" is used rather vaguely by those who enjoy reading such fiction in these ways. But reading Austen's novels for escape tends to offend Austen's admirers in and outside the academy who bristle at the suggestion that her novels are glib and trashy. Reading for escape also involves a way of reading that privileges pleasure over reflection, entertainment over "study," recreation over the labor of analysis. Readers who enjoy Austen's novels in this manner tend to scorn academics for "reading into" Austen's novels all manner of subtleties, complications, and meanings – typically relating to sex, politics, or the unconscious – that perturb their enjoyment. It is doubtful that such readers are really seeking to escape anything in particular, but rather to chill out without the annoyance of pausing or thinking.

Academics, on the other hand, feel the full, opprobrious weight of reading for escape, hence our embarrassment. It's transgressive to read for escape. We're not supposed to read to forget, to elude, to dodge, or to

30 Great Myths About Jane Austen, First Edition. Claudia L. Johnson and Clara Tuite.
© 2020 John Wiley & Sons, Inc. Published 2020 by John Wiley & Sons, Inc.

withdraw somewhere safe. While reading certainly does not preclude pleasure, it is also supposed to have the dignity if not at all times of work then at least of purpose, and it should show the mastery of expertise and a sense of responsibility; it is supposed to produce something – something smart, insightful, and solid. We feel particularly sensitive on the subject of reading Austen for escape precisely because we know that her novels can indeed lend themselves to doing so more than, say, Joyce or George Eliot or George Meredith.

Reading Austen for escape has a long and honorable tradition – still very much in progress – originating with Victorians who saw in Austen's novels a world entirely sufficient to its own forms and rituals, a quieter and gentler time when people lived without strife, conflict, or angst, and when the ordinary relations therefore still yielded interest and satisfaction. That's what they wanted to escape to. What they wanted to escape from was modernity itself. Sometimes the ills of modernity were associated with the shocks of technology and mass media. Contrasting "our modern times, when steam and electricity have linked together the ends of the earth, and the very air seems teeming with news, agitations, discussions" with the "tranquil, drowsy, decorous English day" of "a century since," Sarah Chauncey Woolsey idealizes the relative tedium of life in Austen's fiction – where receiving a single letter is enough to provide a village with months of conversation – to the sensibility of a better, less sensationally harried time: "people did not expect happenings every day or even every year. No doubt they lived the longer for this exemption from excitement, and kept their nerves in a state of wholesome repair."[2]

Austen's perceived readiness to represent the satisfactions of prosaic life appeared attractive when contrasted to contemporary sensational fiction, which was often judged to emerge out of sensibilities so jaded and degraded that only the lurid or extreme subjects could be considered engaging. Accordingly, Austen's novels were escaped to in part because of what they excluded: *St. Paul's Magazine* notes that the "wild pulsation, the stormy embracing, the hand-pressure which bruises, the kiss which consumes" are all "absent from Jane Austen's pages"; Andrew Lang playfully scolds her for being unperplexed by Esoteric Buddhism, Higher Pantheism, High Paganism, Analysis, Passion, Realism, Naturalism, Irreverence, and Religious Open-Mindedness; while the *Temple Bar*, drawing up a considerably shorter list, is grateful simply that "she has nothing to say about evolution and the Jews."[3]

But Austen was a locus of escape not merely because of what was not in her fiction. She was also embraced because her novels are irresistibly interesting, and as such they were an antidote to that most Victorian of maladies: ennui. Anne Thackeray Ritchie's apostrophe – "Dear books!

bright, sparkling with wit and animation, in which the homely heroines charm, the dull hours fly, and the very bores are enchanting" – was widely quoted and reworked in essays, appreciations, and biographies from the 1880s through 1930. Ritchie's tribute is worth pondering, precisely because it celebrates the wondrous immunity to the Victorian malady of ennui. As Ritchie's testimony implies, ennui is always assumed to be our condition prior to reading. The dullness of our homely lives stretches out before us, unrelieved and unanimated and "the most fashionable marriage on the *tapis* no longer excites us very much." But "the sentiment of an Emma or an Anne Elliot comes home to some of us as vividly as ever." Our "friends of pen-and-ink" in Austen's novels are "are always 'at home';" they "never turn their backs nor walk away as people do in real life, nor let their houses and leave the neighbourhood."[4] Austen's novels are read because she manages to make the daily lives she narrates ever desirable, despite their familiarity. It is plain that we often call on our pen-and-ink friends and we are never anything less than gratified to find them at home and ready for us, so that even the bores become bottomless sources of fascination.

Austen has provided thoughtful readers with escape in even more trying circumstances. Take, for example, the English public during World War II, when Austen's novels were in short supply. In April 1943, one London newspaper observed: "It is as pleasant to be told ... that the young men and women in the Forces want to read MISS AUSTEN'S novels, as it is harrowing to learn that they cannot get them." The article continues: "If the best and most reviving literature for times such as these is that which gives a brief escape from thoughts of war then who should stand beside MISS AUSTEN? ... The books are full of the drowsy humming of a summer garden which can deafen the ears even to the humming of the aeroplane overhead."[5] Who could possibly begrudge the men and women in "the Forces" their "brief escape" to drowsy undramatic Austen, their respite from the disruptions of grim war everywhere else around and above them? And yet this respite is intensely permeable, so proximate to what is being escaped from that it cannot really be separated from it: the humming of Austen's gardens is said to be louder than the humming of airplanes overhead, but since Austen's novels actually don't mention any humming gardens, we must infer that the humming breaks through rather than being overwritten by Austen.

The escape provided by the 1940 movie adaptation is similarly porous. The MGM adaptation of *Pride and Prejudice* began production in February 1940, with a screenplay largely by Aldous Huxley, with Greer Garson and Laurence Olivier in the lead roles, and with a predominantly British cast. Despite the ludicrousness of the costumes, despite Mr. Collins's metamorphosis into a librarian (the Hollywood Production Code forbidding irreverent representations of the clergy), despite the fact that Lady Catherine was only pretending to be ornery in order to test the lovers' devotion, the production was a critical as well as a box office success. In November 1940, the MGM *Pride and Prejudice* afforded the reviewer in *The London Observer* "a deal of pleasure" that made him "forget for two blessed hours, that the world wasn't bounded by Longbourn, Rosings, Netherfield, and a wedding ring."[6] A 1941 letter from an Englishwoman in Southampton to director Robert Z. Leonard describes in more detail the grateful escape the film provided:

> My husband is a Naval Officer and a few days ago he had one of his rare afternoons in port and a chance to visit the cinema.
>
> We went to see your film made from the book we know and love so well and to our delight were carried away for two whole hours of perfect enjoyment. Only once was I reminded of our war – when in a candle-lit room there was an uncurtained window and my husband whispered humorously, "Look – they're not blacked out."
>
> You may perhaps know that this city has suffered badly from air raids but we still have some cinemas left, and to see a packed audience enjoying *Pride and Prejudice* so much was most heartening.[7]

It is poignant to consider how Austen provided relief to war-weary people by giving them a manageable elsewhere for two whole hours. But it is also painful to register again how fragile this elsewhere is: the movie helps viewers both to forget the war – "for two whole hours" – while at the same time prompting them to remember its inescapable presence. Seeing a candle on the set points both to how it wasn't necessary to curtain the windows during Austen's time and to the anxious recollection that someone ought to draw the blinds fast before the Luftwaffe spots the light and bombs Pemberley off the map.

These very different "escapist" readers, it must be noted, are hardly inattentive to the course of Austen's novels or to the methods of art. For real impermeable escape, combined with readings of still-thrilling intensity, we must turn to Reginald Farrer's extraordinary appreciation of Austen, written on the centenary of her death in 1917. Farrer celebrates Austen for passing over "all the vast anguish of her time" and committing herself instead solely to the truth of her art. Earlier Janeites longed for the magical wholeness of Austen's lost world of England, but Farrer despised that world, along with Christianity and all of Europe, converting to Buddhism to distance himself from it. For Farrer Austen is a god, "The

Divine Jane," who is infinitely above our world. The Divine Jane has created another world, autonomous from yet contiguous to our own, a kingdom of art that is "hermetically sealed" from our toils and frets. While our world's "tyrannies and empires erupt and collapse" here below, her art remains immortal, and immortally vibrant for us, in large part because of her godlike power for "intense vitalization," endowing characters with commanding liveliness.[8]

It is precisely because Austen is above and apart from the world as we live in it, Farrer claims, that worshippers like himself and his contemporaries, scarred by the trenches and carnage of World War I, can fly "for comfort and company perennially refreshing, to Hartfield and Randalls, Longbourn, Northanger, Sotherton and Uppercross." Escape is both possible and rewarding because Austen's novels are conceived as nonsignifying, as referring to themselves alone. Being at one and the same time vitally engaging and also about nothing other than itself, Austen fiction offers the possibility of a both absorbing and expansive triviality that releases us from the grip of the inevitable, of whatever oppressive reality we are escaping from.

So, in short: yes. Over more than a century and a half, many readers have felt blissfully unashamed about reading Austen's novels to escape one condition or another. For most of these readers, the Austenian world they escape to, however, is intensive, powerful, rich, and alive, not bland or "chill." Is this a correct way of reading her novels? Insofar as a lot of Austenian escape – not all, viz. Farrer – is founded on a nostalgia for an idealized, decorous, peaceful past her novels are thought to celebrate, probably not. Austen thought of herself as modern, after all, and if her fiction predates railroads, electricity, and a host of other noisome ills from which we might seek to escape, it does not predate others, such as commodity culture, the slave trade, revolutionary terror, real estate development, or everyday cruelty. Life within Austen's novels is pretty precarious, especially for women, and it is not surprising that many readers turn to her better to understand and resist their difficulties rather than to seek relief from them. Still, people read for a lot of different reasons, and consolation and refuge are as good as any. Sir Walter Elliot in *Persuasion* always turns to his favorite book, the *Baronetage*, to "[find] occupation for an idle hour, and consolation in a distressed one." Surely Austen is not mocking the wish to find comfort in distress, but rather his choice of reading, which merely reflects him back to himself and thus in some ways only imprisons him further. Austen would surely have thought novels a better if also more challenging choice, for they might help him escape into the real world rather than stay entrapped in his self-important delusions.

Notes

1 J.R.R. *Tolkien, Tolkien on Fairy-stories: Expanded Edition, with Commentary and Notes*, ed. Verlyn Flieger and Douglas A. Anderson (New York: HarperCollins Publishers, 2014), p. 69.
2 Sarah Chauncey Woolsey, *Letters of Jane Austen* (Boston: Roberts Brothers, 1892), pp. iii, iv.
3 *St. Paul's Magazine*, 632; Andrew Lang, *Letters to Dead Authors* (New York: C. Scribner's Sons, 1886), pp. 82–83; *Temple Bar* 64 (1888), p. 355.
4 Anne Thackeray Ritchie, *A Book of Sibyls* (London: Smith, Elder & Co., 1883), pp. 197–229.
5 "Miss Austen for the Forces," *The Times*, Thursday, 22 April 1943, p. 5.
6 C.A. Lejeune, "*Pride and Prejudice*," *London Observer* (3 November 1940). Burke Collection. http://meyerhoff.goucher.edu/library/Web_folder_Jane_Austen_Books/Composition_book_2/ppcb2a58.htm, accessed 17 November 2019.
7 Kenneth Turan, "*Pride and Prejudice*: An informal history of the Garson-Olivier motion picture," *Persuasions* 11 (1989), pp. 140–143. This letter is dated 10 February 1941 and is written by a woman named Betty Howard.
8 Reginal Farrer "Jane Austen, *ob.* July 18, 1817," *Quarterly Review*, (July 1917), reprinted in *Jane Austen: The Critical Heritage 1870–1940*, vol. 2, ed. B.C. Southam (London: Routledge & Kegan Paul, 1987), pp. 249, 246.

Myth
30 JANE AUSTEN WAS A STAR-CROSSED LOVER

Jane Austen's readers always want more. As Henry James complains, "where her testimony complacently ends the pressure of appetite within us presumes exactly to begin."[1] On the one hand, we celebrate how Austen's free indirect style enhances our access to her heroines' thoughts and feelings; on the other, we are eager to hear the author "herself" speaking through her heroine. One way of resolving these competing "pressure[s] of appetite" has been to promote the myth that Austen was nursing an unrequited love.

There are two parts to this myth: that Austen was a star-crossed lover and that her romantic plots recast herself as their fictional heroines, transforming the bittersweet fruits of failed romance into happy endings. Anne Thackeray Ritchie claims in *A Book of Sibyls* (1883) that when Anne Elliot in *Persuasion* (1818) says, "All the privilege I claim for my own sex … is that of loving longest when existence or when hope is gone," she "must have been Jane Austen herself, speaking for the last time."[2] She must have been, but was she? Thackeray Ritchie celebrates writing as a kind of channeling ("What trains of thought go sweeping through our brains!").[3] And she is not alone. There are similar windmills in many others' minds.

William Johnson Cory, a poet and "Uranist" (one of the many intriguing varieties of queer people in Victorian times), wrote in 1889 that "a careful perusal of Jane Austen's *Persuasion*" convinced him that "Wentworth is [Austen's] own lost lover, and a sweet knight of the quarter-deck."[4] On the basis of family history passed down by his grandmother, who knew Austen, Johnson Cory speculated that the mysterious lover was John, the sailor brother of William Wordsworth.

30 Great Myths About Jane Austen, First Edition. Claudia L. Johnson and Clara Tuite.
© 2020 John Wiley & Sons, Inc. Published 2020 by John Wiley & Sons, Inc.

The Great War trench poet Edmund Blunden introduces Austen's "most candid anatomy of woman's love" by asking:

> could she have attained such insight without any personal history to develop it? Could she have depicted ... Anne Elliot without being an Anne at one time or another? ... [W]e may look through the happy ending of Anne's story at the tears of the authoress.[5]

In this myth, Anne speaks the unrequited love that is "really" Austen's and is given the happy ending the author denied herself. That Austen was "veiled" by her characters is a deeply held wish for many readers and a primary way of reading her novels.

This myth tells us much about how readerly attachment manifests as the desire for authorial autobiography, a desire so strong it sometimes sees autobiographical traces in every work Austen creates. Its flagrant conflation of character and author takes us into knotty theoretical questions about the relationship between author, character, and reader. Roland Barthes was seeking to understand this kind of relationship when he wrote his essay "The Death of the Author" (1967).

In examining the myth, we are tracing the figure of the quietly weeping Jane Austen who channels her desire into her heroines and leaves "her anxious and delicate presence within the persons of her dramas."[6] This Jane Austen lies at the melancholy border between a disappointed real-life love and the consolation of aesthetic sublimation. These "tears of the authoress" speak to powerful ideals about literature as some form of sublimation. Again, Barthes is useful here: "Two powerful myths have persuaded us that love could, *should* be sublimated in aesthetic creation: the Socratic myth (loving serves to 'engender a host of beautiful discourses') and the romantic myth (I shall produce an immortal work by writing my passion)."[7]

These myths are coeval with the origins of literature itself. So too is the figure of the star-crossed lover. From Hadrian and Antinous to Dido and Aeneas, Tristan and Isolde, Eloise and Abelard, Romeo and Juliet, these unrequited lovers are doomed never to match up. Such is the power of the romantic myth of sublimation that aesthetic representation of the forbidden or unrequited love is enough to consecrate that love and make it "true." There's the rub: the love "lives" on, even if only as fiction. But what else is there? Such literary tropes are what many people live their lives by, as they give the breath of life to their loves. And so Austen's cinematic updaters work their magic on her failed romances – the homely, realist version of these mythic, epic loves.

The Austen biopics or "biographical romantic dramas" *Becoming Jane* and *Miss Austen Regrets* (both 2007) use Austen's letters to craft the myth anew. *Becoming Jane*'s screenwriter credits Austen's romance with Tom Lefroy as the inspiration for *Pride and Prejudice*.[8] With perfect symmetry, *Miss Austen Regrets* takes her romance with her neighbor Harris Bigg-Wither, who made her an offer of marriage, which she initially accepted but then rejected next morning. The cast and crew of *Becoming Jane* describe their excitement when they discovered Austen's romances. Anne Hathaway, who plays Jane Austen, says "From the moment I read the script I was really passionate about it." Producer Graham Broadbent says he "love[s] the idea that [Jane Austen] had this romantic experience. We never imagine that. We just think of her as a spinstery old lady." His co-producer, Douglas Rae, enthuses for all of them: "We were fascinated by why this woman who had written six of the most successful romantic novels in history had not herself married."[9]

We too are fascinated. The wish to make Jane a married woman first took visual form in 1873 in the so-called "Betrothal Portrait" of Duyckinck's *Portrait Gallery of Eminent Men and Women of Europe and America*, where she sports a ring on her wedding finger.[10] The spinstery old lady was married, it seems. Anne Thackeray Ritchie had it both ways – curiously signing *A Book of Sibyls* as both "Miss Thackeray" and "Mrs Richmond Ritchie." Why not Jane Austen?

When archival sources are used, the idea of the author as a character "behind" the novel suggests that we can retrieve the author intact. But, at most, the author's letters locate the subject who has become material for the novel, and whose thoughts and actions have become so fully transformed by the creative work that the character bears little resemblance to the "original," much less a blueprint for how we should read the novel. This aesthetic transformation is crucial to the novel as an aesthetic form, and to the play of readerly desires and identifications it enables. *Identification* is another term for the affective investment that readers make in characters, which arises from the recognition necessary to bring characters into being.[11] The medium of the letter, too, while part of the historical record, is nevertheless a rhetorical artefact, a form of "life-writing," rather than a neutral source of truth. In any biographical undertaking, be it a scholarly biography or a cinematic romance, "the portrait of the artist" is still a kind of fiction.

So: what are the facts? The one incontrovertible fact is that Jane Austen did not marry. Living at a time when there was enormous pressure to do so, and having received an offer, she nevertheless chose to remain single. Her closest relationships were with members of her family, particularly her older sister, Cassandra.

Jane's earliest surviving letter, dated 9 January 1796, was written to wish Cassandra a happy birthday. The letter describes a ball at Manydown, the home of their neighbors the Bigg-Withers. Here Jane danced with a young Irishman, Tom Lefroy: "I am almost afraid to tell you how my Irish friend and I behaved. Imagine to yourself everything most profligate and shocking in the way of dancing and sitting down together. I *can* expose myself, however, only once more, because he leaves the country soon after next Friday."[12] Later that week, Jane reports that she received a visit from Tom Lefroy the day after the ball.[13]

A few days after that, John Warren, who had also danced with Jane at the ball, presented her with a portrait of Tom Lefroy he had drawn for her. As Claire Tomalin reads it, this "gesture made it quite clear that the flirtation had attracted attention."[14] Nevertheless, the intentions behind such gestures are often unclear, as we know from *Emma*, which features an uncannily similar ritual when Mr. Elton entreats Emma Woodhouse to paint a portrait of Harriet Smith ("it will indeed, to use your own words, be an exquisite possession," [*E*, 45]). Emma mistakenly thinks Mr. Elton is only interested in Harriet. How wrong she is and how much dramatic gold Austen spins from his encomiums, which Emma fails to perceive are an indirect expression of love for the artist herself.

Whether John Warren was in love with Jane Austen we will never know. In any case, knowledge that a woman has a suitor may spur potential rivals to emerge. What we do know is that Austen's rewriting of these biographical materials in *Emma* works against any tendency to read fiction literally – or indeed for too obvious a disguise. Austen is a master of indirection, reporting the gift from Warren "as indubitable proof of Warren's indifference to me."[15] Romantic desires themselves are not straightforward, especially when tangled up in the plots of fiction. (As Emma's epigraph has it, "The course of true love never did run smooth.")

Take the reader's elegiac regret for what might-have-been in Austen's love life. This may not all be sweetness and light. Readerly desires are often perverse. As D.A. Miller reminds us, "our commiseration for the author of *Persuasion* is no freer from schadenfreude than the equally well-contented sorrow people feel on learning of the personal problems of a celebrity."[16]

And what of the other romance reworked in *Miss Austen Regrets*? On 25 November 1802, Jane and Cassandra went to stay at Manydown at the invitation of their friends Catherine and Alethea Bigg. A week later, Jane accepted a proposal of marriage from Harris Bigg-Wither, the sisters' younger brother, who stood to inherit Manydown. But by the following morning she had changed her mind.[17] Austen's niece Catherine Hubback later wrote, "I am sure she had no attachment to him." Catherine had seen some of Jane's letters (later destroyed by Cassandra), in which she said she had accepted the proposal "in a momentary fit of self-delusion."[18]

Caroline Austen, another niece, described Harris as "very plain in person – awkward, & even uncouth in manner."[19] Harris's sense of humor had a mean streak, which Austen may well have appreciated; he joked about deliberately serving a bad-tasting punch to some "disagreeable" friends who had crossed him in business.[20]

Is that all there is? The plot thickens. Another question arises (one we might ask of the process of aesthetic sublimation). How interested was Jane Austen in these marriage plots? They are almost emphatically predictable. Even Blunden concedes that she is not "desperately energetic" in describing the search for a husband, but he then rationalizes it away: "I cannot consider it to be other than a veil for a deep intensity. She was serious, and the search was then, as it is now, among the biggest things in the world."[21] But one reader's certainty is another's wishfulness.

There are other facts and readerly desires that attend fondly to our author (and produce her through other authorial figures, including the spinstery old lady, who lived to be a hoary 42). These other ways of reading are less likely to subordinate Austen's life to the marriage plots of her fictions: the two don't have to fit, and the inevitable happy endings don't have to figure a solution for what might have been. These different possibilities include separating Austen from her marriage plots and producing a queerer reading of how these things might be related.

Where Blunden emphasizes seriousness, the creators of *Becoming Jane* craft a breezy nonchalance for their biographical Austen, who retracts her acceptance of Bigg-Wither's proposal to reserve the prerogative to flirt. But an alternative perspective might weigh the cost of that rebuff, giving credit to her decision to remain single in the face of social pressure and economic hardship (including that of her family of female dependents). This would accord due power to the strange, unnerving social force of Austen's singleness.

Considering these circumstances, an alternative biographical model to the "light, bright and sparkling" Elizabeth Bennet of *Pride and Prejudice* might be found in Emma Watson, the protagonist of Austen's mid-career fragment *The Watsons*. Initially drafted about 1804, when Austen lived in Bath, this fragment details the experience of Emma Watson, who, having been adopted by wealthy relatives, is returned to her impoverished birth family after her benefactor dies. This heroine has a satiric, clear-eyed reading of her social world and an ability to speak back to it; she is a subtly compelling social presence that defies her precarious situation while underscoring it all the more forcefully.

Virginia Woolf was an acute critic of the development of Austen's oeuvre and a keen connoisseur of *The Watsons*. Comparing it to *Mansfield Park*, she remarks how Mary Crawford's "chatter" suddenly seems "flat" when Austen's narrator "strikes one note of her own, very quietly, but in perfect tune." Woolf observes: "From such contrasts there comes a beauty, a solemnity even, which are not only as remarkable as her wit, but an inseparable part of it. In *The Watsons*, she gives us a foretaste of this power."[22]

This precarious heroine, and this unfinished text, bears a charged relation to the singleness that is a structuring feature of Austen's life and work. In subtle ways, *The Watsons* marks Bigg-Wither's rejected proposal in 1802 and her father's death in 1805, and the loss of financial security these events entailed. Her father's death seems to have put an end to work on the manuscript. In this sense, *The Watsons* marks the liminality of her position as a single woman, but also, as Woolf suggests, indicates the power she will display in her later works.

As a single woman, Austen willed her possessions to members of her family, mainly Cassandra. The inheritance included Austen's unfinished manuscripts, among them *The Watsons* – the posthumous legacy of this power.

Notes

1 Henry James, "The new novel," reprinted in *Notes on Novelists* (1914), quoted in *Jane Austen: The Critical Heritage*, vol. 2, ed. B.C. Southam (London: Routledge & Kegan Paul, 1987), p. 231.

2 Anne Thackeray Ritchie, *A Book of Sibyls: Mrs Barbauld, Miss Edgeworth, Mrs Opie, Miss Austen* (London: Smith, Elder & Co., 1883), p. 211.

3 Ibid, p. 212.

4 *Extracts from the Letters and Journals of William Cory: Selected and arranged by Francis Warre Cornish* (Oxford: printed for subscribers, 1897), p. 545. On Johnson's account, see Carl H. Ketcham, "The still unknown lover," *Persuasions*, 11, (1989), pp. 7–11.

5 Edmund Blunden, Introduction, in Jane Austen, *Persuasion* (London: Avalon Press, 1946), p. ix. Originally published in a private wartime edition of 1944.

6 Ibid, p. xi.

7 Roland Barthes, *A Lover's Discourse: Fragments*, trans. Richard Howard (Penguin, 1978), p. 97.

8 *See Kevin Hood, "The art of adaptation: Becoming Jane," The Writing Studio,* http://www.writingstudio.co.za/page1718.html, accessed 2 March *2019.*

9 All quotes from Sally Williams, "Not so plain Jane," *Telegraph* (17 February 2007), https://www.telegraph.co.uk/culture/3663235/Not-so-plain-Jane.html, accessed 2 March 2019.

10 See Claudia L. Johnson, *Jane Austen's Cults and Cultures* (Princeton, NJ: Princeton University Press, 2012), pp. 45–46.

11 See John Frow, *Character & Person* (Oxford: Oxford University Press, 2014), p. 37.
12 Jane Austen to Cassandra Austen, 9–10 January1796, *Jane Austen's Letters*, ed. Deirdre Le Faye, third edition (Oxford: Oxford University Press, 1995), p. 1.
13 Ibid, p. 2.
14 Claire Tomalin, *Jane Austen: A Life* (London: Viking, 1997), p. 116.
15 Jane Austen to Cassandra Austen, 22 May 1801, *Letters*, p. 87.
16 D.A. Miller, *Jane Austen, or The Secret of Style* (Princeton, NJ: Princeton University Press, 2003), p. 75.
17 William Austen-Leigh and Richard Arthur Austen-Leigh, *Jane Austen: A Family Record*, rev. Deirdre Le Faye (London: British Library, 1989), pp. 121–122.
18 Austen-Leigh, *Family Record*, p. 122.
19 Ibid, p. 121.
20 Tomalin, *Jane Austen*, p. 319, n. 3.
21 Blunden, Introduction, p. vii.
22 Virginia Woolf, "Jane Austen," in *Collected Essays*, vol. 1 (London: Hogarth Press, 1980), p. 150.

FURTHER READING

Jane Austen's Life: There is not a lot of documentary material about Jane Austen's life, and even the best biographies resort to novelizing from time to time. Many of Austen's letters are rumored to have been destroyed, and we have nothing in the way of journals or diaries, had they ever existed in the first place. As a result, Austen remains an elusive figure. The first biographies of Austen written by family members, though somewhat hagiographical, remain fascinating. Readers should begin with brother Henry's two biographical notices (1818 and 1833) and nephew J.E. Austen-Leigh's *Memoir of Jane Austen* (1869/70 and 1871). These, along with other family remembrances, have been splendidly introduced and annotated in *A Memoir of Jane Austen: And Other Family Recollections* (Oxford World's Classics, 2002, ed. Kathryn Sutherland). Still very much a family piece, William Austen-Leigh and William Arthur Austen-Leigh's *Jane Austen, Her Life and Letters: A Family Record* (1913) gives a far more detailed picture of Austen's life and family. Deidre Le Faye has considerably revised and expanded this volume in her edition *Jane Austen, A Family Record* (London: British Library, 1989; 2nd ed. Cambridge: CUP, 2004).

Even though they draw most of their facts from *Jane Austen: A Family Record*, many modern-day biographies of Jane Austen provide some new research and new spins. In contrast to the family biographies, Park Honan's *Jane Austen: Her Life* (New York: St. Martin's, 1988) makes a good case for the wideness of Jane Austen's world – and so the guillotining of her cousin's husband, the presence of the militia, and the sugar plantations in Antigua. Claire Tomalin's *Jane Austen: A Life* (New York: Knopf, 1997) does an excellent job of integrating the novels into the life and of complicating the myth of loving family relations in order to show rivalries, tensions, and coolness, along with love. Squarely – extravagantly – revisionist is David Nokes's *Jane Austen: A Life* (New York: Farrar, Straus, & Giroux, 1997) which stresses darker elements of the Austen family – the shoplifting aunt, the suspected adultery of aunt Eliza Hancock with Warren Hastings, the "missing" brother, George who was put out to a family in Monk Sherborne on account of some impairment – epilepsy? deafness? cerebral palsy? – and who is all but expunged from earlier family histories. The best biography to focus on Austen's life as an author is still Jan Fergus's excellent *Jane Austen: A Literary Life* (London: Macmillan, 1991).

Jane Austen's Letters: The first edition *Jane Austen's Letters* appeared in 1884, edited by her great-nephew the first Lord Brabourne. This edition was based on letters in the possession of his mother, Fanny, Austen's beloved niece, who in turn inherited these letters from Austen's sister, Cassandra, to whom most of Austen's letters are addressed. Brabourne frames the letters within his own narrative about Austen's life and silently censors allusions to the body and illness. A scholarly edition of the letters did not appear until 1932, with R.W. Chapman's two-volume *Jane Austen's Letters to her Sister Cassandra and Others* (Oxford: Clarendon Press, revised 1952). Chapman's edition has been further revised, annotated, and well indexed by Deirdre Le Faye in *Jane Austen's Letters* (Oxford: Clarendon Press, 3rd ed. 1995; 4th ed. 2011).

Jane Austen's Texts: Jane Austen was the first English novelist whose collected novels were edited according to modern textual principles. For most of the twentieth century, R.W. Chapman's *The Novels of Jane Austen: The Text Based on Collation of the Early Editions*, 5 vols. (Oxford: Clarendon Press, 1923; revised, 1933) was the authoritative edition of Austen's novels, and though many editors have emended, ignored, and critiqued Chapman's editorial work, it still – with revisions and corrections – forms the basis of many excellent and widely available classroom texts of Austen's novels published by, for example, Broadview Press and Oxford World's Classics, and by W.W. Norton as Norton Critical Editions. *The Cambridge Edition of the Works of Jane Austen* (Cambridge: Cambridge University Press, 2005–2008) is the first collected scholarly edition for the twenty-first century, eschewing Chapman's edition altogether, supplying rigorous scholarly examinations of early published and (where possible) manuscript sources and giving readers textual variants and copious notes. *The Jane Austen Annotated Editions* (Harvard University Press, 2010–2016) are oversized volumes, replete with sumptuous and plentiful color illustrations and marginal notes.

Some students will want to know more about Jane Austen's manuscripts. Although no manuscripts of Austen's six novels remain, we do have manuscripts of Austen's early works, as well as her unfinished works, such as *The Watsons* and *Sanditon*, and other pieces. Kathryn Sutherland has made a superb digital editions of "Jane Austen's Fiction Manuscripts," including some 1000 pages of manuscript, available online at https://janeausten.ac.uk/manuscripts/index.html.

Jane Austen's Afterlives: Lionel Trilling once remarked that opinions about Jane Austen were almost as interesting as the novels themselves. Brian Southam's two volumes remain foundational to the study of the history of Austen's reception from her death until the mid-twentieth century: *Jane Austen: The Critical Heritage* (London: Routledge & Kegan Paul, 1968) and *Jane Austen: The Critical Heritage, Vol. 2, 1870–1940* (London: Routledge & Kegan Paul, 1987). The past two decades have witnessed a sharp increase in the history of Jane Austen's reputation and of her cults. The major works: Deidre Lynch, ed. *Janeites: Jane Austen's Disciples and Devotees* (Princeton University Press, 2000); Kathryn Sutherland, *Jane Austen's Textual Lives: From Aeschylus to Bollywood* (Oxford University Press, 2005); Claudia L. Johnson, *Jane Austen's Cults and Cultures* (University of Chicago Press, 2012); Gillian Dow and Clare Hanson, eds., *Uses of Austen: Jane's Afterlives* (London: Palgrave Macmillan, 2012); Devoney Looser, *The Making of Jane Austen* (Baltimore: Johns Hopkins University Press, 2017).

Jane Austen Criticism: There are so many good critical books and articles on Jane Austen, employing such a diverse range of critical methods, that it would require a book to list and describe them. We refer readers to the endnotes of the essays presented here for the studies to which we find ourselves referring again and again. The following are collections of essays covering historical contexts and critical interpretation that students, scholars, and general readers will find helpful: *The Cambridge Companion to Jane Austen*, ed. Edward Copeland and Juliet McMaster (Cambridge University Press, 1997) covers Austen's novels and letters along with subjects such as class, money, and style; *Jane Austen in Context*, ed. Janet Todd (Cambridge University Press, 2005) provides extensive essays on just about every important background topic touching Austen and her time, ranging from food to dress to agriculture to politics; *The Blackwell Companion to Jane Austen*, ed. Claudia L. Johnson and Clara Tuite (Blackwell, 2009) collects 42 methodologically diverse essays on Austen's genres, texts, social and political contexts, and afterlives. Though somewhat unwieldy, the most comprehensive collection of important older but still important essays on Jane Austen is Ian Littlewood's four-volume *Jane Austen: Critical Assessments* (Mountfield, East Sussex: Helm Information, 1998).

INDEX

Addison, Joseph, 81
Amis, Kingsley, 101
Anstey, Christopher
New Bath Guide, 53
Auden, W.H., 128–29
"Letter to Lord Byron", 128
Austen, Anna (Jane's niece), 67, 151
Austen, Caroline (Jane's niece),
149, 197
Austen, Cassandra (Jane's sister), 4–5,
20, 52, 68, 70, 85, 102,
147–52, 162–63, 180–81,
195–96, 198, 201
Austen, Cassandra (nee Leigh, Jane's
mother), 68, 161
Austen, Charles (Jane's brother),
94, 97
Austen, Edward (Jane's brother). *See*
Knight, Edward Austen
Austen, Eliza (Jane's sister-in-law),
107
Austen, Francis (Frank) (Jane's
brother), 5, 73, 94, 97, 150
Austen, George (Jane's father), 49,
52–53, 69, 97, 114, 161
Austen, George (Jane's nephew),
151–52

Austen, Henry (Jane's brother), 2, 5–6,
69–70, 75, 94, 107, 114–15,
148, 158
Austen, James (Jane's brother), 94,
107, 114
Austen, Jane
anonymity, 2–5, 155–59
autobiography, 193–98
and Bath, 49–54, 109, 180
biographies, 202
class, 52, 160–65, 163, 176,
180, 185
and feminism, 141–46
humor, 19–26, 62, 115–16, 138,
148, 152, 168–73, 182
letters, 50–51, 53, 75, 147–52,
195–96, 201
and literary canon, 8, 27, 31, 66,
81, 88
literary earnings, 67–70
literary practice, 35, 38
literary tourism, 54
money, 128–33
morality, 114–19
musical performance, 112
parodies literary convention, 15,
21–26, 41, 43, 57, 62

---

30 Great Myths About Jane Austen, First Edition. Claudia L. Johnson and Clara Tuite.
© 2020 John Wiley & Sons, Inc. Published 2020 by John Wiley & Sons, Inc.